WHOSE ISLAM?

Encountering Traditions
Rumee Ahmed, Randi Rashkover, and Jonathan Tran, Editors

WHOSE ISLAM?

The Western University and Modern Islamic Thought in Indonesia

MEGAN BRANKLEY ABBAS

STANFORD UNIVERSITY PRESS
STANFORD, CALIFORNIA

Stanford University Press
Stanford, California

© 2021 by the Board of Trustees of the Leland Stanford Junior University.
All rights reserved.

English translation ©2016 by the Board of Trustees of the Leland Stanford Junior University. All rights reserved.

No part of this book may be reproduced or transmitted in any form or by any means, electronic or mechanical, including photocopying and recording, or in any information storage or retrieval system without the prior written permission of Stanford University Press.

Printed in the United States of America on acid-free, archival-quality paper

Library of Congress Cataloging-in-Publication Data
Names: Abbas, Megan Brankley, author.
Title: Whose Islam? : the Western university and modern Islamic thought in Indonesia / Megan Brankley Abbas.
Other titles: Encountering traditions.
Description: Stanford, California : Stanford University Press, 2021. | Series: Encountering traditions | Includes bibliographical references and index.
Identifiers: LCCN 2020041385 | ISBN 9781503606333 (cloth) | ISBN 9781503627932 (paperback) | ISBN 9781503627949 (ebook)
Subjects: LCSH: Islam—Indonesia—History—20th century. | Islamic education—Indonesia—History—20th century. | Islam—Study and teaching (Higher)—Indonesia—History—20th century. | Islam—Study and teaching (Higher)—Western countries—History—20th century.
Classification: LCC BP63.I5 A226 2021 | DDC 297.071/1—dc23
LC record available at https://lccn.loc.gov/2020041385

Cover design: Angela Moody
Cover photos: (*l*) Lowell House Bell Tower, Harvard University, Boston, Massachusetts, Adobe Stock | Crin. (*r*) Minaret, Masjid Babulssalam Pelabuhan Mosque, Makassar, Sulawesi, Indonesia, Adobe Stock | Klodien
Typeset by Motto Publishing Services in 10/14 Minion Pro

To Aatif, of course

*And in loving memory of my grandmother
Shirley Ann Brankley (1935–2020)*

CONTENTS

Preface ix
Acknowledgments xiii
Note on Spelling and Italicization xvii

Introduction 1
1 Building a Modern Islamic College 21
2 McGill University as a "Midwife for the Islamic Reformation" 52
3 A Fusionist Transformation at the Ministry of Religious Affairs 92
4 Islam and Development, Chicago-Style 122
5 The Specter of Academic Imperialism 155
Conclusion: The Future of Islamic Studies 187

Notes 201
Bibliography 229
Index 245

PREFACE

Like most historians, I am rather suspicious of clean-cut origin stories, and the same holds true for the origins of this book. I can tell its story in many ways, and I'm honestly not sure which is the most accurate. This project might have begun toward the end of my second year in graduate school at Princeton University. I had left a seminar frustrated with our class' reductionist debate over whether Fazlur Rahman, the late and well-respected professor at the University of Chicago, should be classified as an academic scholar or an Islamic thinker. I determined that I would later revisit the issue with greater nuance and humility. Or perhaps this project began a year earlier, when I noticed in another seminar that three of the most recent chairmen of Muhammadiyah, the largest Muslim modernist organization in Indonesia and arguably the world, possessed doctoral degrees from American universities. I was fascinated by the pattern, but those around the seminar table dismissed it as mere coincidence. It is also possible that the book's origins stretch back even further to my undergraduate semester studying at Universitas Gadjah Mada in Yogyakarta. With the help of the Australian Consortium for "In-Country" Indonesian Studies, I had enrolled in several Indonesian history courses at the university. I was excited to be learning Indonesian history alongside Indonesian classmates speaking in Bahasa Indonesia, and yet I was also surprised to discover that my course syllabi were dominated by English-language texts written by American and even Dutch historians—texts that most of my classmates could neither read with any fluency nor easily locate in Yogyakarta bookstores or libraries. I wondered why Indonesian college students learned their nation's colonial and postcolonial history mostly from Western academic texts. As an American, I could hardly remember ever reading a history of the United States written by a non-American, with the exception of Alexis de Tocqueville.

Regardless of when the seeds were first planted, this book has its roots in questions about the dynamics of Western academic and Islamic religious authority: Who gets to count as an academic scholar of Islam and for what reasons? How have Western universities shaped Islamic politics and modern Islamic thought since the mid-twentieth century? What would a more ethical relationship between Western universities and Muslim intellectuals, whether in Indonesia or elsewhere, even look like?

These motivating questions emerged from two particular aspects of my life. First, I have spent the past two decades struggling with the many manifestations of American exceptionalism and imperialism. I was fifteen years old on September 11, 2001. I vividly recall sitting in my tenth-grade social-studies classroom when a teacher popped her head through the door to tell us to turn on the television because something major was happening. My class watched, live on television, the two World Trade Center towers collapse and reeled when we saw reports that another plane had crashed about an hour away from my Pittsburgh suburb in Shanksville, Pennsylvania. While 9/11 certainly altered my sense of security, it only magnified my youthful, blind patriotism. I donated all my meager savings to memorial funds. I wore red, white, and blue to school for the next month. Over the next few years, however, disillusionment began to creep in. First, there were our catastrophic wars in Afghanistan and Iraq and then my college history classes on European imperialism, the Cold War, and the modern Middle East. I began to ask myself whether the United States was actually an empire, and if so, then what role did American universities play in maintaining that global dominance. I still believe in the university as a space for critical thinking and intellectual discovery but am also wary that we resemble our British, French, and Dutch colonial predecessors more than we care to admit.

Second, in graduate school I cultivated a respect for faith-driven scholarship. It was a surprising development (even for me) in light of my very secular upbringing. Indeed, beyond a vague notion that my family was Christian because we hunted for pastel-colored eggs and chocolate rabbits on Easter and exchanged presents on Christmas, I had never attended church and knew little about Jesus and the Bible beyond what I had learned in my public high school. Yet it was the *academic* study of religion that shook my certainty in my secular worldview. Learning about Islamic epistemologies and Muslim virtue ethics helped me to see that my definitions of *education* and *ethics* were simply that, *mine*, and that viable and compelling alternatives existed. In the early stages of researching this book, I was particularly struck by the clarity of intellectual purpose and the ethical commitments that drove Wilfred

Cantwell Smith's and Fazlur Rahman's work. While I have occasionally experimented with personal religious practice (primarily Islam), I find it difficult to make any sustained jump into a religious tradition, despite a lingering dissatisfaction about where I stand. I remain a decidedly secular historian, albeit one with unabashed religious curiosities.

While this book is concerned with recent history, I am an archival historian by training and believe in the value of contemporaneous documentary records for reconstructing the past. I thus traveled widely in search of institutional and personal documents about the role of the Western university in modern Islamic thought. Specifically, between 2012 and 2016, I visited the National Archives of Indonesia (Jakarta); the Fazlur Rahman Collection at the International Institute of Islamic Thought and Civilization (Kuala Lumpur); the Wilfred Cantwell Smith Papers at California State University, Northridge (Los Angeles); the Islamic Research Institute (Islamabad, Pakistan); the International Institute of Islamic Thought (Herndon, VA); the McGill University Archives (Montreal); the Princeton University Archives (Princeton, NJ); the Cornell University Archives (Ithaca, NY); the University of Chicago Archives; and, perhaps most importantly, the Rockefeller Archive Center (Sleepy Hollow, NY). Not every archive held materials that were directly related to the book, but all helped me to see the scope of the story I sought to tell. I worked to supplement this archival research with oral-history interviews because they could provide insights into the individual personalities and everyday institutional dynamics that are rarely captured in official documents. Accordingly, I sought out opportunities to conduct interviews with a range of American, Canadian, and Indonesian scholars between 2012 and 2013. These interviews were informal and wide-ranging conversations, which I either recorded digitally or documented through copious note-taking. Because I asked participants to reach far back into their memories to recall what were sometimes mundane university occurrences, the interviews were often more impressionistic than detailed recountings of specific events. I used them mostly to gain a more textured perspective on daily life and to ask for clarification about any perplexing archival finds. I thus rarely cite interviews as the sole source for analysis.

In addition to archival research, I conducted some interviews and observations at the Syarif Hidayatullah State Islamic University (UIN) Jakarta during a research trip to the Indonesian capital in 2013. Yet because of the nature of my research, I wrestled with whether and how to forge more substantial academic connections in Indonesia. I was acutely aware of both the potential for feedback loops and the privileged, albeit contested, position of Western academics at Indonesian Islamic universities. I decided that it would be prudent to adopt a "first do no harm" approach. As a result, I avoided examining contemporary scholars because my analysis could have an unintended impact on their careers. I also strove to write—especially the conclusion—from a self-consciously Western academic perspective. As the following pages surely attest, I continue to struggle, in both theory and practice, with the ethics of such transnational scholarly networks. It is my hope that this book will spark conversation about these difficult issues so that future scholars can make more thoughtful and confident decisions about why and how we wish to study Islam in our twenty-first-century world.

ACKNOWLEDGMENTS

As I write these words in July 2020, we have been living under lockdown because of the COVID-19 pandemic for more than four months. Amid the mounting tragedy and lingering uncertainty about what is to come, I find myself feeling even more grateful for all the opportunities I had to discuss this book project with teachers, colleagues, friends, and students *in person* during the previous several years. I hope that we can all meet up over coffee, attend nonvirtual conferences, travel to archives, and learn together in classrooms sometime again in the not too distant future.

This project was initially conceived alongside my teachers and mentors at Princeton University. Michael Laffan introduced me to the history of Southeast Asian Islam and modeled how to conduct meticulous archival research. His unfailing sense of humor was a welcome respite from the inevitable stresses of graduate school. I am profoundly grateful to Muhammad Qasim Zaman for his insightful feedback at every stage of this project, from when I first discovered the riches of the Ford Foundation archives in his fall 2010 seminar on modern Islamic political thought to his helpful and encouraging comments last year on the book's rewritten introduction. Our conversations have so often filled me with a renewed sense of purpose and excitement about this research. I am also thankful to the other gifted scholars and teachers with whom I had the chance to study while at Princeton. They include On Barak, Kevin Kruse, Bhavani Raman, and Bradley Simpson. I extend a special note of appreciation to the Princeton Writing Program. While I was officially there to learn how to teach writing to undergraduates, the program's administrators (especially Amanda Irwin Wilkins, Keith Shaw, and Khristina Gonzalez) and graduate fellows had an equally significant impact on how I approach my own writing.

Beyond Princeton, I have benefited from the support of many generous individuals at various institutions. At the top of the list is Richard Fox. During my undergraduate years at Williams College, Richard introduced me to Indonesian studies, took me on a study trip to Bali, and nurtured my interest in the country's modern history. He and his wife, Jude, served as trusted advisers during my first year living and studying in Indonesia, and he has continued to serve as a long-distance mentor and friend over the years. Michael Feener kindly agreed to serve as the outside reader on my dissertation committee and even flew halfway around the world to be at my defense. His detailed feedback on the dissertation was enormously helpful as I extensively revised the manuscript over these past five years. I also count myself lucky to have worked alongside an incredible group of scholar-teachers in the SUNY Geneseo History Department between 2015 and 2018. Thank you especially to Cathy Adams, Justin Behrend, Joseph Cope, Tze-ki Hon, Ryan Jones, Kathy Mapes, Michael Oberg, and, of course, Yvonne Seale for your feedback on draft chapters, your consistent encouragement, and your warm collegiality. I am now fortunate to call the Department of Religion at Colgate University my institutional home. In two short years, I have already learned much about the academic study of religion from my new colleagues. A special thanks goes to Chris Vecsey and Georgia Frank for their wonderful mentorship and to Jenna Reinbold, Angela Rudert, Ben Stahlberg, and Brenton Sullivan for helping me settle into the scholarly life at Colgate. I also want to acknowledge my incredible undergraduate students, both at Geneseo and Colgate. Their curiosity and enthusiasm have so often reminded me of why I wanted to become an academic in the first place.

Many other individuals have offered invaluable feedback on various aspects of this book. Leah Klement, my "fellow fellow" from the Princeton Writing Program, has read so many versions of this manuscript that I have long ago lost count. I always look forward to her incisive comments. Sarah El-Kazaz has consistently and kindly pushed me to sharpen my arguments. I thank her for first starting and then continuing our enormously helpful writing group. I also thank other Princeton graduate colleagues for their friendship and support: Usaama al-Azami, Teresa Davis, Catherine Evans, Cristina Florea, Maeve Glass, Saarah Jappie, Radha Kumar, Aaron Rock-Singer, Amin Venjara, and Nurfadzilah Yahaya. I attended many conferences and colloquia that helped me further refine this project, including the Princeton Islamic Studies Colloquium, the Colonialism and Imperialism Workshop (Princeton), the Center for the Study of Religion seminars (Princeton), panels sponsored by the Religion in Southeast Asia Program Unit of the American

Academy of Religion, the Global Asias Conference (Penn State University), and a pair of conferences hosted by the Asian Research Institute (National University of Singapore). For all the probing questions from discussants and attendees, I am thankful.

Over the course of my research, I was fortunate to meet many senior scholars willing to share their own recollections about and experiences in the field of Islamic studies. Howard Federspiel provided me with copies of his papers from graduate school and answered many questions about his years at McGill University's Institute of Islamic Studies. John E. Woods opened his office to me and helped me better understand Fazlur Rahman's role at the University of Chicago and the many facets of studying Islam in Hyde Park. Richard C. Martin sat down over coffee to share his perspective on the history of the insider-outsider problem in Islamic studies and kindly read a draft of chapter 2. Philip Buckley spoke at length with me about the McGill-Indonesia exchange programs during my visit to Montreal in March 2012 and then introduced me to the Indonesian side of the operations during my 2013 trip to Jakarta. I also thank the late Leonard Binder, Bahtiar Effendy, Stephen Humphreys, Fuad Jabali, Paul Walker, and John A. Williams for participating in informal interviews.

I benefited from the warm company and patient assistance of dedicated archival staff across the globe. I thank Margaret Hogan at the Rockefeller Archive Center in Sleepy Hollow, NY, in particular for her help in scouring the foundations' grant files for relevant documents. I also extend my appreciation to those staff members at the American Institute for Indonesian Studies who provided crucial guidance on obtaining my Indonesian research visa in 2013. If it had not been for them, I might still be lost in the maze of the Indonesian bureaucracy. It has likewise been a real pleasure to work with Stanford University Press. I thank the four anonymous reviewers whose comments and critiques were indispensable in helping me to revise the manuscript. I am especially grateful to Emily-Jane Cohen, who guided me through the first stages of publishing; Kate Wahl, who oversaw the transition; and Erica Wetter, who brought the book to final fruition; as well as to my hard-working and attentive associate editor, Faith Wilson Stein, and my meticulous copyeditor, Plaegian Alexander.

My deepest gratitude goes to my family. From a young age, my dad encouraged my love of history through family trips to battlefields, museums, and other historical sites. My mom nurtured my desire to explore the world through reading and traveling. They have both been constant sources of support, even when my budding interests and academic career took me to cities and towns far away from their Pittsburgh suburb. My grandparents, older sister, and extended family of aunts, uncles, cousins, in-laws, and now nieces and nephews have likewise lent words of encouragement and provided opportunities for relaxation over the years. And, of course, this book would not have been possible without the patience and loving support of my partner, Aatif Abbas. From Williamstown to New York City to Upstate New York, it has been quite the journey! Thank you for all the book-related conversations and, more importantly, for building a home with me and our quirky little cat, Slatie.

NOTE ON SPELLING AND ITALICIZATION

This book frequently refers to Indonesian organizational names and terms, which I have spelled according to the post-1972 standard Indonesian orthography. I have updated the spellings of common individual names (e.g., Sukarno rather than Soekarno, Yunus rather than Junus) in the text and bibliography for constancy's sake, but I have retained the original spelling of book titles in order to facilitate any future efforts to locate the cited texts. All translations from the original Indonesian sources are mine, unless otherwise noted. For Islamic terms, I have used common Arabic transliterations rather than Indonesian spellings (e.g., *fiqh* rather than *fikih*, *dawah* rather than *dakwah*) in the text but retained the Indonesian spelling for any book titles or organizational names. All non-English terms appear in italics only the first time they are used in a section in order to make the book more readable.

WHOSE ISLAM?

INTRODUCTION

FOR DECADES NOW, Indonesian Muslims have joked about the existence of a powerful McGill mafia in Jakarta. They laugh about its rumored control over the country's elite Islamic universities and sprawling religious bureaucracy. They exchange sheepish grins about the suspected mob ties of colleagues and friends.[1] While clearly intended as hyperbolic humor, the phrase "McGill mafia" also has a firm foundation in reality. Since the 1950s, nearly 200 Indonesian Muslims have earned graduate degrees at McGill University's Institute of Islamic Studies, and another 1,400 scholars have participated in McGill-sponsored training programs.[2] They include a minister of religious affairs (Mukti Ali), a former rector of the State Islamic University in Jakarta (Harun Nasution), multiple high-ranking religious bureaucrats (Kafrawi Ridwan, Timur Djaelani, and Murni Djamal), and an entire cohort of contemporary public intellectuals. Rectors of major Islamic universities in Jakarta and Surabaya have also cited McGill's institute as the model for the academic programs they aim to build.[3] Indonesian Muslims have other curious entanglements with Western academia. In 1995, the mass modernist organization Muhammadiyah elected Amien Rais (b. 1944), a professor with a PhD in Islamic politics from the University of Chicago, to serve as its national chairman. Although he was the first Muhammadiyah leader with Western academic credentials, Rais was certainly not the last. The next two chairmen, Ahmad Syafii Maarif (b. 1934) and Din Syamsuddin (b. 1958), also held doctoral degrees from the University of Chicago and the University of California,

Los Angeles, respectively. The late twentieth century thus witnessed the rise of an alternative and decidedly academic model of Muslim religious authority in Indonesia.

While this shift was perhaps most visible in Indonesia, it has not been confined to the archipelago nation. On the contrary, Muslim intellectuals from across the globe have transformed Western universities into places where Muslims study and sometimes teach Islam. Their ranks include globally prominent scholars, such as Mohammed Arkoun (1928–2010), originally of Algeria; Naquib al-Attas (b. 1931) of Malaysia; Ismail al-Faruqi (1921–86) of Palestine; Hassan Hanafi (b. 1935) of Egypt; Nurcholish Madjid (1939–2005) of Indonesia; Seyyed Hossein Nasr (b. 1933) of Iran; and Fazlur Rahman (1919–88) of Pakistan. These senior scholars have, in turn, opened the doors of Western academia for countless young Muslims to follow in their footsteps. Some have secured their own faculty positions at Western universities, and others have returned to their native countries to serve as bureaucrats, politicians, and public intellectuals. From their various positions of influence, Western-educated Muslims have used their academic training to fuel their visions of Islamic reform.

This book repositions the Western university as a significant site for the production of Islamic knowledge and Muslim religious authority over the course of the last century. These are typically understood as the functions of madrasas or other explicitly religious schools. As traditional institutions for Islamic learning, madrasas have a long history that dates back, in some regions, to the tenth and eleventh centuries. They have provided advanced instruction in core Islamic disciplines, including Qur'anic exegesis (*tafsir*), hadith studies, logic, Arabic grammar, and especially jurisprudence (*fiqh*) for centuries. Given their centrality to the Islamic intellectual tradition, madrasas have attracted a fair share of academic attention in recent years. Scholars have overturned pervasive stereotypes that madrasas are unchanging bastions of unthinking traditions by investigating their varied epistemological and institutional logics and highlighting their capacities for internal criticism and dynamism.[4] Some have traced colonial-era movements to introduce modern pedagogies and secular subjects into the madrasa milieu.[5] Others have researched how postcolonial madrasas continue to evolve with their changing political circumstances, sometimes choosing to partner with secular developmentalist states and, at other times, fomenting resistance and even rebellion against state power.[6] This literature demonstrates that madrasas and other

Islamic schools remain, without a doubt, important and vibrant intellectual institutions where students learn to embody and shape their religious tradition. However, they no longer exist as the only—or even the primary—spaces where aspiring Muslim scholars study Islam. In the second half of the twentieth century, Western universities emerged as a viable alternative for Islamic religious education.

Studying Islam in Western universities provides Muslim intellectuals with the resources and opportunities to experiment with cross-discursive forms of knowledge. For example, they adopt historical research methods so that they can reexamine Islam's formative period in search of new insights into the faith. They learn about competing hermeneutical theories and devise new ways of interpreting the Qur'an. They study the social sciences in order to better infuse Islamic values into the policy-making process. By merging empirical and normative research, these Muslim intellectuals open up new possibilities for revitalizing Islam in the modern world. However, they also transgress established discursive boundaries and unsettle existing power structures in both the Islamic and Western traditions. The resulting controversies bring a series of fundamental questions to the fore: What exactly constitutes academic versus Islamic knowledge? Are they and should they be distinct intellectual traditions? Which types of scholars belong in which institutional spaces? Who has the power to make such decisions, and with what consequences do they do so?

At its heart, this book tells the story of the contested border between Western academia and modern Islamic thought. While neither absolute nor impenetrable, the border has long been taken for granted. It has existed to separate Muslim intellectuals and the Western academics who study them into two distinct and even rival traditions of inquiry. Yet, by the late twentieth century, the border proved to be so porous that it threatened to collapse altogether.[7] Not only were Muslims studying Islam in Western universities, but Western academics were also teaching at Islamic universities and consulting for Muslim governments. Given its increasingly precarious nature, the border has become a hotbed of activism and controversy. Some have worked to hasten its erasure, and others, fearing an invasion, have endeavored to erect a higher wall and marshal new resources to police it. These movements coexist and often feed off of one another in complicated ways. Ultimately, the collapsing border reveals the possibilities—as well as the perils—of building a more integrated intellectual world.

DUALISTS AND FUSIONISTS IN MODERN ISLAMIC THOUGHT

At the turn of the twentieth century, Muslim leaders across the globe despaired over the state of Islamic education. While traditional madrasas had thrived in the Middle East, South Asia, and—to a lesser extent—Southeast Asia for centuries, the intensification of European colonial rule shook Muslims' confidence in their educational institutions. They feared that madrasas no longer equipped young Muslims with the knowledge and skills they needed to flourish in their rapidly modernizing societies. Given these concerns about intellectual isolation and stagnation, some Muslims began to call for reform. In South Asia, a constellation of education activists—ranging from Deobandi revivalists to the Cambridge-inspired Sayyid Ahmad Khan (1817–98)—rejected the educational status quo and established their own Islamic schools. In the Arab world, prominent Muslim intellectuals, such as Jamal al-Din al-Afghani (1838–97) and Muhammad Abduh (1849–1905), petitioned their fellow Muslims to integrate modern sciences, philosophy, and history into Islamic educational institutions. Despite these early efforts, the fears persisted. The next generation of Muslims continued to worry that Islamic education was woefully out of step with the changing times.

Whether they lived in Cairo or Calcutta, Muslim thinkers diagnosed the root of this crisis as an epistemic framework that I term intellectual dualism.[8] As a system of classifying knowledge, intellectual dualism rests on the contention that the Islamic and Western intellectual traditions exist as two distinct and largely independent discourses. Dualists therefore partition canonical texts, methodological tools, rules of engagement, and metaphysical presuppositions into either the Islamic or the Western tradition. They also bifurcate claims to truth itself. Qur'anic revelation and the values according to which Muhammad lived are understood as "Islamic truths," whereas modern Western philosophy and Newtonian physics are understood as "Western academic" forms of knowledge. This dualist thinking marginalized madrasa-educated Muslims because colonized societies ran according to Western knowledge. After all, European administrators used advances in scientific disciplines to devise new military, transportation, agricultural, and public-health technologies that supported colonial rule. They promulgated European-style law codes and operated courts according to European standards of procedure. They regulated economic transactions on the basis of political and economic theories popular in Europe. The very language of colonial administration was often English, French, or Dutch. If colonized Muslims wanted to succeed, let alone wield influence, in these colonial systems, they needed to master the language—both literal and metaphorical—of European knowledge. In contrast to the great social utility of European knowledge, traditional Islamic education appeared irrelevant for worldly pursuits such as accumulating wealth or attaining justice through the legal system. Consequently, many Muslims feared that dualism, unless checked, would render Islam obsolete in the age of European-style modernity.

Dualism's dominance over the past several centuries should not be mistaken as evidence that it somehow captures the way knowledge inherently works. While possessing some explanatory power, dualist thinking tends to obscure the rich internal diversity of both the Islamic and Western intellectual traditions.[9] It also fails to account for the full extent of their dynamism. As a result, I draw on Alasdair MacIntyre in order to conceptualize intellectual traditions as "essentially historical" in nature.[10] MacIntyre explains:

> A tradition is an argument extended through time in which certain fundamental agreements are defined and redefined. . . . Debates may on occasion destroy what had been the basis of common fundamental agreement, so that either a tradition divides into two or more warring components, whose adherents are transformed into external critics of each other's positions, or else the tradition loses all coherence and fails to survive. It can also happen that two traditions, hitherto independent and even antagonistic, can come to recognize certain possibilities of fundamental agreement and reconstitute themselves as a single, more complex debate.[11]

In other words, traditions are subject to continuous revision, contestation, and even radical change. They can exist in various forms, or not at all, at different moments in time. I apply this same antiessentialist logic to the Islamic and Western intellectual traditions.[12] Neither the contours of the two traditions nor the relationship between them is stable. Dualism therefore exists as only one, historically contingent epistemic framework among other viable alternatives.

The history of intellectual dualism is decidedly modern. Although it is possible to find distant precedents in interreligious polemics from late antiquity and the medieval era, recent research points to the nineteenth century as the crucial incubating period.[13] It was then, at the height of colonialism, that European scholars took advantage of their increased access to Islamic texts and Muslim societies to build the new academic field of Orientalism. These Orientalists approached Islam as "an all-encompassing, determinant, and unchanging cultural entity" that existed as the antithesis of the modern West.[14] This monolithic Islam was despotic, irrational, and drowning in darkness, whereas the West was democratic, rational, and enlightened. While European Orientalists created this civilizational discourse, the essentialist conception did not stay confined to Europe. Rather, it traveled eastward, where it shaped the ways that Muslims approached their own religious tradition. Historian Cemil Aydin argues that many Muslim intellectuals sought "to contest European claims of Muslim inferiority" by reversing Orientalist tropes.[15] They characterized Islam as an innately rational and progressive religion capable of competing with Europe. Although positive in nature, these Muslim arguments depended on an equally essentialist, civilizational definition of Islam that ironically "thicken[ed] the racial discourse."[16] By the late nineteenth century, European and Muslim intellectuals had agreed that Islam was a distinct and unified civilization and that it was in perpetual competition with the West. These shared essentialist assumptions enabled dualism to flourish globally.

While undoubtedly an intellectual construct, dualism was never merely an abstract idea; it also structured educational systems, career opportunities, and even social circles in very tangible ways. Nineteenth-century European colonial officials and Christian missionaries, with very few exceptions, built schools that operated independently from the existing Muslim educational systems in the Middle East, the Indian subcontinent, and Southeast Asia. The languages of instruction were different, as were teacher qualifications and curricular goals. Consequently, Muslim families—whether living in Egypt, India, or Indonesia—faced a stark choice between sending children to modern European-style schools, which provided access to more lucrative professions and powerful social networks, and sending them to a separate system of traditional madrasas that instructed children in Islamic ethics and legal tenets. The existence of these parallel school systems reinforced the explanatory power of intellectual dualism by making the bifurcation of knowledge appear as simple common sense rather than the result of a contingent process. In this sense, dualism was neither natural nor inevitable, but it was, by the late nineteenth century, a reality that shaped the lives of millions of colonized Muslims across the globe. It remains so entrenched in our language and institutions that it is difficult even to write about dualism without reproducing the Islam–West binary.

Upon diagnosing dualism as a serious social ailment, some Muslim intellectuals began prescribing the fusion of the Islamic and Western academic traditions as the best treatment. I call them fusionists, for a convenient shorthand. Fusionists constitute a loose coalition of Western-educated Muslims who reject the dualist bifurcation of knowledge as artificial and instead champion a more unified and universal conception of truth. They strive for commensurability between the two intellectual traditions. According to MacIntyre, such commensurability work "requires a rare gift of empathy as well as of intellectual insight for the protagonists of [one] tradition to be able to understand the theses, arguments, and concepts of their rival."[17] Yet becoming fluent in a second discursive language alone is insufficient; fusionists also must learn to write from within both traditions, "extending each as part of [the] task of integrating them into a single systemic mode of thought."[18] In other words, they must contribute meaningfully to both traditions, even as they weave them together into one coherent and yet enriched design. This ambitious task makes cross-discursive borrowing absolutely indispensable. Fusionists routinely integrate Western academic methods into their normative writings on Islamic reform and likewise infuse Islamic principles and personal faith commitments into their academic research. Indeed, their most important intellectual work occurs at the levels of methodological experimentation and ethical critique. Because they seek to speak simultaneously to Muslim and academic audiences, fusionists transcend the discursive boundary between the Islamic and Western intellectual traditions. A history of fusionist thinking thus helps us see what Nur Amali Ibrahim so aptly calls "hybrid forms of religious practices" and "the hard creative labor that Muslims put in to cope with the continuing hegemony of the West."[19]

Fusionism is closely connected to Islamic modernism but is not synonymous with it. As a movement, Islamic modernism is substantially older. Beginning in the mid-nineteenth century, Muslim modernists set their sights on reimagining the Islamic tradition so that Muslims could better meet the demands of their rapidly changing societies. Modernist thinking rests on three pillars. First, modernists insist that Islam, in its pure form, is a rational and progressive religion. Accordingly, they see their work not as reforming Islam itself but rather as removing centuries' worth of rust to reveal Islam's original dynamism. Second, they stress the importance of the spirit—Islamic values and social ethics—rather than the letter of the law. This emphasis on principles enables flexibility on particular legal and social matters. Third, modernists criticize the practice of *taqlid*, or adhering to interpretative precedent within one's school of law, as little more than "blind obedience" to earlier Islamic scholars. Instead, they advocate *ijtihad*, or returning directly to the Qur'an and Sunnah to derive fresh, reason-based interpretations of these source texts. They see ijtihad as the key for preserving Islam's relevance and vitality in the modern world. Like their modernist forefathers, fusionists share these three commitments. However, they practice their own version of ijtihad that is grounded in Western academic methods and disciplinary frameworks. As this book demonstrates, not all modernists engage in or even accept such cross-discursive ijtihad.

By engaging in fusionist thinking, Muslim intellectuals have contributed new perspectives on two perennial tensions in the Islamic tradition. The first involves the relationship between reason and revelation. Fusionists, like their modernist predecessors, insist that Islam is a rational faith. They repeatedly argue that the Qur'an enjoins humans to exercise their capacity to reason and reflect on the world around them. Because they see reason as a revelatory imperative, fusionists eagerly embrace Western academic disciplines as modern manifestations of human rationality. They are especially drawn to academic methods that address a second major tension: how to balance Islamic claims to universal truth and the reality of relentless social change. As we will see, some employ historical research methods to trace the contextual manifestations of timeless Islamic principles, such as modesty and justice. Other fusionists study literary hermeneutics to consider new interpretative approaches to the Qur'an or explore anthropology to theorize about cultural diversity within Islam. Still others embrace political science and economics as crucial tools for translating Islam's universal principles into effective policies for the contemporary world. Despite these diverse disciplinary interests, fusionists use academic forms of knowledge to imagine an Islam that is both universal in nature and flexible enough to adapt to modern contexts.

In addition to their intellectual contributions, fusionists often wield social and political influence, thanks to their roles as mediators between Western institutions and Muslim communities.[20] They are able to speak both discursive languages and therefore translate between the two spheres. At the international level, fusionists apply for and win Fulbright scholarships and participate in similar exchange programs at American, Canadian, and European universities. They sometimes serve as official diplomats or unofficial representatives for Western development organizations such as the Ford Foundation. Taken together, these linkages constitute a transnational scholarly network that provides Muslim thinkers with access to significant financial and institutional resources. Fusionists also mediate between religious and more secular domestic constituencies in Muslim-majority countries. Their commitment to balancing Islamic universality and social change frequently opens access to high-level posts in developmentalist governments. In Pakistan, Oxford graduate and former McGill professor Fazlur Rahman ran the Islamic Research Institute and served as a close advisor to military modernizer Ayub Khan in the 1960s. In Indonesia, members of the so-called McGill mafia staffed General Suharto's religious bureaucracy for decades. Fusionists use this proximity to political power to craft Islamic policies on a range of important social issues.

Because of their new cross-discursive forms of knowledge and access to political power, fusionist thinkers pose a collective challenge to established models of religious authority that are, for the most part, based on claims to Islamic authenticity.[21] Authenticity, of course, is a constructed and highly contested concept. It purports to capture the essence of a desired identity in something that can be embodied or even owned by certain group members. Islamic authenticity typically involves a perceived continuity with the Islamic discursive tradition and especially with its foundational sources, the Qur'an and the Sunnah. While fusionists insist that their approaches to Islam recapture the rationality and dynamism of the Qur'an and the Prophet's life, they often encounter fierce resistance from fellow Muslims who castigate their cross-discursive scholarship as foreign in origin and hence inauthentic. These conflicts can sometimes claim national and even international headlines. After devoting the better part of the 1960s to advising Ayub Khan, Rahman faced mass protests and even threats to his personal safety because of his academic-style writings on Islamic reform. He was forced to resign as director of the Islamic Research Institute and leave Pakistan altogether, taking up a faculty appointment in the United States instead.[22] In the 1990s, Egyptian scholar Nasr Hamid Abu Zayd (1943–2010) gained international notoriety when Cairo University denied him promotion on grounds that his literary-inspired approach to the Qur'an was un-Islamic. Rather than let the university handle the matter, Islamists seized on the case. They denounced Abu Zayd as an apostate and eventually convinced a court to dissolve his marriage on the basis that he was no longer a Muslim. Abu Zayd and his wife subsequently fled Egypt and went into academic exile in the Netherlands.[23] These controversies underscore the extent to which fusionist thinkers disrupt prevailing intellectual norms and raise difficult questions about what constitutes authentic Islamic knowledge, who possesses it, and how exactly modern Muslims should respond to Western intellectual dominance. The recurring and heated debates over these questions have left an indelible imprint on the politics of Islamic education and Muslim religious authority.

INSIDERS AND OUTSIDERS IN WESTERN ACADEMIA

Fusionism has also fueled debates in Western academic corridors over the very purpose of the post-Enlightenment university. During the nineteenth century, Western universities began to disavow their medieval Christian roots in favor of a secularized, scientific self-image. Specialized research into "isolable problems that could yield answers" largely displaced earlier modes of "large-scale" metaphysical inquiry.[24] As a result, theology gradually lost its status as "queen of the sciences," and disciplinary divisions came to define academic life.[25] It was against this broader backdrop that the so-called insider–outsider problem emerged in the new disciplines of anthropology and religious studies. The insider–outsider problem refers to the complex relationship between adherents of a particular cultural or religious group ("insiders") and their scientific, scholarly observers ("outsiders"). It encompasses a series of interrelated epistemological questions. For starters, is it possible for scholarly outsiders to understand, let alone to analyze, a set of beliefs and practices that they do not share? If it is, then what are the most effective methods for studying the cultures and religions of others? Building on these crucial questions about epistemic access, the insider–outsider problem also compels scholars to weigh the relative authority of insider-versus-outsider modes of knowledge. Should insiders have the power to explain their own culture or religion, or do scholarly outsiders possess the necessary emotional distance from and hence objectivity with which to analyze and even critique?[26] While especially pertinent to anthropology and religious studies, these questions reflect larger intellectual and ethical anxieties about the post-Enlightenment university as a whole.

The insider–outsider problem has divided contemporary scholars of religion, especially the theorists among them, into two generally rival camps.

In one camp are scholars, such as Bruce Lincoln and Russell T. McCutcheon, who draw a sharp distinction between insider and outsider forms of knowledge.[27] They see theological insiders and religious-studies outsiders as "utterly different" because, in contrast to the former's interest in universal and transcendent truths, religious studies functions primarily as a historical discipline.[28] In Lincoln's words, scholars of religious studies should "insist on discussing the temporal, contextual, situated, interested, human, and material dimensions of those discourses, practices, communities, and institutions that characteristically represent themselves as eternal, transcendent, spiritual, and divine."[29] Proponents of this approach characterize theologians as data, not colleagues, and see themselves as "critics, not caretakers," of religious traditions.[30] They are, in many ways, dualists. In the other camp are scholars, such as Robert Orsi, who endow insider accounts with an authority that complements and even counterbalances outsider knowledge. They invite insider voices into the seminar room in an effort to enrich scholarly conversations and challenge academic assumptions. As Orsi writes, "[This] way of approaching religion . . . is meant to eliminate the comfort of academic distance and to undermine the confidence and authority of the claims 'we are not them' and 'they are not us.'"[31] This position stands in direct opposition to the dualist aspirations of the first camp.

The insider–outsider problem arrived comparatively late to Islamic studies, where it took on a particularly postcolonial hue.[32] This delay dovetails with the field's demographic history. Unlike their Jewish and Christian counterparts, who had deep roots in the Western academy, Muslim intellectuals had been direct and sometimes indirect subjects of European empires and therefore had few opportunities to pursue Western-style higher education and fewer chances still to secure faculty positions at European or North American universities. They remained a relative anomaly until the mid-twentieth century. These demographic patterns began to shift in the wake of decolonization. Starting in the 1950s, newly independent Muslim governments in Iran, Pakistan, Indonesia, and elsewhere helped to finance Muslim scholars who aspired to Western graduate study. At the same time, Palestinian exiles and Muslim dissidents from various repressive regimes looked to Western higher education as a way to remake their lives and achieve some degree of stability. Not all these Muslims became fusionists, but their growing presence in Western universities forced the academy to confront difficult questions about the state of Islamic studies as a field. Inevitably, these questions were never only about personal religious commitments; they were always intertwined with colonial and postcolonial power dynamics.[33]

Debates over the insider–outsider problem in Islamic studies have coalesced around two specific moments. The first began in the late 1970s with the publication of *Orientalism* (1978). In his landmark book, Edward Said criticized the Western academic study of Islam as an imperialist discourse reliant on racialized tropes about Muslims' inferiority and their irredeemable otherness.[34] By exposing European and American scholars as custodians of a racist and colonizing discipline, Said helped usher in the age of postcolonial theory. However, he denied any ambition to elevate Muslim (or Arab) insiders over scholarly outsiders, writing, "It is not the thesis of this book to suggest that there is such a thing as a real or true Orient (Islam, Arab, or whatever); nor is it to make an assertion about the necessary privilege of an 'insider' perspective over an 'outsider' one."[35] Despite this clear declaration of intent, some of Said's harshest critics read his argument as a straightforward pro-insider polemic. Bernard Lewis, for example, caricatured Said's critique as akin to suggesting that only Greeks should study classics. He dismissed the position as both "absurd" and "alarming."[36] Other scholars took a more nuanced perspective on the simmering insider–outsider tensions. In the early 1980s, Richard C. Martin invited colleagues to consider what the growing numbers of "Muslims in the classroom on both sides of the lectern" might mean for the field's future.[37] He solicited essays from both Muslim and non-Muslim scholars for his book *Approaches to Islam in Religious Studies* (1985). Although the exchanges were often acrimonious, Said's book compelled a postcolonial reckoning with disciplinary methods and values in Islamic studies.

The second moment unfolded in the wake of the 9/11 attacks. The surging public interest in and fear of Islam conferred a new political salience on the field in the early 2000s. Academic scholars of Islam appeared on cable-news shows and wrote popular-press primers on the Qur'an, Muhammad, and the contemporary Middle East. In this charged political climate, Aaron W. Hughes devoted substantial energy to "provoking" renewed debate over the insider–outsider problem in Islamic studies.[38] Hughes's multiple essays and books argue that, in an effort to defend Islam against malicious attacks, too many academics resort to essentialist apologetics that paint Islam as an inherently peaceful and pluralist religion. Building on Lincoln and McCutcheon's work, he dismisses this brand of scholarship as deeply theological in nature and hence beyond the proper academic scope of religious studies. Hughes reserves his harshest criticisms for Muslim intellectuals who practice what I call fusionism and what he calls "liberal Muslim theologizing."[39] Unsurprisingly, more than a few scholars have challenged Hughes's negative assessment of the field.[40] Because this book's conclusion addresses Hughes and his allies in greater depth, it will suffice here to state that the insider–outsider problem possesses a particular resonance in our post-9/11 era.

Rather than jump headlong into these debates, this book has a different set of aspirations. I trace the history of insider–outsider politics in Islamic studies as a window into the field's discursive norms and authority structures. At the center of this history is, undoubtedly, the ideal of objectivity. Interestingly, academic claims to objectivity generally run parallel to Muslim claims to authenticity. Objectivity, too, is a constructed and highly contested concept. It purports to demarcate scientific, universal knowledge from its subjective, culturally specific imitations. Consequently, the concept of objectivity functions as a potent source of academic authority. Academic scholars frequently make explicit and implicit claims to objectivity in order to garner greater legitimacy and respect within the Western academy. They—or, to break from the objective, third-person posture for a moment, "we"—also criticize scholarly opponents as insufficiently objective, thereby casting them as less-authoritative members of the university community. Fusionists have been lightning rods for objectivity-related conflicts. Critics question the legitimacy of their commensurability work and suggest instead that Islamic religious commitments render fusionists questionable academics at best and beyond the pale of the academy at worst. These conflicts help reveal the often hidden processes behind who gets to count as an "academic" and who does not in Islamic studies. They also hint at submerged and yet substantive alternatives for how to navigate insider–outsider politics in the field.

This book also shines a light on the extent to which so-called academic "outsiders" have become entangled, whether wittingly or unwittingly, in "insider" projects of Islamic reform. As Said demonstrated, Western academics have long possessed cultural, religious, and political presuppositions about Islam that translated into essentialist and disparaging scholarship on Muslim societies. Yet Wael Hallaq argues that Said's focus on Orientalism's representational injustices has led many to overlook the "performative" power—that is, "the remolding, refashioning, and, in short, re-creation of [Muslim] subjectivities"—associated with the Western academic study of Islam.[41] As we will see, Orientalists and their social-scientific counterparts have shaped modern Islamic thought in myriad ways. Countless academic publications have been read, translated, and selectively appropriated by Muslim intellectuals who engage with these works as part of their own religio-political agendas. Prominent professors, such as H.A.R. Gibb, took these interconnections a step further and actively cultivated relationships with Muslim activists, sometimes writing across thousands of miles to offer words of encouragement and advice for reformist endeavors. Some, such as Wilfred Cantwell Smith and Leonard Binder, recruited promising Muslim intellectuals to study Islam at Western universities and then served as their teachers and mentors, and others regularly consulted on Islam-related policies for Western governments and development organizations. Ultimately, Western academics have rarely, if ever, been neutral observers of modern Islamic thought; they are instead active participants in American foreign policy *and* in Muslim movements to reform Islam. These activities blur the distinction between academic "outsiders" and Muslim "insiders" to the point of nearly erasing it altogether.

THE GEOPOLITICS OF FUSIONISM

While fusionist thinking destabilizes discursive norms in both the Islamic and Western academic traditions, its story cannot be confined to intellectual history alone. On the contrary, the history of fusionism intersects at multiple points with colonial and postcolonial geopolitics. It was, after all, the experience of Dutch colonialism that precipitated the dualist crisis at the turn of the twentieth century, and it was amid the Indonesian nationalist movement that Muslim intellectuals began to dismantle dualist structures and thinking. This relationship between ideas and political context is notoriously difficult to define. In recent years, some scholars have stressed the (near) hegemony of Western liberalism and its wide-ranging power to remake Muslim societies according to its own categories and metrics.[42] Others recognize these global power dynamics but emphasize the creative agency and intellectual flexibility Muslims exhibit in navigating our complex world.[43] This book seeks to balance the two positions. On the one hand, I trace how Cold War politics shaped Western academic frameworks and dictated the material resources available to Muslim and non-Muslim scholars alike. I also examine how Indonesian politics empowered some Muslim intellectuals and closed the door on others. Power dynamics certainly circumscribe possibilities. On the other hand, fusionists often respond to global politics and institutional dynamics in unexpected ways. They frequently appropriate academic methods and arguments for projects that would make their Western colleagues rather uncomfortable. Some study and teach at Western universities only later to speak out against their experiences and lead Muslim resistance to Western academic encroachment. As a result, I argue that this brand of soft power is more diffuse and unpredictable than both its policy advocates and scholarly critics often care to admit. It is perhaps for these very reasons that soft power has had such a pervasive and enduring impact on Indonesian Islam.

In the second half of the twentieth century, fusionist thinking became especially intertwined with Cold War development politics.[44] Modernizing military regimes in Egypt, Turkey, Pakistan, Indonesia, and elsewhere staked their political legitimacy on calls for Western-style development. They pursued economic policies designed to increase agricultural production and strengthen the urban middle class and pushed social programs such as increased access to education and family planning. Many fusionists were attracted to this rationalist and pragmatic model of governance. They also possessed a similarly friendly disposition toward the West. The resulting fusionist alliances with modernizing military regimes bolstered their authority as religious bureaucrats and favored public intellectuals. Fusionists used their positions of influence to spread their thinking and push for reforms to Islamic educational, legal, and social policies. In Indonesia, Suharto's New Order state often implemented fusionist ideas that balanced Islam and development. Yet this pro-development posture also had negative repercussions for fusionist thinkers. Traditionalist and especially Islamist opponents criticized fusionists' penchant for authoritarian allies and their willingness to compromise Islamic values for the sake of some Western-inspired definition of development. Oftentimes fusionists were derided as sellouts. These attacks highlight that political power in Muslim-majority countries did not always—or usually—translate into robust claims to Islamic authenticity or religious authority.

Cold War development politics also helped to open space for fusionist thinking on the Western academic side of the border. Beginning in the 1950s, Western governments recruited academics to help fight the Cold War in Muslim societies. They encouraged research on modern Muslim politics, in particular, because it could be used to inform the policy-making process. The political attention produced a boom in Islamic studies. A handful of scholars—such as Wilfred Cantwell Smith at McGill University—used this opportunity to build relationships with Muslim reformers and to nurture the first generation of fusionist thinkers. By the mid-1960s, social scientists began to insert modernization theory into the conversation. As the dominant social-scientific paradigm of the period, modernization theory rested on a Western liberal foundation that encouraged scholars to evaluate other cultures on the basis of their similarity to or difference from postwar America. Many social scientists working on the Middle East concluded that Islam, in all its perceived difference, was an obstacle impeding modernization. They came to believe that Islam required its own Protestant-style reformation. As a result, social scientists started to speak openly about Qur'anic hermeneutics and other topics related to Islamic religious reform. In these ways, the Cold War–era development discourse both spurred Muslim intellectual interest in Western academic disciplines and encouraged Western academic engagement with Islamic reform.

If the development discourse fueled the entanglement of Western universities and modern Islamic thought in the twentieth century, then international aid organizations acted as a collective accelerant. Private philanthropic foundations such as Rockefeller and Ford donated millions of dollars to both academic programs in Islamic studies and major development initiatives in Muslim-majority countries.[45] They funded research-related travel for individual Western academics, financed graduate study at Western universities for promising Muslim scholars, and issued grants to emerging fusionist centers, such as the Islamic Research Institute in Pakistan and the Ministry of Religious Affairs in Indonesia. These private foundations also worked closely with governmental agencies such as the United States Agency for International Development (USAID) and the Canadian International Development Agency (CIDA) to build a pro-development cohort of Western-educated Muslims. Given their financial resources and political influence, these aid organizations acted as powerful mediators that were able to forge connections between Western academics and Muslim intellectuals in Indonesia and beyond.

Western fears about Islamism added a new dimension to Cold War development politics. In 1979, the Iranian Revolution and the resulting hostage crisis persuaded many Americans that Islam could be nearly as dangerous as communism. The assassination of Anwar Sadat by radical Islamists in 1981 only seemed to confirm these fears. While expedient foreign-policy exceptions were made for the Afghan mujahedeen, the Pakistani regime of Muhammad Zia ul-Haq, and the Saudi royal family, the cultural tide was shifting.[46]

The perceived Islamist threat garnered increasing attention from Western governments, aid organizations, and academic scholars. Together, they conducted research on the relationship among Islam, development, and democracy and worked to empower newly designated "moderate" Muslims through exchange programs and targeted development assistance. The 9/11 attacks and the subsequent war on terror intensified these collaborations among American foreign-policy makers, development organizations, Western universities, and fusionist Muslim intellectuals in significant ways. As Saba Mahmood astutely observes, "The United States . . . embarked upon an ambitious theological campaign aimed at shaping the sensibilities of ordinary Muslims whom the State Department deems to be too dangerously inclined toward fundamentalist interpretations of Islam."[47] This political climate made fusionist thinkers into a favored tool of American soft power yet again. However, I suggest that it is too early to write this unfolding twenty-first-century history. Archives in Indonesia, the United States, and Canada are generally closed for the post-9/11 era. Moreover, scholars' careers are still evolving and hence on the line. Instead of wading into these waters without sufficient archival evidence, this book focuses on the twentieth-century roots of what Mahmood terms "the politics of Islamic reformation." After all, the border between Western academia and modern Islamic thought was already collapsing well before 9/11.

THE ROAD AHEAD

To understand the history of any border necessitates investigating both sides of the line. Accordingly, the following chapters weave together into one unified history the seemingly disparate tales of traveling Indonesian Muslims, the Western universities that hosted them, and the state ministries where they worked. To begin, chapter 1 locates Indonesian Muslims as part of a global movement to bridge the gulf between the Islamic and Western intellectual traditions. As the Indonesian Revolution gathered momentum in the 1940s, Muslims of diverse persuasions banded together to establish the Islamic College (later known as the State Islamic Institute [IAIN]) as an institution that would reject dualism and instead equip Muslim students with both Islamic and Western academic forms of knowledge. The vision struck a chord with Indonesian Muslims, and the Islamic College quickly expanded into a nationwide network. Despite these outward signs of success, the original consensus to combat dualism was superficial. Cracks soon began to appear in the governing coalition. This chapter focuses on two particularly prominent Indonesian Islamic thinkers, Mahmud Yunus and Mohammad Natsir, who played critical roles in designing and then running IAIN. I investigate the ways the two scholar-activists cited, criticized, and appropriated Western scholarship in their efforts to construct a distinctly modern form of Islamic thought. Both Yunus and Natsir were committed to overcoming dualism, but they offered two different and perhaps irreconcilable visions for how to accomplish that goal. Compounding these intellectual disagreements were the severe resource shortages and rising intra-Muslim partisanship across the IAIN system in the 1960s. While the mission to integrate Western and Islamic modes of knowledge managed to survive these challenges, the fissures were harbingers of larger conflicts to come.

Shifting to the distinctly different space of the North American academy, chapter 2 tells the story of several Indonesian Muslims who traveled to McGill University's Institute of Islamic Studies to study and teach Islam. Wilfred Cantwell Smith founded the institute in 1951 to facilitate sustained encounters between Western academics and Muslim intellectuals. He hoped that researching and learning together would encourage McGill's diverse scholars to engage in deep interreligious dialogue and to experiment with new research methods for the sake of greater cross-discursive understanding. Smith believed that this fusionist model would revolutionize both Western academic and Muslim approaches to Islam. Several prominent Muslim scholars, including Fazlur Rahman, of Pakistan, and Mukti Ali and Harun Nasution, both of Indonesia, took advantage of McGill's unique intellectual environment to conduct their own fusionist experiments. This commensurability work proved to be exceedingly difficult. In addition to the substantial challenges involved with integrating two intellectual traditions, established Western scholars used the ideal of objectivity as a means to exclude Muslim fusionists from the academic guild. As a result of these objectivity politics, McGill's brand of fusionism gained little traction in Islamic studies, but its model for cross-discursive research did leave a lasting imprint on the many Muslims who passed through the gates of the Montreal campus.

Chapter 3, in turn, follows three influential McGill alumni—Ali, Nasution, and Mohamad Rasjidi—back to Indonesia and examines their efforts in the 1970s to reimagine Muslim politics and reform higher Islamic education. At the start of the decade, Ali and Nasution forged mutually beneficial partnerships with Suharto's developmentalist state and subsequently received appointments as minister of religious affairs and rector of IAIN Jakarta, respectively. They used these powerful positions to spread fusionist thinking. At the ministry, Ali created new opportunities to train Muslims in Western academic methods and forged a transnational scholarly network that connected Indonesian Muslims to Western universities. At IAIN Jakarta, Nasution redesigned the undergraduate curriculum to include more Western-style disciplines and wrote popular fusionist textbooks. Ali's and Nasution's high-profile work attracted resistance from fellow Muslims. Drawing on his own bitter experiences at McGill, Rasjidi emerged as a particularly outspoken opponent of fusionism. He publicly criticized Nasution for adopting Western academic frameworks that, in his eyes, misrepresented Islam to impressionable Muslim college students. He assailed Western academic credentials as inauthentic and as a neoimperial threat to Islam. Despite this vocal opposition, Western-educated Muslims were able to institutionalize their fusionist visions, thanks to the support of Suharto and Western developmentalist allies.

Chapter 4 chronicles the experiences of a second generation of Indonesian scholars who studied Islam at the University of Chicago in the 1970s and 1980s under professors Leonard Binder and Fazlur Rahman. At first glance, Binder and Rahman seem like an odd pair. Binder, a political scientist, was an avid proponent of modernization theory, whereas Rahman was a historian of the Islamic tradition and a prominent Islamic activist in Pakistan. Nevertheless, they collaborated for nearly a decade on a major Ford Foundation–sponsored project titled "Islam and Social Change." The multicountry project combined the social sciences and modern Islamic thought in order to create what Binder and Rahman saw as an authentic Islamic model of development. It also opened up a surprising space for Muslim theological reflection and fusionist research at Chicago. Indonesian graduate students Amien Rais, Nurcholish Madjid, and Ahmad Syafii Maarif capitalized on this space to reconsider the relationship between Islam and development and apply their new ideas to the evolving political landscape back in Indonesia. Together, Chicago faculty members and students demonstrated how porous the purported wall between "normative" Islamic thought and "empirical" social-scientific research and between Muslim "insiders" and academic "outsiders" actually was.

After returning to Indonesia in the early 1980s, the three Chicago alumni quickly ascended the ranks of Indonesian Islamic leadership. Rais and Maarif were elected as consecutive national chairmen of Muhammadiyah, and

Madjid's work as a Muslim public intellectual made his into a household name across the country. Chapter 5 traces their meteoric careers to show that Western-educated Muslims wielded unprecedented authority in the 1990s, but they also faced mounting anti-fusionist criticisms. Muslim opponents, following Rasjidi's example, castigated fusionist thinking as overly Westernized and hence inauthentic, and postcolonial theorists within Western universities attacked the academy as mired in Western cultural presuppositions and imperialist politics. Indonesian fusionists responded to these concerns about epistemological imperialism with new philosophies of cross-discursive engagement. I analyze Rais, Madjid, and Muhammadiyah activist Amin Abdullah's writings to highlight the depth and diversity of these fusionist responses. Still, they were not able to persuade everyone. Many Islamist opponents doubled down on criticisms that Western academics were not neutral scholars but rather situated actors whose ties to Western governments and development agencies rendered them little more than agents of American soft power. While Western-educated Muslims were able to survive and even thrive amid this rising wave of suspicions, the specter of academic imperialism continued to haunt the fusionist project at the turn of the twenty-first century.

Taking a step back from the historical narrative, the book's conclusion reflects on the present and future of Islamic studies as a field. Given the entanglement between Western universities and modern Islamic thought, how should we conceptualize the purpose of academic scholarship on Islam? What are the ethics of conducting research in such an intertwined world? In search of potential answers, I draw from religious studies and postcolonial theory to first identify three possible responses and then evaluate their relative strengths and limitations in the hope that, collectively, they might help us navigate our increasingly integrated and yet bitterly divided world.

1 BUILDING A MODERN ISLAMIC COLLEGE

ON APRIL 10, 1946, Vice President Mohammad Hatta delivered the inaugural address at the Islamic College (Sekolah Tinggi Islam) in Yogyakarta, Java.[1] In an effort to delineate the "nature of an Islamic college," Hatta compared and contrasted the two modes of education available to Indonesian Muslims: Islamic and Dutch. For all but a handful of Muslim youth, Islamic education began at a local mosque school (*langgar* or *surau*), where they first learned to recite the Qur'an and studied the basic teachings of Islam. Hatta praised these mosque schools for "planting the feelings of religiosity" into the hearts and souls of young students and thus establishing a foundation for faith-filled lives.[2] However, Hatta also criticized Islamic schools because their focus on recitation and memorization neither prepared students to become great religious scholars nor instructed students in the practical knowledge necessary for their daily lives. As a result of these twin failures, Hatta noted that many parents, even in the 1940s, were choosing to send their children to secular schools for better career training. Hatta also had words of criticism for Dutch-style secular education. He lamented that secular schools valorized cleverness over faith. If they taught religion at all, it was in a perfunctory manner that did not ingrain Islamic values in Muslim youth. He concluded:

> The reality is that neither of these paths of religious education is satisfactory. The langgar is imperfect; the secular elementary and middle schools are insufficient. Education must be made whole, perfected at the Islamic College. The

Islamic College can deepen [religious] feelings as well as deepen knowledge and broaden perspectives.³

Hatta elaborated that students at the Islamic College must learn philosophy, history, and sociology alongside Islamic disciplines in order to better understand modern society and become more well-rounded leaders. He envisioned the Islamic College as a place where religious and Western knowledge would meet "in a cooperative environment for the benefit of a prosperous society."⁴

In addressing the fraught relationship between modern Western and Islamic education, Hatta spoke from personal experience. Born in 1902, Hatta was raised in a pious Muslim family in West Sumatra. His paternal grandfather was a well-known member of the local ʿulama (religious scholars), and as a young boy, Hatta studied the Qurʾan and other subjects with local Islamic scholars. Yet, for his formal education, he attended a Dutch-medium and predominantly European primary school in Padang. Although the family briefly considered sending the boy to Mecca and grooming him to take over the family surau, Hatta eventually settled on an educational trajectory that was decidedly Dutch. In 1921, the nineteen-year-old Hatta departed for the Netherlands, where he spent the next eleven years studying modern economics in Rotterdam and spearheading the influential Indonesian Association (Perhimpunan Indonesia). Throughout his years in the Netherlands, Hatta continued to live a modest and observant Muslim life, but his intellectual and political worlds were entirely Western and secular.⁵ In the face of this polarizing milieu, Hatta had to forge his own balance between his Islamic faith and his Western education. In this sense, Hatta shared much with other Muslim activists and political figures of his era. Whether emerging from Islamic educational backgrounds or reared within the world of Dutch learning, Hatta's generation of Muslim revolutionaries cobbled together pieces of disparate intellectual traditions in order to build their political and religious worldviews. Their paths were unplanned and eclectic, but they had a common goal: building a modern Indonesia on the basis of both Islamic and Western learning.

With his speech, Hatta expressed a conviction widespread among modern Muslims that intellectual dualism, or the bifurcation of knowledge into separate Islamic and Western systems, represented a dangerous dead end. Indeed, the mid-nineteenth century saw numerous South Asian and Middle Eastern reformers criticize Islamic education as isolated and stagnant. They worried that Muslim students had little exposure to modern scientific and humanistic disciplines, which rendered them incapable of responding to—let alone thriving in—their rapidly modernizing societies. Consequently, they insisted that Muslim students must also master modern Western-style subjects. In north India, Sayyid Ahmad Khan (1817–98) took a major step toward challenging dualism when he established the Muhammadan Anglo-Oriental College in Aligarh in 1875. Modeled after Cambridge University, the college provided instruction in the modern sciences, European humanism, and the Islamic religious tradition in hope of cultivating young Muslims capable of flourishing in both British colonial society and their own Muslim communities. Aligarh represented an important, albeit controversial, early experiment in mixed-curriculum education.[6] Egypt soon emerged as a second center in the struggle against dualism. Often heralded as the founding father of Islamic modernism, Muhammad Abduh (1849–1905) taught works by European scholars, such as François Guizot, and championed reason as central to Islamic thought. He also spearheaded an ill-fated movement to reform al-Azhar, the nine-hundred-year-old seat of Sunni learning, in the 1890s.[7] While Khan and Abduh both encountered opposition from Muslim contemporaries, the next generation of Muslim scholars largely embraced their aim of integrating Islamic and modern Western education. Muhammad Qasim Zaman concludes that "there clearly is a broad and growing agreement within the ranks of the leading ʿulama as well as between the ʿulama and other religious intellectuals that bridging the gulf between different intellectual traditions is desirable and, indeed, a matter of great urgency."[8] With the exceptions of the Taliban and a few other holdouts, twentieth-century Muslims have agreed that intellectual dualism constitutes a major problem that must be overcome.

Focusing on the establishment and early history of the Islamic College, this chapter positions Muslims from the Indonesian archipelago as significant voices in the global agreement to combat intellectual dualism. It was a remarkably broad and yet shallow consensus. To begin, the first part chronicles how Indonesian Muslims from across the ideological spectrum came to see their polarized educational landscape as a serious social ailment. These Muslims forged a broad-based coalition in the 1940s to address this common concern and eventually built the Islamic College for the emergent Indonesian nation. Shifting from macrolevel politics to microlevel intellectual biographies, the second part examines the writings of two prominent Islamic College leaders, Mahmud Yunus and Mohammad Natsir. Yunus and Natsir were both dedicated to the struggle against dualism, but they developed competing and perhaps irreconcilable visions for how to merge the two traditions. These intellectual differences—as well as lingering dualist logics—signaled the fragile nature of the anti-dualist consensus. The third part argues that the campaign against dualism also encountered serious structural hurdles, including fierce intra-Muslim partisanship and chronic, self-perpetuating resource shortages, throughout the 1950s and 1960s. Ultimately, the early decades at the Islamic College represented a period not only of high reformist and nationalist hopes but also of great frustrations.

THREE STREAMS, ONE ISLAMIC COLLEGE

The Dutch East Indies, or what would soon become Indonesia, was home to a strikingly diverse range of intellectual traditions in the early twentieth century. Regional cultures with rich literary, customary, and linguistic practices continued to flourish in Java, Madura, Bali, West Sumatra, Aceh, and many other provinces. These traditions interacted with and influenced one another as they had for centuries, but they had also begun contributing to a nascent nationalist culture based in the lingua franca of the archipelago, Malay/Indonesian. The Dutch carried European religious, philosophical, and scientific ideas with them to their prized colony, and influential Arab and Chinese communities added their expansive intellectual traditions to the mix, especially in port cities and other trading centers. Raised in this imperial cosmopolitan environment, Indonesian Muslims emerged as active participants in the global struggle against dualism. Three streams (*aliran*) were particularly drawn to debates over dualism: Arab-educated modernists, Dutch-educated elites, and a small contingent of modernizing traditionalists. Although they possessed different educational backgrounds and social commitments, these three groups reached a broad consensus in the 1930s–40s that established models of Islamic education were inadequate for modern Muslims because they failed to merge the Islamic and modern Western traditions.

Muslims from the Indonesian archipelago had long traveled to Arab lands for hajj, but the second half of the nineteenth century saw a substantial increase in pilgrimage traffic across the Indian Ocean, thanks, in large part, to the invention of the steamship.[9] The majority of these newly mobile Muslims spent only a few months in the Hijaz and remained reliant on pilgrim guides to see the holy sites and perform the religious rites. Yet the steamships also carried a significant number of Muslim students who were seeking longer-term higher Islamic education in Mecca. These scholarly communities served as crucial incubators for Islamic modernism in Indonesia.[10] Muslim students from the archipelago turned to two Arab-based scholars in particular for inspiration: the Sumatran-born Ahmad Khatib al-Minankabawi (1860–1915), who had resettled in Mecca as an Ottoman-licensed imam and preacher, and the famed Egyptian reformer Muhammad Abduh. The students adopted two interrelated principles from Khatib and Abduh. First, following Khatib's attacks on Sumatran customs such as Minangkabau matrilineal inheritance, Arab-educated modernists sought to cleanse popular Islamic practices of what they saw as unlawful innovations.[11] They invested much energy in criticizing local customs and Sufi teachings as irrational and un-Islamic. Second, inspired by Abduh, they rejected *taqlid*, or adherence to interpretative precedent especially within one's school of law, as little more than a blind and unthinking obedience to past Islamic authorities. Instead, they insisted upon their right to practice *ijtihad*—that is, to return directly to the Qur'an and hadith in order to develop fresh, reason-based interpretations of the Islamic source texts. They pointed to Abduh's legal rulings on banking interest and the consumption of meat prepared by Christians as examples of ijtihad that bravely broke with juristic precedent.[12] Early Indonesian modernists hoped to use these two principles to revitalize Islam in their communities.

At the turn of the twentieth century, Arab-educated modernists began to establish organizations and attract substantial followings in the Indonesian archipelago. Ahmad Dahlan (1868–1923) spearheaded the modernist movement in Java. Born into a family of Islamic scholars, Dahlan received a traditional Islamic education in Yogyakarta and on two separate occasions—first in 1890 and then in 1903—traveled to Mecca to perform hajj and deepen his knowledge of traditional Islamic disciplines. During his years as a student, Dahlan studied under Khatib and read Abduh's writings with great interest. He came to champion a pure and revitalized Islam that was not held hostage to unthinking local traditions. Translating this vision into concrete reforms, Dahlan advocated first to change the *qibla* (direction of prayer) in the Sultan's Mosque in Yogyakarta and then to alter the traditional Javanese date for Eid al-Fitr so that it aligned with more accurate astronomical measures.[13] Dahlan drew on his growing reputation as an outspoken reformer to establish Muhammadiyah in 1912. In its early years, Muhammadiyah sponsored public religious gatherings and engaged in social-welfare work, especially in the educational sphere. It would eventually become the largest Muslim modernist organization in Indonesia.

During the same period, a loose network of Arab-educated modernists often referred to as the Kaum Muda, or the Young Faction, emerged in West Sumatra. They, too, had deep connections to Khatib and Abduh, with many members studying under the former and admiring the works of the latter. The most prominent Kaum Muda scholar was Shaikh H. A. Karim Amrullah (1879–1945), popularly known as Hadji Rasul. Hadji Rasul spent more than seven years living and studying with Khatib in Mecca before returning to West Sumatra and becoming a teacher at a well-known reformist madrasa in Padang Panjang. He soon emerged as a force for Islamic renewal in the region. With Hadji Rasul at the helm, the Kaum Muda criticized Minangkabau customs and local Sufi orders as heterodox and attacked traditionalist ʿulama for their reliance on taqlid.[14] In the late 1920s, Hadji Rasul joined Muhammadiyah, cementing an organizational link between the Islamic modernist movements in Central Java and West Sumatra.

Like most Muslim modernists of the era, Muhammadiyah and Kaum Muda activists viewed intellectual dualism as dangerous and called for the reform of Islamic schools. In Java and West Sumatra respectively, Dahlan and Hadji Rasul pioneered the use of grade-based class structures, standardized textbooks, desks, blackboards, and end-of-the-year examinations. They overturned the traditional model of private-school leadership by the ʿulama in favor of governance boards composed of alumni, parents, and donors and instruction by respected but not revered teachers.[15] Most importantly, they adopted the mixed-curriculum model in hope of bridging the gap between the Islamic and Western intellectual traditions. Muhammadiyah began with a small number of elementary schools in the early 1910s but expanded rapidly to include more advanced madrasas and even its own versions of Dutch elementary and high schools. By 1923, it ran 32 schools. That number skyrocketed to more than 1,500 by 1957.[16] These Muhammadiyah schools taught general subjects, such as sciences, mathematics, and European languages, alongside Islamic disciplines. Yet Muhammadiyah modernists not only integrated Western and Islamic subjects in their own schools but also petitioned the Dutch colonial state to incorporate Islamic instruction into its educational system. They even provided teachers for willing schools.[17] In West Sumatra, the Kaum Muda were not far behind. They had introduced so-called practical and secular subjects, such as agriculture, carpentry, geography, and world history, into their curricula and adopted new streamlined textbooks and modern pedagogical methods by the late 1920s.[18]

Building on Dahlan and Hadji Rasul's pioneering efforts to combat dualism, many aspiring Muslim scholars in the next generation traveled to Egypt in search of a modernist-style education. They were drawn to Cairo because of its reputation as a more modern, politically active, and vibrant city than early twentieth-century Mecca. Consequently, the population of Indonesian students in Cairo exploded from merely a few dozen to approximately two hundred by the early 1920s.[19] The majority of these students studied at al-Azhar, which had recently undergone important changes to make it more accessible to foreign students.[20] A handful also enrolled at the nearby teacher-training college, Dar al-Ulum. Established in 1872, Dar al-Ulum offered an "educational middle way . . . between the traditional and European-type systems."[21] Its students, many of whom were graduates of al-Azhar, took advanced courses in Islamic disciplines as well as introductory classes on modern Western subjects, such as mathematics, history, geography, and the natural sciences. Whether at al-Azhar or Dar al-Ulum, the experience of studying in Cairo exposed Indonesian Muslims to the often intertwined nationalist and modernist movements sweeping the Islamic world. As they protested in front of the Dutch consulate and wrote impassioned essays in their newsletters, the Cairo students articulated increasingly robust visions for a modern Islamic Indonesia.

Cairo's modernist currents also inspired Indonesian students to enlist in the struggle against dualism. Among the most influential educational activists in Cairo was Mahmud Yunus (1899–1982). Born into a family of religious teachers in West Sumatra, Yunus studied with Kaum Muda leaders in his youth and imbibed the movement's commitment to mixed-curriculum education. After working as a teacher for several years, Yunus decided to embark for the Middle East in the mid-1920s to continue his studies. He obtained his *alimiyyah* certificate from al-Azhar and then enrolled in the Department of Arabic at Dar al-Ulum. Yunus used his time there to think deeply and write prolifically about educational reform. He published several textbooks on Arabic-language learning, Qur'anic exegesis (*tafsir*), and Islamic jurisprudence (*fiqh*) in hope of systematizing Islamic education for younger students. He also produced scientific texts in Malay and Arabic, insisting that "it is then obligatory for us to provide our children with the foundations of sciences . . . so that our offspring can expand and develop [the sciences] as high as possible."[22] In 1930, Yunus became the first Indonesian to graduate from Dar al-Ulum.[23]

The return of Mahmud Yunus and other Cairo students to the archipelago in the early 1930s ushered in a second wave of Islamic education reform, albeit this time centered at the collegiate level. Yunus served as head of the Islamic Normal School in Padang, where the curriculum consisted of Arabic-language instruction (20 percent); secular subjects, such as mathematics, geography, history, and English (65 percent); and traditional Islamic disciplines (15 percent). Two other Cairo alumni, Muchtar Lufti and Iljas Ya'kub, opened their own Islamic college, known as Al-Kulijat ul Islamiyah, in 1931 as an institution to train both Islamic teachers and political leaders. They collaborated with Western-educated professionals and traders to finance the school and design its mixed religious and secular curriculum. These two colleges developed alongside a collection of Muhammadiyah institutes of higher education. By 1940, the number of Islamic colleges in West Sumatra alone exceeded a dozen, precipitating calls to consolidate efforts into one unified institution for higher Islamic education.[24]

Arab-educated modernists were soon joined by a second group committed to overcoming intellectual dualism: Dutch-educated Muslims. Although a trickle of elite Javanese had enrolled in medical and teacher-training colleges in the late nineteenth century, the Dutch colonial state only really began to open its education system to native Indonesians in 1901. That year, Queen Wilhelmina declared that the Dutch possessed an "ethical obligation and moral responsibility to the people of the East Indies."[25] This speech signaled an official embrace of what became known as the Ethical Policy, or a new Dutch focus on Europeanizing Indonesian society in the name of colonial benevolence. Spreading Dutch education among the native population became a major colonial priority. The first targets for reform were institutes of higher education, such as the STOVIA medical school and other professional schools for engineering, veterinary science, and law.[26] Then, in 1914, the first Dutch Native School (Hollandsch Inlandsche School) opened so that Indonesian children could receive a European-style primary education over the course of seven years. By 1930, there were over thirty-seven thousand students receiving a full Dutch primary education, which served as the gateway for Dutch secondary and tertiary schools.[27]

The rise of the Dutch education system introduced a new set of cultural and epistemological loyalties into elite Indonesian society. After early struggles with the language barrier, many Western-educated students gained a fluency in and even preference for the Dutch language. They adopted European-style dress and tastes for leisure activities. Beyond these cosmetic changes, many Dutch-educated Indonesians began to embrace modern European ideas regarding education, scientific advancement, and social progress. This growing hunger for Western-style modernity produced a wave of social changes across the archipelago. Dutch-educated youth rose up in protest against traditional hierarchies and especially Javanese aristocratic practices.[28] Some even turned their reformist zeal on the Islamic tradition. For example, in 1918 a Javanese newspaper published an article that denigrated the Prophet Muhammad, which sparked a series of counter-rallies and protests in defense of Islam.[29] Robert van Niel argues that this new generation of Indonesians suffered from "the tremendous psychological and spiritual problems which followed as an aftermath from education that was tuned to a non-Indonesian way of life."[30] In other words, the dualist system produced both social and personal crises.

Whereas many Dutch-educated Muslims adopted secular outlooks, others resisted their schooling-induced religious alienation by searching for paths back to the Islamic tradition. European Orientalists played unlikely roles in this process. Dutch scholar and colonial advisor Snouck Hurgronje (1857–1936) argued that if Europeans desired more moderate Muslims, they should invest resources to help them "reconcile the new ideas which they want with the old ones with which they cannot dispense."[31] Accordingly, Hurgronje mentored several Muslim students, including the brothers Achmad (1877–1943) and Hussein Djajadiningrat (1886–1960), the latter of whom earned a doctorate under his supervision at Leiden.[32] One of Hurgronje's most famous protégés was Agus Salim (1884–1954). Salim, the son of a West Sumatran aristocrat, spent his youth studying in Dutch-medium schools. After topping the Indies-wide high school graduation examination, he hoped to study medicine in the Netherlands, but those plans failed to materialize. Hurgronje stepped in to help the young Salim secure a consular posting in Jeddah instead. There, Salim forged ties with Arab-educated modernists. He made frequent trips to Mecca to study classical Islamic disciplines with his distant cousin Ahmad Khatib, who, in turn, encouraged him to read reformist writings by Muhammad Abduh.[33] Salim was impressed by the twin modernist emphases on human reason and ijtihad. Having reconnected with his Islamic heritage, he became a leading advocate for anti-dualist education.

Seeking to bridge Islamic and Western learning, Salim helped establish the Young Islamic Union (Jong Islamieten Bond [JIB]) in 1925. Erni Haryanti Kahfi characterizes JIB as "the most important organization to oppose the ideological Westernization of the Indies."³⁴ JIB drew the majority of its members from Dutch-educated Muslims and offered them lectures and informal short courses on Islam. Salim himself taught Dutch-language classes on Islam and published articles in the organization's monthly magazine, *Het Licht* (The Light), in order to counter "the feeling of inferiority on the part of Muslim youth" and help "them to value their religion more highly."³⁵ Under Salim's guidance, JIB emerged as an important training ground for a new generation of Muslim intellectuals with knowledge of both the Islamic and Western traditions.

Among JIB's influential activists was Mohammad Natsir (1908–93). Born in West Sumatra as the son of a minor colonial clerk, Natsir attended a series of Dutch-medium schools as a boy. He excelled, graduating at the top of his class at the Dutch Native School in Padang and winning several government scholarships to continue his studies. In 1927, Natsir moved to the bustling West Javanese city of Bandung to enroll in the prestigious general secondary school (Algemeen Middelbare School [AMS]) there. Because the school specialized in the Western classics, Natsir perfected his Dutch, learned English, and even studied Latin. However, it was also during these years in Bandung that Natsir began to deepen his commitment to Islam. He first forged a close relationship with Islamic Union (Persatuan Islam [PERSIS]) founder Ahmad Hassan, receiving private instruction from the reformist thinker and contributing to his magazine, *Pembela Islam* (Islamic Defender). He also joined JIB and became the head of the Bandung branch in 1929. In this role, Natsir traveled frequently to Jakarta as part of a small cadre of Muslim students who studied directly with Agus Salim.³⁶ With Hassan and Salim as his mentors, Natsir began to challenge the secularist underpinnings of the Sukarno-led nationalist movement and articulate an alternative Islamic nationalism for Indonesia.

When he graduated from AMS Bandung in 1930, Natsir faced a stark choice: accept a government scholarship to study law in the Netherlands or pursue his interest in Islamic education and activism in Bandung. He chose the latter and devoted the next decade of his life to teaching and writing about Islam. As a pious, Dutch-educated Muslim, Natsir worked to reconcile Western and Islamic forms of knowledge. He argued that "an educated Muslim does not need to deepen or enlarge the antagonism between East and West. Islam only recognizes the antagonism between truth and falsehood. All that is true must be accepted, even if it comes from the West."³⁷ After completing a teacher-training course, Natsir helped to establish a network of PERSIS-affiliated schools that combined the standard Dutch curriculum with Islamic subjects. He also emphasized instruction in practical skills, such as agriculture and business, as well as in music and the arts. By the late 1930s, Natsir supervised a network of seven-year primary schools, three-year secondary schools, and a two-year teacher-training institute. Its reach expanded beyond Bandung to other towns in West Java.[38] In addition to administering his schools and teaching, Natsir continued to contribute articles on Islamic educational reform to leading Muslim periodicals, ensuring that he had a voice on the national stage.

While Arab-educated modernists and Dutch-educated Muslims composed the majority of Islamic education activists, there was a notable third stream: modernizing traditionalists. In Java, traditionalists are closely associated with the world of the *pesantren*, or privately run Islamic boarding schools that train students (known as *santri*) in classical Islamic texts, such as the legal writings of Imam al-Shafi'i (767–820) and the religious discourses of Abu Hamid al-Ghazali (1058–1111). For centuries, the life of the pesantren revolved around its leading *kyai*, or a respected member of the 'ulama who was often also the local head of a Sufi order. The kyai led prayers, taught advanced students, managed the affairs of the pesantren, and served as an Islamic expert for the surrounding community. It was an individual kyai's reputation that drew advanced students, who sometimes traveled from hundreds of miles away, to a particular pesantren.[39] However, at the start of the twentieth century, the pesantren tradition faced several challenges to its authority. In the Middle East, the abolition of the caliphate in 1924 and the Saudi conquest of Mecca in 1926 created anxieties about whether threatened Islamic traditions would survive the political upheavals. In Indonesia, Muslim modernists continued to gain in popularity and power. Refusing to cede any more ground, Javanese traditionalists came together in 1926 to establish their own organization: the Nahdlatul Ulama (NU). Although it was a modern voluntary association like Muhammadiyah, Nahdlatul Ulama—which translates as the "Awakening of the 'Ulama "—was first and foremost an organization of kyais. Hasyim Asy'ari (1871–1947), a widely respected member of the 'ulama and founder of the Tebuireng Pesantren in East Java, was chosen as its first chairman. NU set its twin mission as protecting pesantren culture and preserving the authority of the Shafi'i school of law. Indeed, in contrast to their modernist opponents, NU traditionalists endorsed taqlid on grounds that the learning and piety of early Islamic scholars far exceeded those of later Muslims. In the 1930s, NU expanded beyond its home base in East Java to include ninety branches and nearly seventy thousand members.[40]

Without a doubt, Nahdlatul Ulama propagated a traditionalist approach to Islam, but many NU leaders refused to equate traditionalism with a static or isolated version of Islamic education. On the contrary, these modernizing traditionalists diagnosed intellectual dualism as a problem and began to implement reforms at their pesantrens. Take Hasyim Asyʿari and his pesantren in Tebuireng as one significant example. Established in 1899, Tebuireng followed the traditional teaching system, which consisted of personal instruction and lectures by a kyai on one specific text, for its first two decades. In 1916, the pesantren adopted a grade-based model of instruction that arranged students into two multiyear levels and required them to pass formal exams to advance to the next stage. Then, in 1919, Tebuireng began to offer a handful of secular subjects, including Indonesian language, mathematics, and geography, to supplement religious learning.[41] While the pesantren remained devoted to training students in the advanced Islamic disciplines, even this well-known bastion of NU traditionalism adapted its curriculum in an effort to mitigate the dangers of dualism.

The most significant modernizing traditionalist was Asyʿari's eldest son, Wahid Hasyim (1914–53). Hasyim received a traditional Islamic education at his father's pesantren, but he also made the effort to learn Dutch and English as a teenager. After a yearlong sojourn to Mecca, he returned to Tebuireng in 1933 with an array of ideas about how to improve the pesantren's quality of education. They included replacing lectures with more personalized tutorials to enable students to exercise more initiative and shifting the pesantren's emphasis from difficult Arabic texts to more practical Islamic subjects written in Latin script. While the father rejected the reforms as too radical, he nevertheless encouraged his son to establish his own school. The result was Madrasah Nizamiyah, an independent school located in close proximity to the Tebuireng pesantren. Under Wahid Hasyim's management, Madrasah Nizamiyah adopted classroom-style instruction and offered a mixed curriculum of secular (70 percent) and religious (30 percent) subjects. It also had its own library with books and magazines in Arabic, Indonesian, and several European languages. In 1938, Hasyim joined the national leadership council of NU.[42] Although his departure from Tebuireng led to the closure of his hybridized school, his new position made him a powerful advocate for Islamic educational reform in traditionalist circles and beyond.

The 1940s was a transformative decade for all three streams of Indonesian Muslims. Japan seized control of the entire archipelago in early 1942, swiftly and unceremoniously ending centuries of Dutch colonial rule. The occupying Japanese forces worked initially to organize and then to mobilize their new Muslim subjects to support their war effort. In 1943, they created the Council of Indonesian Muslim Associations (Majelis Syuro Muslimin Indonesia [Masyumi]) as an Islamic umbrella organization. Given its broad mandate, Masyumi brought modernists and traditionalists as well as Sumatrans, Javanese, and other regional Muslim communities into closer contact. The Japanese also laid the groundwork for two pillars of post-independence Islamic politics. First, they allowed Indonesian nationalists to convene the Investigatory Committee to Prepare for Independence in 1945. It was during one of the committee's meetings that Sukarno (1901–70) brokered his famous compromise between secular and Islamic nationalists over the role of Islam in the new state. He proposed the multipronged Pancasila as a grand ideological synthesis. It consisted of five foundational principles: the belief in one god, international harmony, the unity of Indonesia, democratic consultation, and social justice for all Indonesians. The first principle, belief in one god, guaranteed a role for religion in the country's governance in order to placate Islamic nationalists but was also sufficiently broad to encompass non-Muslim minorities. Pancasila thus made Indonesia into a multireligious rather than a secular, or an Islamic, state. Second, the Japanese also established the precursor to the Indonesian Ministry of Religious Affairs. This religious bureaucracy was tasked with managing places of worship, administering the hajj, and supervising religious schools.[43] It became even more powerful after independence.

In the midst of these major political changes, the three Muslim streams remained focused on their struggles against intellectual dualism and eventually converged on a tangible goal: to build a modern Islamic college. In November 1944, Masyumi established an official planning committee and named Mohammad Hatta its chairman. Other committee members included Mas Mansur (Muhammadiyah), Mohammad Natsir (JIB), and Wahid Hasyim (NU). Despite their differing religious affiliations, the men reached a quick consensus and managed to open the doors of the Islamic College in Jakarta on July 8, 1945. It welcomed students from both the Islamic and Dutch-style educational systems and offered a mixed curriculum of traditional Islamic disciplines and modern Western subjects to young Muslims.[44]

Within two months of its birth, the infant college was swept up in the surging tide of the Indonesian Revolution. The first wave struck on the morning of August 17, when Sukarno, with Hatta by his side, walked into the courtyard in front of his Jakarta home and declared Indonesian independence. The Dutch predictably refused to accept the declaration and instead asked their British allies to receive the Japanese surrender and secure the islands on their behalf. In early 1946, Dutch troops were able to land in Java and reoccupy Jakarta, forcing most Indonesian nationalists to flee the city. Despite the unparalleled significance of these events, Masyumi did not forget about the nascent Islamic College. They rather took the new institution with them on the run, relocating it nearly three hundred miles to the east in Yogyakarta. When it reopened in April, Sukarno attended the ceremony, and Hatta delivered the inaugural address. The revolution also failed to sink Muslim aspirations to expand the Islamic College. Only eighteen months after the relocation to Yogyakarta, Masyumi convened meetings about transforming it into a full-scale university. In March 1948, the newly renamed Islamic University of Indonesia (Universitas Islam Indonesia [UII]) enrolled its first students, but classes were soon interrupted again when the Dutch military captured Yogyakarta in mid-December. By the time classes resumed in late 1949, the new Indonesian state had its own plans for the college. It nationalized the UII religion faculty and created the State Islamic Institute (Perguruan Tinggi Agama Islam Negeri [PTAIN]) in its stead.[45] In July 1951, PTAIN began to accept student applications for its inaugural semester. It seemed like nothing—not even a bloody anticolonial war and the intense pressures of state building—could shake Indonesian Muslim commitments to their Islamic College.

One reason why Muslim leaders remained so steadfast in their commitment to PTAIN was that they saw the school as integral to the Indonesian nationalist project itself. College founders believed that the mixed-curriculum education they offered would equip pious Muslims with the knowledge necessary to contribute to nation building. In his 1946 address, Hatta made this mission explicit by stating:

> In an independent Indonesia, many ʿulama will participate in debating national affairs. However, if they do not possess a broad knowledge of society and the state, then they will not be able to fulfill their responsibility. The state and its regulations are human activities; therefore, the state will only be able to endure if its regulations are in line with the social requirements of each era. In constructing a state, people provide faith, their own individual knowledge, and also their own aspirations. How awkward will the position of the ʿulama be in these debates if they are only armed with Qurʾanic verses and hadith

and not with real knowledge about society. This requires higher education. This higher education must be provided by the Islamic College.⁴⁶

In other words, Hatta argued that modern Western learning was essential for meaningful participation in national decision-making. Wahid Hasyim echoed these sentiments in 1951, when, as minister of religious affairs, he encouraged PTAIN students to work toward improving the "very weak" situation of the Muslim community as a way of bettering the nation as a whole.⁴⁷ In the same speech, Hasyim articulated another nationalist aspiration: PTAIN would help soothe ideological divides that threatened national unity. He hoped that bringing Western and Islamic-educated Muslims together under one roof would enable the two populations to grow toward one another rather than develop in separate and perhaps hostile directions.⁴⁸ Other official statements portrayed the college as part of the Indonesian state's plan to reduce the need for Muslim students to travel abroad for their educations and to ensure parity for secular and Islamic higher education.⁴⁹ In these ways, PTAIN would ideally bind the Muslim community more tightly to the Indonesian nation.

TWO EARLY CHALLENGES TO INTELLECTUAL DUALISM

PTAIN's revolutionary mission drew many star Muslim intellectuals to its campus. Prominent Muslim scholars such as K. H. Mohammad Adnan (1889–1969), K. H. Fathurahman Kafrawi (1901–69), Mukhtar Yahya (1907–96), and T. M. Hasbi Ash-Shiddieqy (1904–75) devoted substantial portions of their careers as administrators and faculty members to developing the institution. Yet, within this constellation of influential Indonesian Muslims, Mahmud Yunus and Mohammad Natsir shone especially bright. These two college founding fathers clearly shared the commitment to overcoming dualism, but their writings reveal a more complicated story. To begin, Yunus and Natsir both retained certain dualist logics that impeded their efforts to integrate the Islamic and Western intellectual traditions. They also espoused very different visions for reconciling the two modes of knowledge, thereby raising questions about the future of the anti-dualist coalition.

Mahmud Yunus

Yunus devoted his long career to tackling dualism through education reform. As we have seen, he used his years in Cairo to work toward improving instructional materials and pedagogical methods in Indonesian classrooms. He then spent most of the 1930s and 1940s serving as a school administrator and publishing dozens of textbooks in his native West Sumatra. By the 1950s, Yunus was arguably Indonesia's foremost scholar of Islamic education. He held national leadership positions, including an appointment to the PTAIN planning committee. He also designed and ran PTAIN's sister school in Jakarta. At the heart of Yunus's work was his conviction that any Islamic education worthy of the name consists of two elements: spiritualism and materialism. In his book *The Principles of Education* (1962), he declared in straightforward language that "the purpose of Islamic education is to prepare children so that, later in adulthood, they are competent to perform worldly work and spiritual practices [*amalan achirat*]."[50] Yunus aimed to strike a careful balance between these two elements. This philosophy of balance underpinned his efforts to combine Islamic and secular subjects in Indonesian schools.

Drawing on his two-pronged definition of Islamic education, Yunus criticized traditional pesantrens and madrasas as "very narrow" and hence "lacking" in scope.[51] Specifically, he lamented that too many Muslims equated the purpose of Islamic education with worship alone, forgetting that the Qur'an and the Prophet also instructed Muslims in worldly matters such as trade and statecraft. This partial vision led Islamic scholars to teach only Arabic grammar, Qur'anic exegesis, Islamic jurisprudence, and hadith studies to the exclusion of the natural sciences, economics, politics, and other social sciences. Yunus argued that this overemphasis on spirituality at the expense of materialism gave rise to a perilous intellectual imbalance among Muslim students. He wrote: "As a result [of the narrow definition of education], the Muslim community became weak and incapable of defending its independence. Finally, the Muslim community was colonized by stronger nations, a situation that persisted for hundreds of years until the Second World War."[52] In order to fortify the Muslim community against further threats, Yunus implored his fellow Indonesian Muslims to train their children in both religious and secular disciplines.

Yunus diagnosed modern Europeans with the opposite problem: they had reduced education to nothing more than the individual's pursuit of material prosperity. He acknowledged that earlier European philosophers such as Plato and Kant had understood that education was primarily an ethical and spiritual matter concerned with improving the character of the individual and building a more just and humane society. In the medieval and early modern eras, European schools tended to value individual knowledge and spirituality over more "worldly" concerns, such as securing productive jobs and contributing to the economy. Yet he argued that these priorities had shifted in the nineteenth century. Modern Europeans began to lionize material rather than spiritual achievements and therefore devoted the majority of classroom time to natural and applied sciences at the expense of spiritual and moral disciplines, such as philosophy, ethics, and religion.[53] Yunus characterized this development as "dangerous" because "if a nation prioritizes materialism and seizes [wealth] in all possible ways, then it will not be disinclined to seize that wealth from weaker nations and to colonize them."[54] Whereas overemphasizing material goals had created moral decay and a lust for conquest in the West, ignoring them had led to societal degeneration and a susceptibility to conquest in the Muslim community. According to Yunus, any imbalance between the material and spiritual purposes of education bred debilitating social diseases.

Yunus encouraged Muslims to recapture the proper balance between spirituality and materialism by returning to the teachings of the Qur'an. It was a classic modernist argument. For Yunus, the first step was to warn against an infatuation with modern Western knowledge that blinded young Muslims especially to the moral deficiencies of Europe and the United States. In 1957, he wrote:

> The fog of Islamic education in this era exists because the Muslim community has been overly influenced by Western education so that they believe that Islamic education is already obsolete and incompatible with the modern era. However, they have only been influenced by seeing the extrinsic shell and shadow of Western education and have forgotten, or are not even acquainted with, the quintessence of genuine Islamic education.[55]

After attacking the tendency to idolize Western-style education, Yunus's second step was to re-introduce Muslim students to the true principles and rich history of Islamic knowledge. He cited verses from the Qur'an to outline a simple and elegant guide to spiritual and worldly excellence. He also conducted three years of extensive research on the history of Indonesian Islamic education in order to write a comprehensive book that would familiarize young Muslims with their own history. Throughout his career, Yunus framed his work as an education reformer—even his advocacy of incorporating secular subjects into Islamic schools—as a fulfillment of core Islamic teachings rather than a retreat from them.

In the mid-1950s, Yunus had the opportunity to implement his reformist vision as dean of the new Government Religious Academy (Akademi Dinas Ilmu Agama [ADIA]) in Jakarta. Designed exclusively for Muslim bureaucrats, the academy sought to fill the lacuna of religious teachers and other employees at the Ministry of Religious Affairs. Yunus prioritized two learning outcomes for ADIA students. First, he stressed the importance of Arabic-language instruction. Ever since his years in Cairo, Yunus had criticized traditional Arabic instruction as too focused on educating students through reciting and translating, rather than through reading, writing, and speaking.[56] Yunus therefore made Arabic the medium of instruction and examination in all Islamic subjects in order to encourage students to develop an active knowledge of the language. This emphasis on Arabic fluency, as well as the high number of Arab-educated faculty members on staff, gave ADIA a distinctly "Middle Eastern color."[57] Second, Yunus required students to devote over 30 percent of their coursework to "general knowledge" (*ilmu-ilmu umum*) subjects, including Western philosophy, English language, and education studies.[58] He hoped that this mixed curriculum would broaden students' intellectual horizons. These "general knowledge" classes remained separate from Arabic instruction and religious subjects, serving as a supplement to ADIA's core Islamic curriculum.

At ADIA and his other institutions, Yunus endorsed the mixed-curriculum model because he believed that modern Western-style subjects, especially education studies, could enhance the existing strengths of Islamic education. Indeed, he frequently praised the ability of traditional Islamic schools to instill faith and personal ethics in young Muslims. He identified physical instruction in prayer and the use of exemplary prophetic stories as commendable teaching methods because they conveyed essential religious knowledge to young Muslims in manners that were both accessible and long lasting.[59] However, he worried that other traditional pedagogical approaches such as lectures and memorization were ineffective in reaching children and adolescents. To remedy these weaknesses, Yunus drew on recent research into developmental psychology to argue that Muslim educators must provide age-appropriate lessons on Islam. He prepared guidelines for Islamic teachers on when to introduce key theological and legal tenets so that children could understand and internalize their meanings.[60] In *Special Methods for Religious Education* (1965), Yunus also exhorted teachers-in-training to adopt modern pedagogical strategies to improve student engagement with Islamic subjects rather than bore them with rote memorization. He outlined ten predominately American methods, such as cooperative class projects and interactive question-and-answer sessions.[61] Yunus believed that Muslim educators could and should borrow from Western education theory to further their own Islamic educational aims.

During his decades-long career, Yunus advocated for education reforms designed to dismantle intellectual dualism, but he also reproduced certain dualist logics in his scholarship and administrative work. His approach to education as a balance between spiritualism and materialism acted as a double-edged sword. On the one hand, he used his theory to widen the scope of Islamic education and make room for secular-style subjects. It thus provided the philosophical basis for advocating mixed-curriculum education. On the other hand, Yunus tended to define spiritualism and materialism as two distinct and self-contained categories that could be weighed against one another but nonetheless remained on their respective sides of the scale. The natural and social sciences were, in his estimation, ideologically neutral tools that would complement but not substantively affect Islamic subjects.[62] For example, he encouraged Muslim educators to adopt Western pedagogies but denounced Western capitalist and colonial mentalities. He did not seem to worry that American classroom practices might carry traces of these American sins. This view overlooked the real possibility that the two elements might blend together—that is, that Islamic metaphysics and epistemologies could influence student understandings of so-called secular subjects and that modern Western metaphysics and epistemologies could, in turn, impact Islamic values. Instead, Yunus retained dualist assumptions about the bounded nature of knowledge. He used a similar dualist logic to organize his mixed-curriculum schools. At the Islamic Normal School in Padang and ADIA in Jakarta, young Muslims studied both Islamic and "general knowledge" subjects, but they did so in separate classes, from separate textbooks, and in order to fulfill separate requirements. In this sense, Yunus wanted to expose students to both intellectual traditions but continued to see them as discreet systems of knowledge.

Mohammad Natsir

Natsir also spent decades wrestling with the problem of intellectual dualism. In the 1930s, he wrote prolifically about the relationship between Islam and the West and helped to build the PERSIS-affiliated school system where young Muslims studied both Islamic and modern Western-style subjects. He served on the Preparatory Committee for the Islamic College and was named the inaugural college secretary in 1945. Soon thereafter, he emerged as a major political figure in the Indonesian Revolution, working closely alongside Sukarno and Hatta for two years as the minister for information. He was elected chairman of Masyumi in 1949 and even served as the prime minister of Indonesia for seven months in the early 1950s. According to his biographer Audrey Kahin, Natsir possessed a certain "ambivalence regarding the influence of Western powers and Western thought . . . [He] was torn between admiration and embrace of the 'positive sides of Western culture' and a strong opposition to Western imperialism."[63] Building on Kahin's observation, I argue that this ambivalence had its roots in a conflict between his theory and practice. Natsir engaged in what scholars Dietrich Jung and Cemil Aydin identify as a civilizational discourse about Islam.[64] Popular among European Orientalists and Muslim modernists alike, this discourse positioned Islam as "an all-encompassing, determinant, and unchanging cultural entity" that was in perpetual competition with the West.[65] Natsir's essentialist vision of Islam and the West made him a dualist at least in theory. However, he ignored any strict bifurcation between the Islamic and Western traditions in practice. Like many of his modernist and Islamist contemporaries, Natsir frequently cited European Orientalists to defend Islam as a quintessentially modern faith. This decidedly hybridized approach to knowledge stood in tension with his dualist theorizing.

During the mid-twentieth century, Natsir consistently argued that Islam represented a distinct and totalizing civilization that was capable of competing with the West. He first developed these ideas as a JIB activist in the 1930s. In a formative essay on "Islam and Culture," Natsir defined Islam not merely as a religion (*agama*) but as "one culture with an incredible significance in history from ancient times to the present."[66] He argued that in contrast to Christian persecution of scientists, Islam flourished in the medieval period because it respected human reason, possessed a questioning spirit, and encouraged an unfettered search for truth. Natsir thus concluded that Islamic civilization was more advanced and progressive than its Western counterpart. To support this claim, Natsir wrote a series of articles on great medieval Islamic scholars for the Islamic magazines *Panji Islam* (Banner of Islam) and *Pedoman Masyarakat* (The Community's Compass). In one February 1937 essay, he described the Persian philosopher Ibn Miskawayh (932–1030) as a pioneer in the field of psychology because his writings presaged many of

Sigmund Freud's ideas by nine centuries. At the conclusion of the Ibn Miskawayh piece, Natsir wrote:

> If our youth are examining the books of Vienna's most famous psychoanalyst Sigmund Freud, then please also investigate as an example [Ibn Miskawayh's] *Tahdhib al-Akhlaq*. Hopefully, this will increase the appreciation that our Muslim community has for our scholar from this earlier period who, until now, only gets appreciation from "other people." And hopefully, [this] will become a small medication for treating the sickness of "low confidence" that weakens the soul and that generally is present in our Muslim community these days.[67]

In this manner, Natsir encouraged Indonesian Muslims to see themselves as part of a universal Islamic civilization and to look to its achievements—not those of the West—as guides for their individual lives and for the collective future of Indonesia.

Natsir continued to advance this civilizational conception of Islam as chairman of Masyumi. Pushing back against secularist moves to restrict the role of religion, he wrote "Islam as an Ideology" to advocate for making Islamic values the basis of the new Indonesian state. The essay quickly became a pillar of the party's platform. Natsir refused to accept the secularist definition of religion as "solely a system of worship between the One, All-Powerful God and his creation" because it limited Islam to personal and private affairs. Instead, he proudly defined Islam as "a philosophy of life or an ideology" that—like Christianity, fascism, or communism—guides its followers in all their endeavors.[68] Because Islam encompassed every aspect of life, it should serve as the foundation for politics. The Qur'an, according to Natsir, offered Muslims indispensable guidance on political issues such as the qualities of an ideal Muslim leader, the rights and responsibilities of the governed, and mutual social obligations. He argued that these Qur'anic injunctions were timeless but also flexible. Muslims could thus use their God-given powers of reason to implement these principles in ways appropriate to their social contexts.[69] Notwithstanding this interpretative flexibility, Natsir's image of Islam was essentialist in nature.

Although he represented Islam as a discreet and totalizing ideology, Natsir nevertheless looked beyond Islamic source texts and even Muslim scholarship to establish this very definition. One of his favorite sources was British Orientalist H. A. R. Gibb (1895–1971). Natsir opened the abovementioned 1936 essay with a quote, printed in both the English original and Indonesian translation, from Gibb's *Whither Islam?* (1932): "Islam is indeed much more than a system of theology; it is a complete civilization."[70] He cited the same Gibb quote in the second paragraph of "Islam as an Ideology."[71] Natsir borrowed liberally from other Western Orientalists as well. In an article from 1937, he praised the intellectual contributions of Ibn Sina (980–1037) on the basis that his books could be found in Oxford University's library and that British Orientalist Alfred Guillaume credited him with transmitting Aristotle to the West.[72] Natsir read and reviewed Dutch Orientalist writings on Indonesian Islam for his fellow Muslims. As Michael Feener notes, Natsir "rel[ied] heavily on modern Western authorities for his understanding of Islam."[73]

In many ways, Natsir was no outlier. Gibb was a remarkably popular source for early twentieth-century Muslim thinkers across the globe. His book *Arab Conquests in Central Asia* (1923) appeared in Turkish translation as early as 1930.[74] Egyptian Islamist and Muslim Brotherhood leader Sayyid Qutb (1906–66) also referenced *Whither Islam?* to underscore what he saw as Islam's unsurpassed ability to unify mankind.[75] In Indonesia, other Muslim thinkers were similarly attracted to the allure of Western academic citations.[76] A quick perusal through the pages of the Medan-based Islamic magazine *Gema Islam* (Islamic Reverberations) reveals the extent to which Western scholarship on Islam was enmeshed in Indonesian Muslim writings. The magazine's articles were littered with footnotes referencing Dutch historians, French and British Orientalists, and Western philosophers. The editor, Haji Abdul Malik Karim Amrullah, or Hamka for short, engaged in historical arguments on the roots of Indonesian Islam with Western Orientalists.[77] Referencing the works of Orientalists enabled these writers to show fellow Muslims that they, too, possessed the modern and cosmopolitan sensibilities necessary to participate in global scholarly conversations and sometimes even to best their European counterparts. The latter also bolstered their credentials as courageous defenders of the faith.

While not unique in his close engagement with Western scholarship, Natsir did represent a new trend in modern Islamic thought: recognizing some Western academics as objective authorities on Islam. When referencing Gibb in his 1936 essay, Natsir explained to his Muslim audience why they should trust the citation:

> Such is the acknowledgement by man of letters [*pudjangga*] and historical expert Prof. H.A.R Gibb in his well-known book, *Whither Islam*. It is an acknowledgement from a person who is uninfluenced by feelings of religious

fanaticism, who is free from dogmatic emotions, and who explains with a constant transparent certainty that is based on careful and thorough research.[78]

It was an unequivocal recognition of Gibb's supposed objectivity.[79] Natsir also singled out Belgian historian Henri Pirenne (1862–1935) for his objective scholarship. According to Natsir, Pirenne's book *Muhammad and Charlemagne* challenged a prevailing historical consensus that the Middle Ages began with the fifth-century fall of the Roman empire. In contrast, Pirenne identified the Muslim conquests of southern Europe as more significant for historical periodization because Islam had altered the very nature of Roman civilization, whereas earlier invaders had merely assimilated into Roman ways of living.[80] Natsir endorsed his revisionist narrative, writing:

> That position was not a voice that arose from a petty or spiteful heart and not even one influenced by a religious fanaticism; rather, it arose from long research and investigation that was careful, fair, and had the courage to oppose and expose that which many people have long considered as a truth based on scientific knowledge that did not need to be discussed again. This is the voice used by someone with the right to call himself an expert and is indeed recognized as such: Prof. Herni Pirenne, former professor at the university in Gent.[81]

This praise for both Gibb and Pirenne was undoubtedly self-interested; their arguments about the strength of Islamic civilization furthered his own political and religious agendas. Nevertheless, Natsir's words heralded an emergent respect for the ideal of objectivity. He communicated that some Western scholars could transcend religious and cultural influences and, through careful research, arrive at historical truth.

Why, despite arguing for the autonomy and all-encompassing nature of Islam, did Natsir and other Muslim contemporaries defer—even if only momentarily—to Western Orientalists? While it is impossible to know his motivations with any certainty, I suggest that Natsir cited Gibb not because he was unable to support his vision of Islamic politics without the British Orientalist but rather because he presumed that Gibb would augment his own authority. French historian Remy Madinier reaches the same conclusion, arguing that "Western thinkers, in the eyes of Masyumi writers, were seen to lend more credibility to their arguments."[82] After all, the primary purpose of quotations is to enhance an author's trustworthiness by avoiding the appearance of interpretative idiosyncrasy or personal bias. If Natsir was not interested in these benefits, then he could have simply declared Islam a complete civilization on the basis of his own authority and saved himself the effort of translating Gibb. While this citation practice presumably strengthened the persuasiveness of their arguments in the short term, the tendency of Natsir and his Muslim contemporaries to seek outside verification had unintended consequences in the long term. It signaled, first, that Western scholars possessed valuable knowledge about Islam and, second, that Muslim insider knowledge of Islam was potentially insufficient even in the eyes of fellow Muslims. This practice, despite writers' efforts to defend Islam against the West, opened the door for more Western academic participation in modern Islamic thought.

Ultimately, while they agreed that Muslim students should study both Islamic and Western subjects, Yunus and Natsir envisioned the relationship between the two intellectual traditions in fundamentally different ways. During his decades as an education reformer, Yunus consistently pushed for the inclusion of modern Western disciplines such as developmental psychology and language pedagogy in Islamic education on grounds that they were useful supplements to traditional Islamic subjects, but he never aimed to change the content of Islamic subjects themselves. In contrast, Natsir and some of his Masyumi colleagues practiced a hybridized form of Islamic interpretation that actually granted legitimacy to Western academic knowledge of Islam. This approach was not merely a push—like Yunus's reforms—for more mixed-curriculum institutions; it represented a new, and more academic, way of knowing Islam. This was a substantial difference, but Yunus and Natsir do not appear to have argued in public about the strengths of their respective positions. Likewise, other opponents of dualism rarely if ever engaged in open debates in the 1950s and 1960s over the proper use of Western disciplines. Indonesian Muslims simply allowed their agreement about the dangers of dualism to mask the profound intellectual disagreements floating just beneath the surface.

PARTISAN POLITICS AND ENTRENCHED DUALISM

In 1960, Sukarno issued a presidential order to combine PTAIN in Yogyakarta and ADIA in Jakarta into a national Islamic higher-education system to be known as the State Islamic Institute (Institut Agama Islam Negeri [IAIN]). Government officials had high hopes for IAIN. They sought to raise the system's standards so that they were on par with Egypt's al-Azhar and India's

Aligarh.⁸³ Sukarno reaffirmed these aspirations two years later when he declared in a speech that "IAIN, as an institution of higher education, must ignite the fire of Islam [*menggali api Islam*] so that it can contribute to the aspirations of building a just and prosperous society."⁸⁴ These words were not empty rhetoric. In the early 1960s, the Indonesian state invested money and other resources into the system. It even guaranteed IAIN graduates either the funding to continue their studies or the right to work for the government as religious teachers or Ministry of Religious Affairs bureaucrats.⁸⁵ While this governmental attention provided reason to be optimistic, the 1960s was also a challenging time at the State Islamic Institutes. The campus climate was rife with partisan tensions that sometimes overshadowed IAIN's intellectual mission, and dualism was so entrenched that combatting it proved to be an uphill battle.

Like the country at large, IAIN suffered from fierce partisan conflicts with roots in two national political developments. First, there was Masyumi's split into separate modernist and traditionalist parties. Masyumi's broad-based coalition had begun to unravel immediately after the military phase of the revolution ceased. In December 1949, Natsir was elected chairman at the party's fourth national meeting in Yogyakarta. It was "a watershed congress" that saw young modernists consolidate control at the expense of traditionalist 'ulama.⁸⁶ NU leaders began to complain about feeling forced to take a backseat to modernists in party leadership and cabinet appointments. The tensions came to a head in 1952. After nearly three years as minister of religious affairs, Wahid Hasyim announced that he would not accept reappointment, leaving NU without a clear candidate. Modernists in Masyumi recognized an opening to secure the ministry for themselves and nominated K. H. Fakih Usman (1904–68) of Muhammadiyah. NU read this move as a betrayal and soon thereafter seceded from Masyumi altogether to establish its own traditionalist political party.⁸⁷ The second crisis unfolded in the late 1950s, when Sukarno announced his plans to build a "Guided Democracy" (*Demokrasi Terpimpin*). It was Sukarno's response to Indonesia's fractured and tumultuous political landscape. The decade had seen cabinets and prime ministers rise and fall at a dizzying speed. Between 1950 and 1955 alone, the country had six different prime ministers. Sukarno devised Guided Democracy as a way to bring a heavy-handed order to this political quagmire. He limited the scope for political opposition, constituted a pragmatic rather than a party-based business cabinet, and consolidated power in his own hands by claiming the twin roles of coalition maker and "guide" behind Guided Democracy. Sukarno insisted that these actions would bring greater political stability and unify the Indonesian people around the principle of "mutual cooperation" (*gotong royong*).

Under Sukarno's new authoritarian-leaning system, the fortunes of the country's two major Islamic parties, the post-1952 modernist Masyumi and the traditionalist Nahdlatul Ulama, diverged quite dramatically. Masyumi entered into open opposition. Natsir attacked Sukarno's concept of Guided Democracy, arguing that it was merely an attempt to forge a "democracy without an opposition."[88] He also proposed to make Islam, rather than Sukarno's cherished Pancasila, the basis for the Indonesian state. As a result of its outspoken opposition, Masyumi was excluded from Sukarno's cabinets and quickly sidelined in the new political landscape. This isolation worsened when Masyumi leaders became entangled in a regional rebellion against Sukarno that broke out in Sumatra in 1958. Even Natsir threw in his lot with the uprising, relocating his family to West Sumatra and then spending months on the run from the Indonesian military. He was eventually captured and would languish in prison until 1966.[89] Masyumi as a whole was stigmatized as a party of traitors and counterrevolutionaries and officially banned in 1960. Nahdlatul Ulama, in contrast, cooperated with Sukarno at nearly every stage of Guided Democracy. In exchange for their support, NU leaders secured high-level cabinet posts and control over the coveted Ministry of Religious Affairs. Sukarno then offered to make NU the primary representative of "religion" in his new NASAKOM—short for nationalist (*nasionalis*), religious (*agama*), and communist (*komunis*)—government in 1960. Although virulently anticommunist, NU accepted, thereby ensuring its continued access to political power and state financial resources.[90]

IAIN continued to grow amid this political turmoil. In March 1962, Sukarno named NU-loyalist K. H. Saifuddin Zuhri (1919–86), an adept political strategist and vocal proponent of NU cooperation with the president, as minister of religious affairs.[91] Zuhri's ministry directed substantial resources to expanding IAIN from its initial centers in Yogyakarta and Jakarta into nearly every province in Indonesia. It also encouraged local Muslim communities to establish pious endowment bodies (*badan waqf*) to raise a portion of the funds necessary to build IAIN facilities.[92] Thanks to these efforts, IAIN quickly proliferated across the Indonesian archipelago. In the mid-1960s, the ministry opened seven new State Islamic Institutes in Banda Aceh, Surabaya,

Ujung Padang, Banjarmasin, Padang, Palembang, and Jambi. Each housed at least four faculties.[93] In addition to these full-fledged IAINs, dozens of branch campuses arose across Java, Sumatra, and the other Outer Islands. Student demand also increased. Between 1960 and 1968, the student population at IAIN Yogyakarta alone grew nearly fivefold from 696 to 3,345 total, and the number of faculty similarly exploded from 29 permanent and 27 temporary faculty members to 84 permanent and 137 temporary professors.[94]

NU took advantage of the State Islamic Institute's rapid growth by appointing party loyalists to valuable administrative and faculty posts. In 1960, R. H. A. Soenarjo (1908–96), a Dutch-educated lawyer and former NU minister of the interior, was named as the rector of IAIN Yogyakarta. He was a close associate of Wahid Hasyim and a long-time proponent of more integrated Islamic education.[95] H. Soenardjo bin H. Abu Ngusman (1916–96), former NU minister of trade, was selected as the rector of IAIN Jakarta in 1963. Many new IAIN campuses also fell under NU control. In response to this one-party dominance, modernist and unaffiliated students began to complain about corruption and "NU-centric activities." The long list of allegations included admission preferences for NU-affiliated students, lowered exam standards for NU activists, favoritism in the hiring and promotion of NU faculty, and intimidation of non-NU students on campus.[96] IAIN gradually became yet another partisan battlefield where modernists and traditionalist fought one another for influence.

Some IAIN professors got caught in the partisan crossfire. In late 1962, several NU student-activists wrote a letter to President Sukarno in which they denounced Mahmud Yunus and eight other IAIN Jakarta faculty members as counterrevolutionaries. These accusations could carry serious consequences at the time. Faculty members accused of holding counterrevolutionary and anti-Sukarno views were frequently removed from government employment and even arrested for political sedition. Fortunately for Yunus, the accusations were quickly proven false when police investigators determined that NU student-activists had forged aspects of the letter and its accompanying evidence. He was not punished, but neither were his student accusers, who escaped sanction thanks to pressure from NU leadership.[97] The Yunus incident demonstrated the fragility of academic freedom, especially for outspoken modernists, on NU-dominated campuses.

These brewing intra-Muslim tensions erupted into open conflict on October 10, 1963, when a group of IAIN Yogyakarta students staged a protest during the annual open senate meeting. After entering into the meeting chanting and holding placards, the students denounced IAIN leadership for running a corrupt and inefficient administration and for transforming the public institution into nothing more than an NU fiefdom. On the basis of these damning criticisms, the students declared that they would no longer accept the authority of the IAIN administration or the Ministry of Religious Affairs. Students at IAIN Jakarta rose up in protest against NU domination shortly thereafter. The demonstrations produced a swift backlash. IAIN and ministry leaders immediately demonized the protests as a counterrevolutionary uprising against Sukarno and accused the student protestors of being merely puppets manipulated by subversive, ex-Masyumi figures. They shut down both the Yogyakarta and Jakarta campuses for more than two months. Minister Zuhri only agreed to resume classes in late December after visiting each campus and delivering firm speeches about discipline, unity, and progress. At least two Yogyakarta protest leaders were arrested, and by September 1964, no fewer than fourteen IAIN students were on trial for holding a protest without proper permits and approvals. In addition to the harsh legal punishments, many protest leaders were stripped of their positions on the student council, and some were expelled from the IAIN system altogether.[98]

NU also punished faculty members, such as Kafrawi Ridwan (1932–2019), for supporting the October 10 incident. Ridwan had been educated at the modernized Gontor pesantren in East Java and then studied at IAIN Yogyakarta in the 1950s. He accepted an appointment as a junior lecturer at his alma mater in 1960.[99] During the October 10 protests, Ridwan circulated faculty petitions criticizing the NU-dominated administration and was subsequently arrested. He spent four months in jail. When he was finally released in February 1964, many of his fellow faculty dissidents, including Zaini Dahlan and Achmad Chotib, had already been transferred from the more prestigious Yogyakarta and Jakarta campuses to recently established provincial IAINs in Sulawesi or Sumatra. Ridwan himself was dispatched to Aceh.[100] The professional exile of these junior faculty members negatively impacted IAIN efforts to bridge the gap between the Islamic and Western intellectual traditions. At IAIN Yogyakarta, Ridwan and other young activist-professors had helped to organize a seminar on incorporating Islamic education into the curriculum at Indonesia's secular universities in July 1963. The seminar featured five days of presentations and concluded with the release of a collective statement that endorsed a "spiritual and scientific approach" to Islamic instruction at the university level.¹⁰¹ There is little evidence that NU traditionalists targeted modernists because of their opposition to dualism, but the intense partisanship was surely enough to dissuade some from taking any additional intellectual risks.

The NU-dominated administrations clearly discriminated against modernist professors and students, but it is important not to overstate the extent to which NU treated IAIN as a simple extension of its pesantren network, as some modernist rivals have claimed.¹⁰² Both modernist *and* traditionalist scholars continued to combat dualism during the turbulent 1960s. IAIN leaders, who were mostly affiliated with NU, constructed a mixed curriculum that required students to progress through a sequence of Islamic and Western-style disciplines. For example, students in the Shariʿa Faculty in 1960–61 were required to take advanced fiqh courses as well as classes in psychology, sociology, and the English language. Education majors studied sociology, anthropology, comparative religion, health sciences, education methods, and English alongside their Islamic disciplines.¹⁰³ It was an ambitious mixed curriculum that placed high expectations on IAIN students and faculty members alike.

IAIN's curriculum posed a major challenge for incoming students, most of whom were raised in a strictly bifurcated educational environment. Few could read all the assigned texts, which included materials in Arabic, English, and Indonesian. An even smaller number was ready to engage with both the nuances of marriage fiqh and prevailing methods for sociological research. Because the majority of potential students were simply unprepared for an integrated curriculum, IAIN was compelled to construct a network of preparatory schools. Yogyakarta had opened its first preparatory school for pesantren graduates in the 1950s. It provided students with predominantly Islamic educational backgrounds the opportunity to receive instruction in "general" subjects and acclimate themselves to a graded, exam-based schooling system. Some students remained in IAIN preparatory schools for three years. As the student population soared in the 1960s, IAIN required more preparatory schools to help incoming students transition to the mixed curriculum. Yogyakarta was coordinating eight additional preparatory schools by 1963.¹⁰⁴

To cater to the other side of the student spectrum, IAIN also offered intensive instruction in elementary Arabic for first-year government-school graduates so that they could acquire the language skills necessary for in-depth Qurʾanic, hadith, or fiqh study.¹⁰⁵ This explosion of bridge programs demanded substantial financial resources and faculty energy, but more significantly, it underscored the manifold obstacles that IAIN faced in teaching its mixed curriculum.

Once enrolled, IAIN students continued to encounter intellectual hurdles and resource shortages tied to the entrenched nature of dualism. The language of textbooks represented one serious barrier. There were so few Indonesian-language translations available in the 1950s and 1960s that IAIN instructors often relied on Arabic and English texts.[106] However, government-school alumni could not read the advanced Arabic of many Islamic texts, and classic works of Western social science, history, and even Orientalism were written in European languages that very few incoming students could read with any fluency. To address these language problems, Muslim intellectuals worked to translate books from Arabic and English into Indonesian and wrote basic textbooks of their own. This textbook work was important for IAIN student success but detracted from faculty members' abilities to produce original research. The IAIN system likewise struggled to build and maintain library collections in such a range of subjects. The integrated curriculum required extra resources in an era when the Indonesian economy was in a tailspin.

The IAIN system also suffered from a deficit of Muslim scholars conversant in both Islamic and modern Western disciplines. While all Indonesian universities faced faculty shortages in the 1950s and 1960s, the situation at IAIN was worse. The majority of Indonesian scholars had been trained in only one of the intellectual traditions. Dutch-educated scholars, even if they were pious Muslims, were usually only self-taught in the Islamic sciences and therefore had limited exposure to the languages and methodological principles of fiqh, tafsir, and other traditional Islamic disciplines. In contrast, NU traditionalists and even Arab-educated modernists had cursory exposure at best to the Western social sciences and humanities. Given this shortage of bidiscursive faculty members, students lacked the intellectual role models to show them how to merge the two traditions of knowledge effectively. Dualism—like partisan conflict—had its own momentum that was difficult to reverse.

Partisan tensions and resource shortages were the most visible obstacles facing the IAIN system in the 1960s, but there were more fundamental problems buried just below the surface. Specifically, Indonesian Muslims disagreed over how exactly to combat dualism and to what extent they should integrate Western academic disciplines into the Islamic intellectual tradition. Many modernists—including Mahmud Yunus—envisioned Western disciplines primarily as useful supplements to traditional Islamic ones. Consequently, they endorsed a mixed-curriculum model in which Muslim students continued to study traditional Islamic disciplines but then augmented them with separate coursework in so-called practical Western subjects, such as education theory, psychology, and sociology, in hope that the latter would serve as tools to translate Islamic values into the modern context. A smaller but notable number of Muslim intellectuals followed Mohammad Natsir in practicing a more intense form of intellectual integration. They drew on Western academic scholarship to produce new interpretations of Islam and new modes of religious authority. For the most part, Yunus's approach dominated IAIN culture in the 1950s and 1960s.

Ultimately, IAIN joined Islamic colleges across the globe in using the mixed-curriculum model to challenge dualism. IAIN required students to take courses in traditional Islamic subjects like fiqh and tafsir and in modern Western disciplines such as sociology and psychology in order to bridge the gulf between the Islamic and Western intellectual traditions. Yet there was an irony behind this approach to combatting dualism. Instead of attacking the Islam–West binary, IAIN continued to categorize certain courses as belonging to one tradition or the other. IAIN administrators seemingly accepted this ontological division as natural. Even the anti-dualist metaphor of "bridging the gulf" rests on an underlying dualist logic; it locates the Islamic and Western traditions on opposite banks of a river and implies that only a feat of engineering can connect them. Such lingering dualist assumptions would not continue to go unchallenged. As Indonesian Muslims traveled to the West in greater numbers for higher education, they began to imagine ways to more fully integrate the two intellectual traditions, and they demanded that IAIN take notice.

2 MCGILL UNIVERSITY AS A "MIDWIFE FOR THE ISLAMIC REFORMATION"

AT 7:30 IN THE MORNING on August 17, 1957, Sukarno strode to the podium on the Presidential Palace steps to deliver his annual Independence Day address. He spoke for nearly two hours, commemorating Indonesia's hard-won revolution and expounding on how Guided Democracy would solve the country's political problems. He concluded his remarks with a flag-raising ceremony and a performance of the national anthem. Sitting only a few feet away and sweating profusely from the equatorial sunshine were two men from McGill University: Professor Wilfred Cantwell Smith and Principal Cyril James. James later admitted that "since the speech was in Indonesian and the people of this country are very little inclined to applaud, we had very little notion of what he was talking about until the ceremonies were over and we were handed English copies of the text."[1] Despite appearing utterly out of place, Smith and James were actually special guests of the president. Sukarno had invited them to Indonesia as a way to reciprocate the hospitality they had shown when he visited McGill in June 1956. They spent two weeks in the country, meeting with Indonesian professors and touring much of Java and Bali. In his personal account of the trip, James wrote effusively about Indonesia, emphasizing the health and enthusiasm of its citizens, the beauty of its diverse cultures, and the "strong and attractive personality" of Sukarno.[2] Smith was more subdued. Although he, too, had described his first trip to the archipelago in 1956 as "tremendous" and "richly rewarding," he was somewhat shaken by the political tensions he detected during this second visit.[3]

Still, for two men with little previous knowledge of Indonesia, the country was now firmly on their intellectual maps.

Thanks in part to this personal connection to Sukarno, McGill University's Institute of Islamic Studies grew in stature among Indonesian intellectuals. In 1957, Mukti Ali earned his master's degree, making him the institute's first Indonesian graduate. Eleven years later, Harun Nasution became the first Indonesian to receive a doctorate at the institute. Both eventually rose to prominent positions in Indonesian Islamic politics, with Ali serving as minister of religious affairs and Nasution as rector of the IAIN in Jakarta. By no means were Ali and Nasution the only Indonesian Muslims to study in Montreal. They were joined initially by Anton Timur Djaelani (MA, 1959), Tedjaningsih Djaelani (MA, 1959), Mochtar Naim (MA, 1960), and Kafrawi Ridwan (MA, 1969). Then, beginning in the 1970s, a steady stream of high-achieving Indonesian scholars of Islam began to pass through the gates of the McGill Institute of Islamic Studies.[4] By the turn of the twenty-first century, approximately 200 Indonesians had pursued a terminal master's or doctoral degree at McGill, and an estimated 1,400 additional IAIN instructors and staff had received short-term training in teaching and research methods.[5] Clearly, the institute possessed qualities that attracted many well-educated Muslims from Indonesia and other Muslim-majority countries, but what were they? Why did so many Indonesians travel to Montreal—of all places—to study Islam? How has McGill influenced their understandings of Islam, and in turn, how has their presence at McGill impacted the Western academy?

Wilfred Cantwell Smith founded the McGill Institute of Islamic Studies as a space of encounter between Western academics and Muslim intellectuals. He envisioned that Western scholars would learn from their Muslim colleagues to see Islam as a lived religion whose adherents possessed very real hopes and fears about the future of their faith. Muslim scholars, in turn, would study academic methods from their Western counterparts and learn to use them as powerful new lenses through which to see and reform Muslim societies. In the process, Smith hoped to make Islamic and Western ways of knowing Islam mutually comprehensible and ideally even commensurable. This hard intellectual work gave rise to a new epistemic framework that I term "fusionism." Fusionism rests on the assertion that knowledge cannot be divided into either the Islamic or Western intellectual tradition but is instead unified. Fusionist thinkers recognize no boundaries. They push beyond the early efforts to combat dualism, which we examined in chapter 1, by seeking to merge academic research methods with Islamic faith commitments. They likewise insist that pious Muslims can produce high-quality academic research on Islam and that Western academic scholarship can strengthen Islam as a religion. By encouraging fusionist experiments, the institute helped produce some of the twentieth century's most dynamic Muslim thinkers.

Although McGill's cross-religious encounters fostered fusionist creativity, they also bred conflict. Muslim scholars sometimes struggled to adapt themselves to Western academic norms. They battled for the authority to speak—and, more importantly, to be heard—as both academics and engaged Muslims, and sometimes they lost those fights. Instead of conceptualizing these struggles as personal tales of intellectual triumph or defeat, this chapter uses the moments of friction to reveal the structures of academic authority within mid-twentieth-century Islamic studies. At the heart of this academic culture was the ideal of objectivity. I follow historian Peter Novick in classifying objectivity as "an essentially contested concept . . . the exact meaning of which will always be in dispute."[6] In other words, academics have long strived for objectivity, but the concept's abstract nature has produced consistent and even radical disagreement over its exact meaning and the ways to achieve it. Novick shows that this contestation is not a bug in the system; rather, it is integral to the concept itself. In the mid-twentieth century, objectivity functioned as a primary mechanism for establishing and wielding power within the Western university. Accordingly, faculty and students at the McGill Institute—as well as their interlocutors at other universities—defined and redefined, claimed for themselves and denied for others, the mantle of objectivity. For them, to be objective was to be a genuine academic, and that academic identity carried with it the authority to speak, write, and teach about Islam.

In order to grapple with the politics of objectivity, this chapter examines the first decade of intellectual encounters at the McGill Institute of Islamic Studies. Part one locates the institute's mission in the broader landscape of post-World War II Islamic studies. While founder Wilfred Cantwell Smith shared much with his contemporaries, he also challenged the dominant definition of objectivity by rejecting what he saw as a false dichotomy between scientific research and religious convictions in the study of Islam. In part two, I argue that Smith expected McGill Muslims to approach Islam as both objective scholars *and* subjective Muslims. Given the difficulty of this task, Muslim faculty members and students struggled to discipline themselves to the demands of institute culture. The resulting tensions produced conflict but also facilitated fusionist creativity. Part three examines how Fazlur Rahman, Mukti Ali, and Harun Nasution, in particular, used academic methods to craft fusionist forms of knowledge at McGill. Finally, part four investigates the broader academic impact of McGill's fusionist experiments. Because fusionist thinking generally failed to gain traction in Western universities, established academics continued to use objectivity to police the border between academic and religious (usually Muslim) knowledge about Islam.

WILFRED CANTWELL SMITH AND THE MCGILL VISION (OR, HOW IT FEELS TO BE A GOLDFISH)

The fields now known as Islamic studies underwent a period of spectacular growth and transformation in the 1940s and 1950s. Before the mid-twentieth century, North American scholars of Islam paled in comparison to their better trained and more prestigious colleagues in Europe. Only a handful of the top research universities, such as Princeton and the University of Chicago, employed experts on the Middle East, and even their programs focused on ancient civilizations that predated Islam. The few scattered Islam specialists in North America were almost invariably Christian missionaries. Indeed, the first American journal devoted to Islam, *The Moslem World*, was launched by the Hartford Theological Seminary in 1911. Its subtitle was *A Quarterly Review of Current Events, Literature, and Thought among Mohammedans, and the Progress of Christian Missions in Moslem Lands*.[7] The outbreak of World War II was a catalyst for major change. During the war years, American academics served their country by teaching more men to speak Asian and Middle Eastern languages and producing crucial intelligence on contemporary Muslim societies. This nascent knowledge base would be even more critical to waging the Cold War because the United States and its allies required academics to help them compete with the Soviet Union in molding the so-called Third World.[8] American experts on Africa, Asia, and the Middle East were suddenly in high demand. Over the course of a single decade, Islamic studies had evolved from being an esoteric and largely forgotten corner of the academy into a booming and politically relevant field.

Nongovernmental and philanthropic organizations accelerated this shift. In 1949, the American Council of Learned Societies (ACLS) published a damning report on the state of Near/Middle East Studies. It judged existing programs "pitifully inadequate for a nation which is already a super-power in the economic, political, and military spheres."[9] ACLS committee members decried what they saw as the near dearth of professionals with knowledge of the contemporary Middle East. They called for "the immediate creation of large university centers of specialized training and research in the Near Eastern fields" to fill the void.[10] The plea fell on sympathetic ears. Over the next two decades, philanthropic foundations such as Rockefeller and Ford poured unprecedented sums of money into area studies. Ford alone donated nearly $70 million to such programs between 1952 and 1963.[11] The foundations' seemingly bottomless coffers enabled centers for the study of Islam to flourish at Harvard, Princeton, Columbia, Michigan, Stanford, Johns Hopkins, and Berkeley. These extraordinary new resources also encouraged many of Europe's leading Orientalists to relocate to North America. Although the influx of European faculty members ensured a degree of continuity with the discipline of Orientalism, Islamic studies witnessed a rebirth in postwar North America.

Founded in 1951, Wilfred Cantwell Smith's Institute of Islamic Studies at McGill University was undeniably part of this Cold War intellectual milieu. The institute received hundreds of thousands of dollars from the Rockefeller and Ford Foundations. Smith met frequently with foundation officials and had close connections to the Canadian diplomatic core. His own brother Arnold Cantwell Smith (1915–94) served as Canada's ambassador to Egypt and then to the Soviet Union in the early 1960s. David Webster explains McGill's ties to Cold War politics: "Though it proudly flew Canadian colours, [the McGill Institute's] role within the North American area-studies complex paralleled that of the Canadian government within the Western alliance. . . . It helped enmesh countries like Indonesia in a Western-centered world while offering Canada as a less self-interested partner."[12] McGill scholars thus acted as "unofficial diplomats" in helping transmit Western ideas about religious modernization to Indonesian Muslims.[13] However, the Cold War genealogy of area studies is only part of the institute's story. I argue that the contested ideal of objectivity and related debates over insider–outsider politics were more integral to the institute's vision for Islamic studies.

By the mid-twentieth century, many scholars of Islam defined objectivity against the images of two constitutive others: Christian missionaries and Muslim "apologists." H. A. R. Gibb drew this negative self-portrait most clearly and authoritatively. Gibb was a towering figure in the study of Islam; he served as professor of Arabic at Oxford University before accepting an endowed chair at Harvard University in 1955, where he ran the new Middle Eastern studies program. As we saw in chapter 1, his work was read widely by Muslim intellectuals across the globe. Gibb used the introduction to his popular book *Mohammedanism* (1949) to juxtapose the previous generation of Orientalists with his own. He wrote that earlier scholars, especially Christian missionaries and Muslim apologists, had been encumbered by the "intellectual and emotional limitations of [their] period" and then assured his readers that his own book would "serve the interests of neither."[14] Such attempts to sever the long history of religiously motivated studies of Islam put Christian scholars on the defensive. For example, in the preface to his *The Call of the Minaret* (1956), Anglican priest Kenneth Cragg (1913–2012) felt compelled to defend the Christian inspiration behind his book against "some [who] will say that such obligations will disqualify objectivity."[15] Even the famed French Orientalist Louis Massignon (1883–1962) encountered criticism from younger scholars who derided his spiritual affinities for Sufis and self-proclaimed religious insights into the Qur'an.[16] However, Cragg and Massignon were exceptions to the new rule. Through programmatic statements such as the one Gibb made in *Mohammedanism*, mid-twentieth-century Orientalists derided Christian-inspired scholarship on Islam as a remnant from a forsaken missionary past that stood in stark opposition to the objective, academic standards of the present.

Western scholars routinely used even harsher language to denounce the supposed Muslim equivalents of Christian missionaries: apologists. Gibb complained that "one looks in vain for any systematic analysis [by Muslims] of new currents of thought in the Muslim world. Almost all the books written in English or French by Muslim writers, on the other hand, turn out to be apologetic works, composed with the object of defending Islam."[17] He also argued that apologetics prevented the majority of Muslims from attaining "the level of current thought."[18] Other prominent professors agreed. For example, Gustave von Grunebaum (1909–72), the Austrian-born professor of Islam at the University of Chicago and then UCLA, characterized contemporary Muslim historiography as "crude" and outside the bounds of critical academic scholarship.[19] These oft-repeated criticisms of so-called Muslim apologetics highlight academic disdain toward religiously motivated scholarship in general and the deep distrust of scholarship sympathetic to Islam in particular.

In contrast to what they saw as Muslim apologists' knee-jerk defenses of Islam, many mid-twentieth century Orientalists associated objectivity with an abiding suspicion toward traditional Muslim narratives and sources.

German-born Orientalist Joseph Schacht (1902–69) exemplified this skepticism. Schacht's *The Origins of Muhammadan Jurisprudence* (1950) was a revisionist investigation into the historical authenticity of the Sunnah and hadith. The book will be discussed in more depth in part three, but for now, I want to examine just a few of its guiding principles. Schacht proposed the rule that "every legal tradition [hadith] from the Prophet, until the contrary is proved, must be taken not as an authentic or essentially authentic, even if slightly obscured, statement valid for his time or the time of the Companions, but as the fictitious expression of a legal doctrine formulated at a later date."[20] Building on this skeptical posture, Schacht crafted the ex silencio rule deeming that any hadith not mentioned in earlier relevant legal discussions must be fabricated.[21] He also frequently characterized early Islamic scholars as devious. For example, he wrote that they often "cleverly disguised" false hadith with their "favourite device" of borrowed chains of transmission (*isnad*).[22] Many of Schacht's contemporaries viewed his work as the epitome of objective scholarship. Indeed, when W. Montgomery Watt (1909–2006) wrote a biography of Muhammad that aligned more with traditional Muslim accounts than Schacht's history, Alfred Guillaume, von Grunebaum, and Schacht himself all questioned Watt's objectivity and seriousness as an academic because he did not embrace a similar skepticism toward Muslim sources.[23]

Many Western academics also associated objectivity with advancing civilizational critiques of Islam. Gibb's work was again emblematic because it diagnosed two supposedly fundamental ailments afflicting Muslim societies. First, Gibb represented Arab culture and Islam as essentially backward. In one well-received book, he argued that "the Arab mind" was so attracted to "simplicity and concreteness" that it produced "the aversion of the Muslims from the thought-processes of rationalism."[24] Second, Gibb believed that Islamic civilization was in decline and that the academic historian's task was to excavate the roots of its decay. He identified the ninth and tenth centuries as the apex of Islamic civilization but then characterized post-twelfth-century Islamic history as a stagnant period when "originality and vitality were gradually crushed out of existence" and "no new currents of thought entered into the Islamic community to stimulate intellectual speculation."[25] Only the colonial encounter with Europe helped to reignite Muslim creativity, but Gibb feared that even that outside catalyst would not enable modern Muslims to truly revive the religion.[26] In a similar vein, von Grunebaum diagnosed Muslims as suffering from an undeveloped and uncritical self-identity that led to decline.²⁷ Although these civilizational critiques were clearly built on Western cultural presuppositions, they still set the standard for "objective" scholarship in the postwar era.

Because the prevailing definition of objectivity involved religious neutrality and skepticism, many Orientalists doubted whether Muslim scholars could produce research that met their academic standards. These doubts informed staffing decisions at some Western universities, perhaps most notably at Princeton. As chair of Princeton's Department of Oriental Studies, Phillip Hitti (1886–1978) was reluctant to hire faculty members from the Near East because he feared they could not adjust to Princeton academic and teaching standards.²⁸ He held this view despite his own background as a Lebanese Christian. Over a decade later, T. Cuyler Young (1900–76), who succeeded Hitti as chair, voiced a similar hesitancy about Muslim faculty. In a 1962 letter to a colleague, he wrote:

> The administration is thinking seriously of making an appointment here in the field of Islamic thought, if possible a Muslim of some standing and reputation. I have indicated to the president that such persons are very difficult to find. The older generation is for the most part still riding an apologetic horse and this we certainly do not want. On the other hand, to have a good intellectual Muslim scholar of reputation on the staff would be a great gain. . . . In your opinion, is it a wild-goose chase to think of such a man and a Muslim?²⁹

Young clearly had his doubts that any man could be both a good scholar *and* a Muslim, and evidently, this concern was shared widely enough that Young openly expressed it to colleagues. Some Muslims and Arab Christians did manage to obtain academic appointments in the 1950s and early 1960s, but they were mostly graduates from the American University of Beirut and hence products of Western education from a young age.³⁰ In postwar academia, there was very little space for Muslims with Islamic educational backgrounds or overt religious commitments.

Wilfred Cantwell Smith (1916–2000) pushed back against these dominant trends to articulate a dissenting version of objectivity. He held fervently that objectivity, while essential for academic research, was also woefully insufficient for the study of religion and demanded instead passion, empathy, and investment from scholars of Islam. Smith had discovered these principles gradually over the course of his formative intellectual years. Raised in a devoutly Protestant family during the Great Depression, Smith had been first exposed to the Islamic world at the age of sixteen, when he traveled to Egypt with his missionary mother. He found the trip inspiring. With his sights set on becoming a Presbyterian minister, he enrolled at the University of Toronto to study Hebrew and Arabic but also found himself increasingly attracted to left-wing Christian socialists.[31] He graduated from Toronto in 1938 and moved to England to continue his study of Christian theology at Cambridge and Islamic history at Oxford under none other than Gibb. Smith soon became immersed in the leftist student movement then prevalent in British universities. In 1940, he left war-torn Britain for India to research his dissertation and, more importantly in Smith's eyes, to assist Indians in freeing themselves from the yoke of British imperialism. Thanks to financial support from churches in his native Canada, Smith began serving in Lahore as a missionary who was nonetheless increasingly uncomfortable with evangelicalism. He taught Islamic history at Lahore's Forman Christian College and was enthralled by its intellectual and interreligious milieu. He also became an avid devotee of Jawaharlal Nehru, embracing his vision for a pluralist, modern, and socialist India. He even visited Nehru during one of his long bouts in prison.[32]

Although a man of faith, Smith was not always a maverick when it came to objectivity. On the contrary, when he published his first book, *Modern Islam in India: A Social Analysis* (1946), he wrote unequivocally in the preface: "I am a socialist with pronounced ethical convictions; and I believe in the scientific method."[33] To Smith, the scientific method meant a Marxist structural analysis of society. While he did not consider himself a communist because he remained a deeply committed Presbyterian, he believed that economic interests and class politics were the real driving forces of history.[34] Smith therefore adopted a reductionist approach to Indian Islam that sought to explain Muslim religious developments primarily in economic terms. For example, he attributed both the sharp nineteenth-century spike in prophetic biographies and Iqbal's fascination with the self to the fact that "capitalist society is preeminently individualist."[35] Similarly, he argued that "religion [was] not the efficient cause of communal riots" but rather explained communal violence as a form of class conflict.[36] In contrast to the Orientalist tendency to explain all Muslim politics through the lens of an essentialized Islam, Smith framed Indian Islam as little more than the ideological byproduct of class struggle.

Soon after publishing *Modern Islam in India*, Smith watched in shock at the paroxysm of violence unleashed by the partition of India and Pakistan.[37]

The events inspired an about-face on the "scientific method" and the study of religion more generally. In 1951, he reflected:

> Many outside observers, failing to understand the [Islamic] ideal, gave all their attention to the [mundane, human factors], the circumstancing agencies, the material and efficient causes. Consequently, they could describe and analyze, but could hardly understand or appreciate what was going on. The present writer speaks with involvement, since he was one of them: calling attention to the economic, sociological, and psychological causes implicated in the movement, he failed adequately to comprehend the integration of these into significantly Islamic history.
>
> One of the advantages, however, of studying contemporary rather than past history, is that one may fairly quickly learn where one is wrong. The economic, sociological, psychological, and other factors conditioning the separatist movement were there, operative, and important; only, they did not add up to explain the full cataclysm of what happened in 1947, nor the vibrant stamina and creativity of Pakistan in the constructive years since.[38]

Transformed, Smith now argued that materialist explanations of Partition were unable to capture the passion and dynamism behind religious movements. He wrote *Pakistan as an Islamic State* (1951) to correct the mistake. The slender volume positioned religious aspirations rather than economic interests as the driving impetus behind the creation of Pakistan, and yet Smith still managed to avoid treating Islam as a monolithic and transhistorical agent in history. He argued instead that it was the act of striving toward Islamic perfection, of debating how to translate the prophetic ideal into a modern state, and of expounding on the best interpretations of the Qur'an that made Pakistan Islamic. Smith used this aspirational model of Islamic history to challenge both the reductionism of the social sciences and the essentialism of his Orientalist colleagues.

Smith crystalized his critiques of the prevailing conceptions of objectivity as a young faculty member at McGill University. In an early exchange with Principal Cyril James, Smith explained his views on the scientific study of religion:

> Our method, current in some of our universities and attuned to the dominant philosophy of our time, is the scientific, the objective. It is an indispensable first step; but in my view is not adequate to this particular field [of religion],

and perhaps to all fields where persons as persons are involved. To be uncharitable, the student has been compared to a fly crawling on the outside of a goldfish bowl, who makes accurate and complete observations on the fish inside, measures their scales painstakingly, and indeed contributes much to a detailed knowledge of the subject, but who never asks himself, and never finds out, how it feels to be a goldfish. The Islamics scholar of this type is, to my thinking, but a technician whose services become valuable only when used by a student of much more profound intent.[39]

In other words, Smith argued that the dominant mode of objectivity prioritized a critical distance and an omniscient perspective for analysis rather than encouraged scholars to explore the emotions, passions, and experiences of the goldfish. This methodological approach rendered academics incapable of understanding the interiority of religious faith. In Smith's assessment, objectivity offered a partial view of religion at best and a hollow knowledge at worst. It therefore fell short of its own claims of impartiality and analytical depth. In contrast, Smith aspired to restore the "link between rationality and personality which it is one of scientific objectivity's avowed aims to cut."[40] He insisted that the subjective was an integral domain if scholars were to grasp the whole truth of human and especially religious experiences. Consequently, Smith proposed fusing objective research methods and subjective modes of understanding into a single method for the study of religion.

Smith established the McGill Institute of Islamic Studies to help transform Western academics from metaphorical flies into near-goldfish. His first step was to insist that the institute's staff and student body be half Western and half Muslim in composition. Indeed, he envisioned that "part of [the institute's] very significance will be that its results will emerge from what is perhaps the first time in history that representatives of these two civilizations will have sat down together to serious, protracted, and mutual pursuit of understanding."[41] For the Western "representatives," Smith hoped consistent and sustained interaction with Muslim colleagues at McGill would teach them to study Islam empathetically and understand its subjective force. This process would, in turn, enable Western academics to take Muslim views of their own religious tradition into account and produce research capable of communicating both to fellow Western academics *and* Muslims of faith. For Smith, this latter point was absolutely critical; he frequently asserted that no work on any religion could be considered valid unless members of that religious community recognized the writing as at least partially reflective of their practices and beliefs.[42]

Smith also implored Western academics to use their study of Islam to reflect on their personal religious convictions. Admittedly, he assumed that the institute's Western participants were, like him, engaged Christians and called on them to abandon their "theological isolationism." He explained to James that "to my mind, few greater services could be rendered the Church in the mid-20th century than that of providing it with serious and creative opportunities to wrestle with . . . the issue of alternative world faiths."[43] Smith worked to model this vision of engaged Christian scholarship in his own writings. He wrote openly about how his encounters with Muslims had both deepened his Presbyterian faith and made him question certain Church tenets on non-Christians. Smith extrapolated from his experiences to suggest that studying Islam could help overturn the West's exclusivist religious culture and cultivate in its stead a more open, universalist ethos. He believed that the institute could and should help forge this new Christian culture.

For McGill's Muslim representatives, Smith envisioned the institute as a space for learning how to balance their subjective insider knowledge of Islam with an objective, outsider perspective. To bring this vision to fruition, Smith actively recruited both Muslim faculty members and graduate students from across the Islamic world and especially from South and Southeast Asia. He helped many secure financial support from the Rockefeller, Ford, and Asia foundations, whereas others were sent on behalf of modernizing governments such as those in Pakistan, Iran, and Indonesia. This diverse group of Muslims would, according to Smith's aspiration, think together "in the dispassionate atmosphere of honest and informed religious inquiry, and away from the pressures and localisms of their own milieu."[44] They would study academic research methods such as historical analysis, philology, and the phenomenology of religion and learn about Western modernity firsthand. This cross-cultural immersion would provide them with opportunities to adapt modern modes of knowledge for their own Muslim communities. Smith had high hopes for the institute's Muslim scholars. In May 1951, he wrote to James, "At its highest—if you will not smile at the exaggerated ambition—I would foresee our programme conceivably acting as a kind of midwife for the Islamic Reformation which is struggling to be born."[45] In other words, the institute would not only study the modern Islamic world but mold it.

LIVING AS GOLDFISH AT MCGILL

As founding director, Smith was the heart and soul of the McGill Institute of Islamic Studies, and he used that stature to set a specific, demanding vision for McGill's Muslim scholars. On the one hand, he sought committed and engaged Muslims capable of representing their corner of the Muslim world to Western colleagues. On the other hand, he also expected that McGill's Muslims would adopt academic research methods to formulate creative, self-critical approaches to Islam. Smith thus wanted them to be both insiders and outsiders, or to embody a simultaneously subjective and objective role vis-à-vis modern Islamic thought. This vision placed a double burden on Muslim scholars. They already had to submit themselves to the disciplining process of the Western university in order to participate in and contribute to academic conversations, but they now had to meet Smith's more particular expectations as well. Laden with cross-cultural and barely (after all, the institute opened in 1951) postcolonial power dynamics, this disciplining process enabled some Muslim scholars to adapt and integrate into Western academia but also produced alienation and, at times, resistance to Smith, McGill, and the academy at large.

From the outset, Smith recruited Muslim scholars to teach and study at the institute largely on the basis that they were Muslim. On May 26, 1951, he explained his plans to James:

> To achieve its objectives, the Institute would invite scholars of major significance from the Muslim world, to expound and explain Islam, and to interpret it in terms meaningful and illuminating to those educated in our cultural ways. They would do this by lectures, in seminars, and by their writing and research.... The Muslim visitors would, it is planned, represent a variety of disciplines ... and a variety of geographic areas ... to give a picture of Islam that would be, to as great a degree as feasible, comprehensive as well as authoritative.[46]

According to Smith, Muslim faculty members were to represent their region or school of thought to Western colleagues. The institute often engaged in tokenism of this kind. Smith introduced Muslim professors according to their identities as traditionalists or modernists rather than in terms of their research specializations.[47] He even spoke about the nonpracticing Turkish socialist Niyazi Berkes as a "creative Muslim mind."[48] Daud Rahbar, a Pakistani scholar who spent two years as a visiting professor at McGill in the 1950s, summarized the Muslim faculty's obligation to represent their culture and religion succinctly. He wrote, "To be *an informant* on the culture of the Muslims was a privilege."⁴⁹ Clearly, Smith framed the roles of a Western versus a Muslim scholar as essentially different. The former had to imagine what it was like to be a goldfish; the latter were tasked with authenticating whether those imaginings were accurate.

Although he encouraged McGill Muslims to represent their faith, Smith did not want them to adopt an apologetic stance to defend that faith. Building on H.A.R. Gibb's criticisms of Muslim apologetics, Smith wrote empathetically but disparagingly about what he saw as this dominant intellectual trend in the Muslim world. He conceded that apologetics were a natural human reaction to the threats of colonialism and to the rapid social changes introduced by Western-style modernity, but he also castigated the practice as corrosive. In *Islam in Modern History* (1957), he argued that "the basic disruption of apologetics is that it has diverted the attention of contemporary Islamic thinkers from their central task—the central task of all thinkers: to pursue truth and to solve problems."⁵⁰ He lamented the apologetic approach to history in particular, writing that Muslims used it "almost explicitly to nourish and to support one's predilections . . . not to analyze or to understand the past, but to glorify it; that is, to glorify oneself."⁵¹ For Smith, apologetic defenses of Islam did not forestall the onslaught of Western-style modernity but instead produced intellectual stagnation and social stasis.

In addition to criticizing Muslim apologetics, Smith used the institute to model an alternative: self-critical analysis. He argued that certain academic methods could offer Muslims a more objective and hence critical approach to their history. In one 1956 report, he wrote:

> The really major service that we can, and I think have begun to provide, lies in the field of self-awareness on the part of Islam. If we can train Muslim personnel with an increased self-critical understanding of the contemporary crisis through which they and their culture are passing and if we can produce books that will disseminate and stimulate further afield in the Muslim world such a self-critical understanding, then certainly we shall feel that our effort has been worthwhile.⁵²

In many ways, Smith wanted Muslims to adopt the Orientalist model of history writing as Islamic critique. He believed that by pinpointing past intellectual failures and identifying the roots of civilizational decline, Muslims could use their critical self-awareness to draw lessons for their contemporary contexts. In Smith's eyes, both the tragedies and triumphs of Islamic history could inspire Muslims to construct a more viable and vibrant modern Islam. Institute faculty encouraged this self-awareness by stressing historical analysis and framing subjects such as theology and law as historical entities susceptible to change across time and space.

Smith evaluated Muslim scholarship on the basis of his subjective–objective vision, often publishing critical book reviews in which he complained about the absence of one posture or the other. Smith disparaged Uthman Amin's and Zafarullah Khan's contributions to the published proceedings of a Harvard conference on Islam and the West as "apologetic" and as "add[ing] virtually nothing to what was previously known."[53] However, less than a year later, Smith criticized Muslim contributions to Kenneth Morgan's *Islam: The Straight Path* for the opposite offense: the essays were "without splendor and without anguish."[54] Although acknowledging that the essays were by no mean failures in the historical or descriptive senses, Smith deemed them woefully devoid of spirit. He pointed to Egyptian historian Shafiq Ghurbal's work as an example: "Ghurbal's historical survey is, we have already indicated, excellent and creative. He is to be congratulated upon it. However, if he had not done this, a Westerner would perhaps have done so soon. . . . There is no reason why a non-Muslim might not in principle have the same sort of perspective."[55] Ghurbal's failure was that his essay was *only* objective and thus lacked that burning insight that comes from faith. According to Smith, Muslims needed to merge the objective and subjective in order to communicate the vitality of Islam to non-Muslims and to inspire Muslims to enact religious reforms.

To create an environment where Muslim scholars could develop this distinct approach to scholarship, Smith worked actively to cultivate a closely knit, interreligious community at McGill. During its early years, the institute was housed in a large stone mansion approximately a quarter mile away from the main McGill campus, straight up Mount Royal. The steep hike between campus and the institute guaranteed a degree of isolation from the wider McGill community but also fostered a sense of solidarity within the institute itself. Smith and other faculty members were known to provide rides to the institute during the long, hard Montreal winters, and it was not uncommon for various professors to invite students to their houses. Smith himself hosted Christmas parties at his home, designating one Western student to dress up as Santa Claus every year. In turn, Smith encouraged Muslims to use the institute's space to hold Friday prayers, and he required all students to attend Muslim funerals in Montreal.[56] Howard Federspiel, a doctoral student at McGill in the late 1950s, noted that "probably we were closer as a group than most academics and I knew my professors better than most graduate students know theirs elsewhere."[57]

Smith also created consistent opportunities for intellectual encounter and exchange at McGill. He implemented two unique policies: major seminars and daily teas. First, the institute convened two wide-ranging seminars each semester on topics such as Islam in the modern world and the meaning of Islam in history, with the expectation that all faculty members and students attend at least one and ideally both. While the seminars were led by one professor, other faculty members contributed to discussion and collaborated on shared research questions.[58] The sessions were often lively affairs. In October 1958, a visiting Rockefeller official counted twelve staff members and sixteen students in attendance at one major seminar.[59] Smith extended this collaborative model to smaller classes by assigning each faculty member a "co-professor" who would attend sessions as an expert participant in the course. Second, Smith established the tradition of daily 4 p.m. teas during which faculty members, students, and visitors discussed contemporary events and scholarship. Smith assigned a Muslim and a non-Muslim graduate student as partners to prepare tea each week in an effort to facilitate friendships across national and religious differences.[60] While attendance at the daily teas was optional, it was required at one formal tea each week when a professor or visitor would lead the discussion. One visiting Rockefeller official joked that these teas "occasionally expanded to a sort of informal inquisition visited upon hapless guests . . . all very pleasant really."[61] Thinking and researching collectively were at the heart of institute culture.

Smith's conscious efforts to foster dialogue across cultural and religious lines had the unintended consequence of essentializing and even pigeonholing McGill scholars as either Western or Muslim. After all, Smith chose a *Western* student to be Santa Claus and designated one *Westerner* and one *Muslim* as afternoon tea partners. Although Western and Muslim were clearly not equivalent terms, Smith and others associated with the institute deployed them as parallel and generally unproblematic categories. They assumed that the two categories were mutually exclusive, even though an African-American convert did study at the institute in the late 1950s.[62] The classification scheme also failed to address faculty members and students who were neither Western nor Muslim, like Japanese scholar of religion Toshihiko Izutsu (1914–93). For the most part, Smith and his colleagues seemed unconcerned about these questions and how the Western–Muslim dichotomy positioned scholars on the basis of only one aspect of their identities. This binary was an ironic blind spot for Smith because he used his later years at the institute to argue against religious essentialism in *The Meaning and End of Religion* (1962).[63]

At the structural level, the essentialized Muslim versus Western categories influenced how Smith hired and brokered contracts with professors. During the 1955–56 academic year, he frequently wrote about his search for a "non-Muslim second" to assist him in the administration of the institute, implying that Muslim scholars were somehow less suitable for institutional leadership.[64] Smith also argued that Muslim faculty members should not be offered McGill's usual five-year professorial contracts with nearly automatic renewal but should rather be limited to one-time, five-year visits.[65] He repeatedly stressed that, after their stints at McGill, Muslim professors would ideally return to their home countries to disseminate their new research methods and serve as much-needed intellectual catalysts for an Islamic revival.[66] However, in late 1956, Smith began to have second thoughts about limited appointments for all Muslim faculty. He crafted a distraught letter to Rockefeller official John Marshall in defense of retaining Fazlur Rahman and Niyazi Berkes, writing, "So far as the moral responsibility of having our men go back to the Muslim world is concerned, you may be quite sure that this weighs on my mind more heavily than on anyone else's—and especially more heavily than on the minds of the Muslims themselves." After detailing numerous attempts by other universities to poach Rahman and Berkes from McGill, Smith continued, "It would seem to me quite unfair if McGill were debarred from offering permanent appointments to men whom other universities on this continent could, and would, take on as permanent members of their staff."[67] Smith eventually won the battle with Rockefeller to keep Rahman and Berkes on a more permanent basis, but he never abandoned his paternalistic hope that Muslim faculty settle in the Islamic world and teach their fellow Muslims a more modern way of understanding Islam.

Smith set exceedingly high expectations for McGill's Muslim scholars. They were to embrace their religious subjectivities as Muslims and adopt an objective and self-critical scholarly posture. They were to return to the Muslim world as reformers and contribute to Western academic conferences and publications. Unsurprisingly, Smith often found himself disappointed with the results. By 1954, he was already asking himself, "To what extent is the training the Institute offers justified in the case of students who will never be first rate?"[68] Although Smith believed that the investment in Muslim students was warranted considering their life-long engagement with Islamic thought, he nevertheless conveyed that the improvements the institute was witnessing were often negligible. In 1955, he characterized the struggle to acclimate a Muslim student to "the world of critical academic analysis of his own culture" as "crucial" but also "so demanding in terms of energy" that he wondered whether to lower it on the institute's priority list.[69] It was a low moment, but Smith persevered with his lofty vision.

Smith expected Muslim students and faculty members to acculturate themselves to his vision. Some were less than willing—or less than able—to undergo the disciplining process. Mohamad Rasjidi (1915–2001) was one such example. Born in Yogyakarta, Rasjidi attended a combination of Muhammadiyah and Dutch schools as a boy and then, in 1931, relocated to Egypt. Once in Cairo, Rasjidi first enrolled at al-Azhar, then at Dar al-Ulum, and finally at Cairo University, where he enthusiastically studied Western philosophy under Arab professors with French degrees. He returned to Indonesia in 1938 and was quickly swept up in the national revolution. In 1946, he was appointed as Indonesia's first minister of religious affairs but served for less than a year, thanks to constant cabinet fluctuations.[70] He later worked as the Indonesian consul in Egypt, served as a Ministry of Foreign Affairs official in Jakarta, and taught at several Islamic universities in Indonesia.[71] However, Rasjidi never forgot his inspiring experiences studying under French-educated professors in Cairo. He pursued opportunities to obtain a doctoral degree at the Sorbonne under Louis Massignon and eventually secured financial support from the Rockefeller Foundation. In December 1955, Rasjidi spent approximately three weeks in Cairo working with Massignon and then proceeded to Paris to submit his dissertation and take his doctoral examinations. It was a brief exposure to Western academia, largely mediated through the enigmatic figure of Massignon. Nevertheless, Rasjidi passed his exams in late March 1956, becoming the first Indonesian to earn a doctorate in Islamic studies.[72]

Rasjidi's newly minted doctorate opened doors. Within months of returning from Paris, he met Smith during the Canadian's first visit to Indonesia.

Smith was impressed and shortly thereafter commenced a campaign to get Rasjidi to McGill. In June 1956, Smith wrote to the Asia Foundation to request funds for Rasjidi's appointment, explaining that "I found him a man of quality, highly interested in the kinds of problems that we at this Institute are trying to tackle, interested in the intellectual, moral, and social problems of Islam in Indonesia in its new, independent, and modern form. . . . He would contribute to our work."[73] Although Rasjidi initially turned down Smith's offer in favor of the ambassadorial post in Pakistan, he accepted a "look and see" five-year appointment two years later, when Masyumi's, and hence, his own, political fortunes sank. In the fall of 1958, Rasjidi joined the McGill Institute.

During the 1950s and 1960s, Rasjidi deepened his familiarity with Western academia and learned to navigate some of its implicit norms. He cultivated his talents at academic networking. In 1958, he contributed an essay on "Unity and Diversity in Indonesia" to Colgate University professor Kenneth Morgan's *Islam: The Straight Path*. This collaboration fostered a friendship between Rasjidi and Morgan, who, in addition to his work as a professor, served in various leadership capacities in the Connecticut-based Edward W. Hazen Foundation. Together, they helped broker a Hazen-McGill scholarship program for Indonesian students from Rasjidi's own University of Indonesia.[74] He also translated Earlham College professor David Elton Trueblood's *Philosophy of Religion* (1957) into Indonesian. His adaptation of Trueblood's work, titled *Falsafat Agama* (1965), deployed internal Western criticisms of Marxism, Freudian analysis, and positivism to delegitimize these modern philosophies and hence stem the surging tide of secularism in Indonesia.[75]

Nevertheless, Rasjidi also struggled against McGill's intellectual currents. A Rockefeller official noted that Rasjidi was "painfully shy, he rarely said a word but [Smith] stated that his rare comments reflect a shrewd and precise mind."[76] He was reportedly unhappy at the institute and often felt outshined by other Muslim faculty members.[77] By 1960, Smith himself speculated that Masyumi's downfall had left Rasjidi so deeply discouraged that he had simply succumbed to passivity and defeat.[78] These problems were particularly acute in terms of Rasjidi's ability to publish. During his five-year contract at McGill, he only managed to publish one chapter, titled "Islam," in the edited volume *The Meaning of Life in Five Great Religions* (1965). Intended as a general introduction to Islam, the chapter neither put forth a sustained argument nor contained footnotes. Rather, Rasjidi devoted much of the essay to explicating what he saw as a series of major Islamic teachings, which he represented as straightforward and eternal. He also took time to defend Islam against common Western criticisms, such as charges that Muslims are fatalists, use violence to spread the religion, and oppress women.[79] None of these passages aimed for original textual interpretation or critical historical analysis. Instead, the essay was Rasjidi's attempt to communicate, as a Muslim, some of the core values of Islam to non-Muslim readers.

Rasjidi's fidelity to "eternal" Islamic teachings rendered him a misfit in an academic environment committed to revisionist historiography. This disjuncture resulted in a direct confrontation with Joseph Schacht in 1958. During a lecture Schacht delivered at the institute, Rasjidi spoke out against the Orientalist's assertion that the Prophet Muhammad had never possessed legislative political authority but rather had relied on pre-Islamic Arab customs of arbitration to settle disputes in Medina. The innovative interpretation elicited enthusiastic responses from McGill's other faculty members, but, as Rasjidi understood it, Schacht—drawing primarily from a tenuous linguistic argument over the difference between a *hakim* and *qadi*—was attacking the precedent of prophetic Medina as the ideal Islamic state. Rasjidi refused to sit quietly and instead challenged the linguistic basis of the argument during the seminar. Schacht, in turn, issued a strong rebuke, retorting that Rasjidi did not have a deep enough understanding of the matter at hand. The exchange quickly escalated from an academic disagreement into a challenge to Rasjidi's position at McGill. Rasjidi recalled that Niyazi Berkes "launched a *fitna* [sedition] campaign" against him, charging that the Indonesian was too orthodox for McGill.[80] In response to the accusations, Smith cancelled classes and convened a meeting of institute faculty and students in order to examine the accusation and Rasjidi's position.[81] Although Rasjidi spent another four years at McGill after the incident, the encounter with Schacht and the interrogation, as Rasjidi saw it, by Smith and other institute faculty left such a bad taste in his mouth that he repeated the story to biographers decades later. McGill, in turn, declined to renew his contract in 1963.

Whereas Smith hoped that Muslim faculty would adopt a self-critical approach to Islam, Rasjidi learned another lesson altogether from his time at McGill: how to embrace the derogatory term *apologist*. In 1972, Rasjidi addressed Smith's criticisms of Muslim apologetics directly:

> Dr. W.C. Smith says that apologetics are found in all Islamic countries, especially Egypt. . . . Why do Westerners dislike apologetics? The reason is that apologetics have opened up new points of view for the Islamic community

> and have provided new evidence that Islam and its sources—the Qur'an and Sunnah—have very strong principles. In contrast, the principles from what is now called Western culture were already known by Islam before they were discovered by the Western world....
>
> Apologetics represent a great progress in thinking about Islam. Apologetics are based on Western knowledge itself, such as that regarding ethics, economics, governance, international relations, etc. Someone who comprehends Islam and then reads the Encyclopedia of Social Sciences will surely feel as though a majority of the Encyclopedia's contents are an application of Islamic teachings.[82]

With these words, Rasjidi turned the academic denigration of apologetics on its head. Instead of signaling the stagnation of Islamic thought, apologists uncovered new aspects of the religion. Rasjidi also argued that apologists' mastery of academic disciplines put them in the ideal position to appreciate Islam's innate modernity and to proclaim its truth to doubting Muslims and critical Westerners alike. In many ways, Rasjidi's time at McGill had led him to the same conclusions that Mohammad Natsir had reached at mid-century: Muslims should only master academic knowledge in order to beat the West at its own game. After returning to Indonesia in the mid-1960s, Rasjidi drew upon his firsthand encounter with the academic study of Islam to develop sophisticated critiques of Orientalism and Western-educated Muslims—both of which we will examine in chapter 3.

Rasjidi was not the only Muslim scholar who scraped up against McGill's unique academic culture. Ismail al-Faruqi (1921–86), the Palestinian-American intellectual who would eventually help pioneer the global Islamization of Knowledge movement, also arrived at the institute in 1958.[83] Faruqi developed a mixed reputation at McGill. On the one hand, faculty colleagues and students alike stressed that he possessed a remarkable mind. Smith reported to Rockefeller officials that "there is no question but that he has an unusually good intellect and quite unusual energy."[84] Over the course of only three years at McGill, Faruqi completed two major book projects, one a wide-ranging cultural history of what he termed "Arabism" and the other a critical examination of Christian theology and the field of comparative religion.[85] The latter was published with McGill University Press and contained a preface by Stanley Brice Frost, the dean of the McGill Divinity School.

On the other hand, Faruqi was often seen as angry, uncooperative, and even combative. Howard Federspiel recalled that Faruqi would skip the institute's weekly teas even when Smith had asked him to host the discussion for the day.[86] At other times, he came to the teas primed for confrontation, especially with Indian scholar Asaf Ali Asghar Fyzee (1899–1981) and British scholars who tried to defend colonialism, especially in his native Palestine.[87] Some of his colleagues worried openly that Faruqi's temperament caused his scholarship to suffer. Having joined several of Faruqi's seminars, one Rockefeller observer noted:

> [Faruqi's] representation was nothing if not forceful; indeed, the "seminar" soon became primarily a podium for the ideas of its leader. These were both fascinating and challenging—and a superb introduction for one intending a career in the Near East. Yet emotion and patriotism as a substitute for objective analysis eventually began to pall, and the last month of the seminar was somewhat repetitious. Greater and uncommitted direction was obviously required, but was not forthcoming.[88]

The observer thus questioned whether Faruqi could constrain his political passions enough to be an objective scholar. Smith shared these concerns, characterizing Faruqi as "not entirely clear in his emotions or always judicious" and as possessing "certain Arab biases."[89] Colleagues routinely called him anti-Western. At McGill, Faruqi's anticolonial perspective was often seen as a breach of academic discipline and even integrity.

One of Faruqi's favorite targets of criticism was Japanese scholar Toshihiko Izutsu. Izutsu was interested in linguistic methods and arrived at the institute hoping to use semantic analysis to understand the ethical system outlined in the Qur'an. Smith was captivated by Izutsu's linguistic methods, but Faruqi and other Muslim faculty members were substantially less impressed. Federspiel described how Faruqi, Rasjidi, and others relentlessly criticized Izutsu "because he came out with this pre-computer rendition of taking the terms out [of] the Qur'an and running them through a program, and [they] thought that this was the worst use of technology possible and that you'd be damaging God's word by doing that."[90] According to Federspiel, these debates went on at afternoon teas, in seminars, and at nearly every other place where Izutsu could be found. Shortly after Faruqi left the institute, he published a scathing review of Izutsu's *The Structure of Ethical Terms in the Koran* (1959). He criticized the Japanese scholar for what he saw as several grievous misinterpretations of the Qur'an—such as representing Islam as tribal, "world-denying," and built around a fearful Allah—that merely repeated

Western prejudices. Consequently, Faruqi labeled the book "an extension of the Western spirit, of the most unworthy intellectual aspect of the spirit, [namely] logical positivism or reductionist analysis, into a field 'Islamics' which has known well the hatreds of religious enmity, of fanaticism and of political imperialism."[91] It was a harsh indictment by a Muslim scholar who had just spent three years studying alongside Western academics at McGill. Clearly, the encounters fostered by the institute resembled, at times, less an intellectual exchange than a head-on collision.

FUSIONIST THINKING AT MCGILL

McGill's unusual academic culture certainly generated friction, but the resulting tension could also be creative in nature, especially for fusionist thinkers. At McGill, fusionists learned to work through two traditions of knowledge—the Western academic and the Islamic—and two modes of truth—the objective and the subjective—simultaneously. They used a variety of academic methods to locate new, cross-discursive truths about Islam. While Smith built the institute as a laboratory for these cross-discursive encounters, McGill Muslim faculty members and students conducted their own experiments that produced diverse results. During its first decades of operation, Fazlur Rahman, Mukti Ali, and Harun Nasution emerged as among McGill's most ardent and influential fusionists. Countering the prevailing assumption that religious commitments were antithetical to objectivity, each of the three men developed a distinct way of merging academic objectivity and Islamic faith. An in-depth examination of their approaches underscores the strength and diversity of fusionist thinking at McGill.

Fazlur Rahman

During his years at the institute, Fazlur Rahman (1919–88) earned a reputation as the rising star among the Muslim faculty. However, McGill was not his first academic appointment. Born in the northwest-frontier region of present-day Pakistan, Rahman received his initial education under the guidance of his father Mawlana Shahab al-Din, who was a member of the local Deobandi 'ulama. He committed the entire Qur'an to memory by the age of ten. Rahman continued the traditional Deobandi course of study but also, with his parents' encouragement, pursued modern Western-style education in Lahore. In 1946, Rahman relocated to England to pursue a doctorate at Oxford University. He devoted his studies to unraveling the complex theories of medieval

Muslim philosophers on human reason, the soul, and the nature of prophecy. Rahman finished his thesis on Ibn Sina only three years after his arrival at Oxford and soon thereafter found a faculty position in the Department of Oriental Studies at Durham University, where he continued his research on Islamic philosophy. In 1953, he took leave from Durham to accept a one-year visiting appointment at the McGill Institute. Toward the end of his time in Montreal, Rahman reported to Rockefeller Foundation officials that he "was most enthusiastic about his year at the Institute of Islamic Studies and felt that it did a great deal for him."[92] Smith was likewise committed to securing him a long-term appointment to the institute faculty. After several years of negotiations, Rahman returned to McGill on a more permanent basis in 1958.

At McGill, Rahman moved away from his earlier focus on Islamic philosophy in order to engage in more wide-ranging historical research. He wrote the first draft of his sweeping history of Islam as a religious tradition, which he later published as simply *Islam* (1966). He also began to research the conceptual history of the Sunnah and hadith. For both of these projects, Rahman embraced self-critical historiography as a way not only to contribute to academic debates over early Islamic history but also to articulate a historically rooted vision for Islamic reform. As a dedicated fusionist, he insisted on the commensurability of academic methods and Islamic faith to both academic and Muslim audiences.

Rahman set his sights on ongoing Orientalist debates over the historical authenticity of hadith in the early 1960s. As the most important source of Islamic teachings and law after the Qur'an, the hadith canon had long attracted the attention of academics who wanted to treat it not as sacred literature but as any other human text with a discernible history. Scholars such as Ignaz Goldziher (1890), D. S. Margoliouth (1914), and Alfred Guillaume (1924) wrote books that criticized wide swaths of hadith literature as forgeries produced decades and even centuries after the death of the Prophet Muhammad. However, in 1950, Joseph Schacht set the new bar for hadith criticism with his widely influential work *The Origins of Muhammadan Jurisprudence*. Schacht credited Islamic legal scholar Imam al-Shafi'i with developing the concept of the prophetic Sunnah. He argued that Muslim scholars in the decades before al-Shafi'i had relied more on the free exercise of personal opinion (*ra'y*), local custom, and often the actions of companions of the Prophet for behavioral models. Al-Shafi'i rejected this status quo as inconsistent and insisted that the Sunnah of the Prophet could not be subordinate to any other source, with the possible exception of the Qur'an itself. Schacht thus characterized al-Shafi'i as "the first lawyer to define Sunnah as the model behavior of the Prophet, in contrast with his predecessors for whom it was not necessarily connected with the Prophet, but represented the traditional, albeit ideal, usage of the community."[93] Because the prophetic Sunnah only acquired its unquestionable normative status in the wake of al-Shafi'i, Schacht argued that "a considerable number of legal traditions, which appear in the classical collections, originated after . . . Shafi'i"—that is, two centuries after the death of the Prophet.[94] In other words, because they postdated the Prophet, most hadiths were merely forged reports designed to boost the authority of their fabricators.

Schacht presented his revisionist history of the Sunnah and hadith in the authoritative language of an objective academic: as impartial, scientific truth. He based his arguments on several modes of historical evidence and argumentation. First, he reconstructed the largely undocumented views and practices of early jurists on the basis of al-Shafi'i's own representations. Second, looking at surviving legal texts, Schacht reasoned that if an earlier scholar did not cite a relevant hadith when a later scholar did, then the given hadith was a post facto forgery. Third, if a hadith referenced political events or theological debates that had not yet arisen at the time of the Prophet, he deemed the content anachronistic and hence inauthentic. Although Schacht claimed that his methods were scientific, each of them relied on unexamined presuppositions. Were al-Shafi'i's representations of his opponents accurate? Would a legal scholar always use all available hadith to support his ruling, or could he be satisfied with only several examples? Would pious Muslims willingly put words in their beloved Prophet's mouth? These interpretative assumptions clearly shaped Schacht's findings. Yet his conception of objectivity did not leave room for the possibility that his own assumptions molded his research—that his skepticism could be as powerful an influence in historical research as belief was.

Whereas Mohamad Rasjidi openly rejected Schacht's revisionist historiography, Rahman praised his methods as "unassailably scientific and sound" and subsequently integrated many of Schacht's findings into his research.[95] Specifically, he deployed Schacht's anachronistic principle to demonstrate that many hadiths, especially those related to political obedience and fatalistic determinism, were inventions of later generations who merely projected their own concerns back to the Prophet.[96] He generally accepted Schacht's argument that if a later version of a hadith contained more detail than an earlier version, then the details were likely fabricated embellishments. Rahman even confirmed Schacht's revisionist chronology by agreeing that "by far the greater part of the *content* of the Sunnah was the result of the freethinking activity of the early legists."[97] In the name of objective historical research, Rahman overturned traditional Muslim understandings of hadiths, accepting instead their inauthenticity and even desacralization. As a fusionist, he believed in the truth-value of academic research over established religious orthodoxies.

While Rahman lauded many of Schacht's methods as objective, he challenged the Orientalist's conceptual history of the Sunnah on grounds that it was simply unreasonable. According to Schacht, "Sunnah" had simply meant the normative practice of the Arab community until al-Shafi'i tied the concept exclusively to the Prophet. By implication, Schacht asserted that the Prophet's actions were only elevated to an absolutely normative status a century and a half after his death. Rahman characterized this argument as "a shallow and irrational scientific myth of contemporary historiography."[98] He maintained that it was a logical absurdity that Muhammad's followers, who had abandoned their homes, waged war, and transformed their lives according to Muhammad's teachings, would not take careful notice of his behavior and consider it exemplary. To support his position, Rahman cited the Qur'an and early Muslim writings as evidence that the earliest Muslims had believed in the prophetic Sunnah.

After countering Schacht's theory, Rahman advanced his own conceptual history of the Sunnah. He argued that Muslims before al-Shafi'i had not originally tied the Sunnah to hadith but had instead relied on reason, communal consensus, and "creative agency" to capture the spirit of Muhammad's teachings. Their Sunnah was more akin to a continual reinterpretation of the prophetic example in light of the realities of daily life. Rahman called this dynamic understanding of the Prophet's example the "living Sunnah." As a logical extension of this idea, Rahman argued that the early generations of Muslims saw the Sunnah and ijtihad as intimately interrelated and that it was only the canonization of hadith that drove a wedge between them.[99] By reconnecting the two concepts, Rahman placed ijtihad on equal footing with the Sunnah as a source of Islamic law. This argument had significant benefits for modernists who had been advocating for the renewed exercise of ijtihad for decades.

Rahman constructed his history of early Muslim jurisprudence in accordance with academic methods and prevailing standards of evidence, but he was also deeply aware of and invested in the religious implications of his research. In the preface to *Islamic Methodology in History*, Rahman wrote, "It is obvious, therefore, that this work has not only a purely historical value but can be of great practical consequence and can indicate the way for further Islamic developments."[100] For Rahman, the practical lesson from his history was that hadiths were not the straightforward records of the Prophet's teachings but rather represented a set of historically contingent interpretations of the prophetic Sunnah. When Muslims overlooked this reality, the consequences were dire. Rahman explained:

> This [hadith] content arose actually in history and has its full significance only within that historical, situational context. Divorced from that situation and eternalized, it blocked and could not fail to block progress in all the spheres of life: political and moral principles, spiritual life, intellectual activity, and education.[101]

If eternalizing hadith had produced grave problems, Rahman suggested that a contextual approach could undo some of the damage. It could overturn hadiths that ran counter to the spirit of the Qur'an and the Prophet's life, like those that encouraged political passivity in the face of corrupt or oppressive rulers. Likewise, because hadith canonization had "stifled [the growth and flowering of Islamic culture] at its very roots," a return to the "living Sunnah" could recapture the dynamism of the early Muslim community.[102] Rahman thus believed that academic research could reinvigorate modern Islam.

Through academic research, Rahman believed that Muslim and non-Muslim scholars alike could understand the Sunnah historically. While he recognized that the motivations driving the search for historical truth were often starkly different for Western academics and for pious Muslims, he did not question whether those differing motives and presuppositions seeped into methodological choices. Rather, Rahman believed in the objectivity of academic methods, maintaining that historical truth was one and the same from all perspectives. In *Islamic Methodology in History*, Rahman wrote: "I, for my part, am convinced, as a Muslim, that neither Islam nor the Muslim Community will suffer from facing the facts of history as they are; on the contrary, historical truth, like all truth, shall invigorate Islam for—as the Qur'an tells us—God is in intimate touch with history."[103] Committed to the unified truth of history, Rahman believed that historical research would clarify and even reform faith and that faith, in turn, would inspire historical research. As a dedicated fusionist, Rahman saw historical research into the Islamic past as both a scholarly imperative and a Muslim obligation.

Mukti Ali

In 1955, Mukti Ali (1923–2004) became the first Indonesian to enroll at the McGill Institute of Islamic Studies. He spent only two years earning his master's degree at McGill, but the brief experience introduced him to the field of comparative religion. It was a formative discovery for a man now remembered as Indonesia's "Father of Comparative Religion."[104] Ali traveled a winding path to the institute. Raised in a pious Central Javanese family, he attended a combination of Dutch and Islamic schools, eventually settling on modernized Islamic education (complete with grade levels, desks, and some nonreligious subjects) in his high school years. Looking back at his early education, Ali acknowledged that the strength of his modernized pesantren was its ability to instill faith and values in its students, but he was frustrated by its reliance on "learning through the methods of memorization and recitation without the energy of criticism."[105] In 1947, Ali enrolled in the Islamic College (later IAIN) where he developed an interest in Islamic modernism. However, when the Dutch army recaptured Yogyakarta in 1948 and forced the college to suspend its operations, Ali joined a Muslim militia to fight for Indonesia's independence.[106]

As the Indonesian Revolution entered its final months of military confrontation with the Dutch, Ali decided to embark on the international leg of his intellectual journey. He studied in three separate countries in the span of only five years. In 1950, Ali traveled to Mecca to perform hajj and pursue his newfound interest in Islamic reformism. Yet he became quickly disillusioned with the city's "medieval" atmosphere and its strictly traditional educational opportunities, so he relocated yet again—this time to Pakistan. Between 1951 and 1955, Ali worked part-time at the Indonesian embassy and studied Islamic history at the University of Karachi. While he eagerly read Western academic scholarship on Islam for the first time in Karachi, he later noted that the level of education in Pakistan was only slightly higher than that in Indonesia and that he regretted his lack of methodological training.[107] By a stroke of good fortune, Ali met Smith during one of the latter's trips to Pakistan, and arrangements were quickly made for the Indonesian scholar to move to Montreal.

When he arrived at McGill, Ali finally located what he called a satisfying model of Islamic education. His courses no longer only focused on the acquisition of facts but also encouraged students to explore answers to "how" and "why."[108] Smith left a particularly strong impression. In his memoirs, Ali fondly recalled that Smith, despite his busy schedule as the institute's director, took the time to pick him up at the airport when he first arrived in Montreal.[109] He also stressed Smith's acumen as a teacher. In addition to noting "the amazing way [Smith] taught," Ali reflected:

> Before studying in Canada, I knew nothing about the study of Comparative Religion. My specialization in Pakistan was Islamic History. Therefore, although at McGill I studied with many professors, such as Niyazi Berkes from Turkey, William Bagley from Britain, Prof. Bahy from Egypt, I paid more attention to Prof. Smith's courses. I cannot explain why. There are some reasons, of course. The first regards the system of study that we used; and second, I liked his method of analysis . . .
>
> Most important of all was that Prof. Smith introduced me to a new approach in the study of Islam. He used comparative analysis in religious works, meaning trying to look at one religious phenomenon from all its aspects. If I may name it, that approach was a "holistic approach" about religion—an approach that greatly affected my path of thought or even in a wider context, changed my attitude towards understanding humanity.[110]

Thanks to Smith, Ali developed a profound interest in both comparative religion and fusionist approaches to Islam. In his own words, he believed "it was an obligation of Muslim intellectuals and ʿulama to marry the two systems of education."[111]

While Ali's memoirs presented McGill as the culmination of his long search for Islamic knowledge, contemporaneous documents hint at a more complicated and even difficult experience at the institute. He had some trouble adjusting to McGill's academic culture. In a report to Asia Foundation scholarship officials, Smith described Ali as "not brilliant" and noted that "he had considerable difficulty at first" but "has done increasingly satisfactory work" in his second year at McGill.[112] While trying to highlight Ali's improvement, the underlying message betrayed the depths of Ali's struggles as Smith mentioned problems with both exams and essays. Smith had so little confidence in Ali's abilities that he advised the graduate student to pursue a decidedly unambitious bibliographical project on Muhammadiyah as his master's thesis. For his part, Ali likely omitted these challenges from his later memoir because he retrospectively remembered the real significance of his time at McGill as introducing him to an alternative model of Islamic scholarship. However, it is clear that he required time to appreciate and eventually adopt the properly critical posture of a Smithian academic.

Although Ali—like many of his fellow Muslims at McGill—had struggled to adjust to Western academic norms, he still found his encounter with Western academia transformative. He returned to Indonesia in 1957 intent on persuading his fellow citizens about the value of comparative religion. He obtained an initial appointment at Mahmud Yunus's ADIA. Then, in 1960, Ali secured a full-time professorship at IAIN Jakarta and was soon thereafter asked to establish the first IAIN Department of Comparative Religion in Yogyakarta. As the inaugural dean, he worked to spread his own enthusiasm for the new field. He wrote eloquently about its great potential as "one of the most profound and extensive endeavors ever undertaken by the world of academia to understand the inner meaning (*batin*) of life, the nature of thought, and the inclination of the heart."[113] He also helped design the curriculum and even wrote an introductory text, *The Study of Comparative Religion: A Discussion of Methods and System*, that was often assigned to students. Drawing inspiration from his studies with Smith at McGill, Ali used the text to construct a fusionist approach to comparative religion that was simultaneously objective and subjective in nature.

Because comparative religion was relatively new to Indonesian Muslims, Ali devoted a substantial portion of the short text to explaining what he saw as its scholarly purpose and research methods. He emphasized the field's universalist and scientific aspirations "to recover and to determine the fundamental structure behind religious experiences and concepts by analyzing similarities and differences among religions."[114] He explained that this work required scholars to collect empirical data and use systematic research methods. Accordingly, Ali outlined major disciplinary approaches to religion, including philology, anthropology, and sociology. He introduced important scholars of religion such as Max Müller and Emile Durkheim and provided a primer on evolutionary theories about primitive and monotheistic religions. He consistently framed comparative religion research as an intricate and professional process that, although challenging, could attain a degree of objectivity.[115]

Moreover, Ali took pains to differentiate comparative religion from religious apologetics. On the third page of the text, he stated unequivocally: "comparative religion is not apologetics. [It] is absolutely not a tool to defend one's own beliefs and religion."[116] Ali explained that beginning in the nineteenth century, a handful of Western academics, including Müller, recognized this important distinction and managed to "free themselves from apologetics."[117] Ali lamented that Islamic scholars, in contrast, had never risen above apologetic writing on other religions. Citing Gibb's assessment of modern Islamic thought, he noted that even Syed Ameer Ali's popular *The Spirit of Islam* (1891) was tainted with this common Muslim limitation. Ali concluded that "there simply are no original works [by Muslims] on non-Islamic beliefs and religions that are written based on firsthand research in our modern age."[118] He attributed this shortcoming not to some essentialist Muslim provincialism but to the experience of colonialism. European scholars had more resources to travel and research whereas Muslims both lacked these advantages and felt compelled to defend themselves against European conquest. Hoping to rectify the intellectual imbalance, Ali implored his fellow Muslims to conduct their own academic—rather than apologetic—research on other religions to escape their dependence on Western scholarship.[119]

Although he encouraged Muslim scholars to eschew apologetics in favor of objectivity, Ali also maintained that comparative religion research would serve the interests of the Muslim community. To support this argument, he denied that objectivity ever required scholars, "even for a moment," to separate themselves from their personal beliefs. On the contrary, Ali asserted that scholars were free to hold tightly onto their own faiths as long as they approached other faiths with sympathy and respect.[120] It was a Smithian rejection of the objective-subjective binary. Indeed, Ali framed comparative religion as a way for Muslims to deepen their faith in Islam, explaining how studying earlier revelations could shed new light on forgotten Islamic teachings and clarify the nature of Qur'anic finality.[121] He also stressed the field's potential benefits for Islamic missionary work but emphasized that comparative religion could only help if Muslims sought knowledge about other religions and cultivated a genuine sense of sympathy and responsibility toward non-Muslims. If they met these emotional prerequisites, then Muslims could use their comparative study of religions to develop a simpler vocabulary to articulate Islamic teachings to others and to learn to solve problems with non-Muslim neighbors, thereby making Islam more attractive to potential converts.[122] Ultimately, Ali believed that the objective and subjective elements of comparative religion complemented one another.

Harun Nasution

In his memoirs, Harun Nasution (1919–98) states that he "found [*mencari*] Islam at McGill."[123] It was a surprising declaration for a well-educated and well-traveled Indonesian Muslim. Nasution was born in Sumatra to a pious Muslim family and attended a Dutch Native School from the age of seven to fourteen. He had hoped to continue his Dutch education, but his parents enrolled him instead in an Islamic high school in Bukittinggi. Nasution later recalled his teenage frustrations with traditionalist Islam, especially rituals such as the need to perform ablutions before touching the Qur'an. His traditionalist parents grew concerned about their son's faith and decided to dispatch the adolescent to Mecca. Nasution, however, soon became disappointed in Mecca's traditionalism as well. He described the city as a woefully unmodern place. Its streets were full of dust but vacant of cars, and its schools lacked desks and chairs. Disenchanted with the reputed heart of the Islamic world, Nasution cajoled his parents with threats of becoming a driver in order to gain their permission and financial support to relocate to Cairo.[124] He arrived in Cairo in 1938 and managed to gain entrance to the Faculty of Usuluddin at al-Azhar, but even al-Azhar was unable to satiate Nasution's desire for a deeper sense of learning. He worried that "after I graduate from al-Azhar, I would obtain a teaching license (*ijazah*) even though my religious knowledge is minimal."[125] As a result, he began to supplement his studies at al-Azhar with courses at the American University of Cairo.

Beginning with the outbreak of World War II, global politics repeatedly interrupted Nasution's education. When the Japanese invaded Indonesia, his parents were no longer able to finance his foreign education. Nasution withdrew from both al-Azhar and the American University and found work as a translator, first for the British troops stationed in Cairo and then for a private corporation. In 1947, he joined the staff of the Indonesian consulate in Cairo, working alongside Foreign Minister Agus Salim and Egyptian Consul Mohamad Rasjidi to secure Arab support for the country's struggle against the Dutch. This initial position opened up more opportunities for Nasution in the new Indonesian diplomatic corps and resulted in subsequent postings to

Jakarta, Riyadh, and Brussels.[126] However, Nasution—like most other Arab-educated Indonesians—was a registered member of Masyumi. He also harbored a contempt for the Indonesian Communist Party (Partai Komunis Indonesia [PKI]) and voiced some sympathies for the regional rebellion in his native West Sumatra. By the late 1950s, these political views marked Nasution as an anti-Sukarno dissident. He was unceremoniously fired from the Brussels embassy and placed on a blacklist. Worried that he would be arrested if he tried to return to Indonesia, Nasution decided to move back to Egypt. He made the best out of a bad situation by enrolling in a private Islamic college. There he began to read Western Orientalist scholarship and became interested in rationalist approaches to Islam. It was an enlightening but also anxious two years. Fortunately for Nasution, the McGill Institute was searching for more students from the Indonesian archipelago, and Rasjidi remembered his former consular colleague and passed his name along to Smith.[127] Nasution arrived at McGill in September 1962.

Although he had pursued advanced Islamic education in both Mecca and Cairo, Nasution chose to credit the institute with finally offering him "a broad view of Islam." In his memoirs, he wrote:

> At McGill, I realized that Islamic instruction within and outside Islam were quite different. The lectures had dialogue. All courses were in seminar format. I genuinely felt the benefits. I not only received the lessons but was engaged in understanding them. There, for the first time, I understood Islam viewed from its various aspects.[128]

At the institute, he read works by South Asian Muslims and European Orientalists and began to see Islam as a diverse and dynamic intellectual tradition. He wrote his master's thesis on Masyumi's conception of the Islamic State, tracing its historical development and the lessons that could be derived from the party's downfall.[129] Most significantly, McGill was the place where Nasution proclaimed his adherence to Muʿtazilism. A once powerful but long defunct school of theology, the Muʿtazilites maintained that God and His injunctions were accessible not only through revelation but through human rationality as well. They also argued that humans possessed an unfettered capacity to exercise free will on the grounds that if God punishes humans for their transgressions, then they must be fully responsible for those actions. Inspired by Muʿtazilite teachings, Nasution emphasized that at McGill, he "came to see Islam in a rational manner."[130] Ultimately, this Muʿtazilite rationalism served as the basis of Nasution's fusionist thinking because it enabled him to embrace academic research methods and the ideal of objectivity as integral parts of—rather than threats to—his Islamic faith.

Nasution's doctoral dissertation sought to answer the question of which—if any—school of Islamic theology the much-respected Egyptian reformer Muhammad Abduh followed. Nasution compared Abduh's approach to the relationship between reason and revelation with the teachings of the Ashʿari, Maturidi, and Muʿtazilite schools of theology. As a self-proclaimed Muʿtazilite, Nasution unsurprisingly concluded that Abduh most closely aligned with Muʿtazilism. Nasution even went a step further, arguing that the thrust of Abduh's reforms required the reformer to adopt a Muʿtazilite orientation. Nasution wrote:

> In view of his endeavor to introduce reforms into the Muslim community, Abduh could not but follow the Muʿtazilite theology with its belief in the great power of reason and man's independence and its doctrine of man's free will and free act. Only in terms of such a theology could his ideas of reform see realization. The Ashʿari theology with its distrust of the power of reason, its great reliance on revelation, and its doctrines of disguised fatalism . . . could not be an adequate basis or vehicle for his ideas of reforms.[131]

The implications of Nasution's argument were clear. If Abduh had been a Muʿtazilite, then the legions of Indonesian modernists who looked to him as an inspiration should also embrace Muʿtazilite teachings. Yet Nasution knew that this was no simple suggestion because the vast majority of Indonesians, like other Sunni Muslims, were adherents to the Ashʿari school of theology, which had developed in the ninth century in direct opposition to Muʿtazilite principles. By connecting Abduh to Muʿtazilism, Nasution hoped to persuade his fellow Muslims to overcome their historical distaste for Muʿtazilites and take their ideas, especially their high respect for human reason, seriously once again.

Although his dissertation sought to use Abduh to resurrect Muʿtazilism, Nasution articulated his reinterpretation of the Egyptian reformer not through personal theological claims but with the language of academic objectivity. His introductory chapter explained his choice to use his advisor Toshihiko Izutsu's linguistic theory of "focus-words" to discern Abduh's theology. He assured his readers that this systematic linguistic method would enable him to "discover the real nature of [Abduh's] theology."[132] He thus made claims to the complete and objective truth about Abduh. In this manner, Nasution argued not only that human reason lay at the heart of Abduh's theology but also that human reason in the form of systematic academic methods was the only genuine means through which to study and understand the Egyptian reformer's ideas. As a fusionist, Nasution viewed reason as both Islamic and academic.

In late January 1969, Nasution disembarked from an empty decommissioned hajj transport ship at the Tanjung Priok harbor in Jakarta. After six years of graduate studies at McGill, he now possessed his doctoral degree, and yet, in Jakarta, he had no family, no house, and no sufficient income to support himself and his wife. He quickly accepted a faculty position at IAIN Jakarta. Over the course of the next several years, Nasution continued to emphasize the importance of human reason for revitalizing Islam. He published several books and essays on the topic, hoping to expand the Indonesian discussion of theology to include Muʿtazilism. The bibliographies for these books featured a diverse range of authors, including classical Arab scholars, Muslim modernists, and Western Orientalists.[133] However, he did not publish his dissertation on Abduh because he realized that its argument would alienate too many of his modernist colleagues.[134] He left that battle for another day.

ACADEMIC CRITICS OF FUSIONISM

By flinging open the doors of Western academia to Muslim intellectuals, the McGill Institute of Islamic Studies served as a creative space where scholars could merge religious convictions and purportedly objective academic methods in pursuit of a unified truth. As a result, fusionist thinking thrived at the institute, but it also faced powerful resistance from established Orientalists beyond McGill's campus. The critics were adamant that academic research required the absence, or at least the suspension, of religious motivations in the research process. They protected a stark juxtaposition between objectivity and religious faith on the grounds that religious convictions crippled scholarly skepticism and the willingness to follow evidence and critical analysis to their logical and sometimes radically unorthodox conclusions. In their eyes, fusionists were no different than the Christian missionaries or Muslim apologists of past generations. These critics simply rejected fusionist claims to objectivity and denied their identity as genuine academics. Given their numbers and stature at the time, they were able to challenge the academic authority of fusionism and marginalize the McGill model within the broader field of Islamic studies.[135]

In the 1950s and 1960s, Rahman emerged as one of McGill's most distinguished Muslim faculty members and as the institute's single most prominent fusionist. As we have seen, Rahman used academic methods to diagnose problems he saw as plaguing modern Islam and to revise understandings of early Islamic history. Specifically, *Islamic Methodology in History* (1965) and *Islam* (1966) were the products of this creative endeavor to merge historical and Islamic religious truths; he addressed both books to Western and Muslim readers, hoping to push the former to "learn to know something of what Islam does to a Muslim from the inside" and the latter to "look more objectively at his religious history."[136] Despite these repeated claims to objectivity, Western scholars of Islam continued to pigeonhole Rahman as a Muslim thinker rather than a full-fledged fellow academic. Even friendly reviewers such as R. B. Serjeant and Annmarie Schimmel appraised Rahman's work not in terms of his historical arguments but rather "to see how a Muslim scholar of his type and attainments in modern Pakistan" positions himself.[137] Rahman's scholarly voice was thus deemed inescapably Muslim, casting him consistently as an informant rather than a colleague.

While Rahman's works contained a sophisticated methodological and philosophical apparatus, some Western scholars not only underscored his inescapably Muslim identity but furthermore assailed him as inadequately "academic." In a review of *Islamic Methodology*, Joseph Schacht wrote:

> The way in which the author uses the results of modern Western scholarship in order to make his point is open to grave objections. The only consistent and valid alternative to the traditional picture of the origins of Islamic law and jurisprudence is indeed that seen in its general outline by Margoliouth and worked out in detail by Professor Brunschvig and by me over the last 15–20 years. Dr. Fazlur Rahman has realized this, but in order to make his programme acceptable to his traditionalist-minded readers, he presents them, instead of the real alternative, with an imaginary, watered-down one which he tries, by verbal gymnastics, to bring into agreement if not with traditional doctrine, at least with traditionalist feeling.[138]

Schacht thus accused Rahman of bending historical truths to fit the demands of Pakistani Islamic politics. Claiming his own authority on hadith history as absolute, Schacht did not even take the time to engage with and actually critique Rahman's nuanced understanding of the "living Sunnah" because, in Schacht's estimation, the book was "not a work of scholarship" but instead a glimpse into contemporary Pakistani thought. Rahman was a source, not a fellow scholar whose ideas warranted close examination. On this note, fellow Orientalist John Burton agreed. In his review of Rahman's *Islam*, Burton wrote: "His intention, he says, has been to attempt 'to do justice to both historical and Islamic demands'—surely a self-contradictory, and hence, impossible programme. Historiography respects none save objective historical standards and can enter into no alliances."[139] For both Schacht and Burton, Rahman's religious motivations foreclosed on the possibility that he could use sound methods and produce objective scholarship. They denied Rahman's fusionist claims to be both a faithful Muslim and an objective academic, insisting that Rahman could be one or the other but never both. In many ways, they subscribed to intellectual dualism.

Opposition to fusionism extended well beyond McGill's Muslim faculty and eventually rendered Smith a target of criticism as well. Although he enjoyed a reputation as an accomplished scholar of Islam, Smith's endeavor to merge religious commitments and historical research produced more than a few raised eyebrows. In a review of *Islam in Modern History*, Albert Hourani questioned whether Smith's own personal convictions about the essence of faith unduly shaped his analysis of the contemporary Islamic world.[140] Moreover, many scholars of religion voiced serious doubts about Smith's oft-repeated dictum that no observation about a religion is valid unless confirmed by believers. They argued that such reverence toward religious insiders threatened the academic obligation to be skeptical and critical. For example, Mac Ricketts assailed the dictum as "inadequate" and attacked the objectivity of Smith's entire methodological project on grounds that it was "extremely amorphous, subjective, and even romantic."[141] Nevertheless, the criticisms directed against Smith's fusionism were substantially different than those aimed at Rahman. Even if they were vocal in their disagreement with Smith's methodological assumptions or historical analysis, reviewers took Smith's scholarship seriously enough to refute it with reasoned arguments rather than deny that it qualified as academic writing at all. Unlike Rahman, Smith benefited from the shared assumption that he was a member of the academic guild rather than a representative of some "Othered" tradition.

In 1963, Smith decided to resign from McGill to pursue his growing interests in comparative religion as director of the Center for the Study of World Religions at Harvard University.[142] There, Smith focused on exploring the religious history of mankind and developing an interreligious theology. He also continued to foster fusionist thinking and interreligious encounters among his students. Yet Smith's new disciplinary affiliation meant that the force of his methodological interventions fell beyond the scope of Islamic studies. This change in primary audience had its benefits for Smith because he often found more fertile ground for fusionism in religious studies than he ever had in Orientalist circles. He was able to train a generation of Harvard Divinity students who have made substantial impacts on their own fields. Nonetheless, Smith continued to face staunch opposition to his vision that historical methods and religious faith could—and perhaps must—go hand in hand. In the late 1970s, Donald Wiebe warned that Smith's work represented "the dangers of subjectivism" in the academic study of religion because his overly personal and relativist framework seemed "to require the student to undergo conversion to the tradition being examined" to reach any real understanding of it.[143] While respected, Smith remained a lightning rod for academic criticism for his unconventional approaches to objectivity.

In addition to the criticisms leveled against Rahman and Smith, the fusionist movement suffered other setbacks tied to the difficulty of spreading the vision. Smith's most devoted students at McGill did not publish enough to exert any methodological influence on the field. Even during his time as director, Smith recognized the institute's weakness in this regard. He lamented to Rockefeller and Ford Foundation officers that McGill lacked top-caliber students and at times even questioned whether the output justified the time and financial investment. At one particularly low period in 1955, Smith wrote to foundation officials: "I have only a precarious hold on the conviction that I can find other Westerners (Muslims are not so difficult to get) who see the problems and have the training and qualifications to pitch into the solving of them . . . What then? Does one give up because one has attempted too much?"[144] Although Smith did not abandon the fight for fusionism, he seemed to be waging a losing war. Even his second-in-command and eventual successor as director of the institute, Charles Adams, possessed neither the passion for fusionist thinking nor the academic stature to ensure the continuation of Smith's vision after his departure for Harvard. In the early 1970s, an internal Ford evaluation reported "difficulty in identifying any noted North American scholars who received their graduate training at the McGill Institute."[145] Compared to academic stars produced at Princeton, Harvard, and Chicago, McGill's Western students often found employment as government officials or professors at lesser-known universities. As a result, the definition of objectivity that reigned at Gibb's Harvard or Schacht's Columbia continued to dominate the field of Islamic studies.

Furthermore, the critiques of fusionism fueled a consensus in the 1960s and even the 1970s that the McGill Institute had overreached in its endeavor to produce capable Muslim academics. Ford officials and external academic consultants agreed that it was simply too difficult to communicate the purpose and spirit of academic inquiry to the vast majority of Muslims. One foundation officer wrote: "I'm sure these fellows [Muslim students] were a trial to McGill and to people who earnestly tried to make good graduate students and Ph.D.'s out of them. But that wasn't the best hope for them and some at least have returned to Islam [sic] to influential positions and [with] a taste for enlightenment."[146] While Smith's vision may have been a noble dream, many believed that Muslims remained ill-suited to become academics in the waking world.

Under the leadership of Wilfred Cantwell Smith, the McGill Institute of Islamic Studies served as a critical incubator for fusionist thinking. Muslim scholars such as Rahman, Ali, and Nasution wrestled with ways to integrate the Islamic and Western intellectual traditions. They developed methodological approaches that balanced objectivity and subjective religious convictions. They used critical historical analysis not only to reconstruct the past but also to reimagine the future for Islam. By thinking as academics and faithful Muslims simultaneously, they demonstrated—with varying degrees of persuasiveness—how the two traditions of knowledge could be made commensurate. However, the intellectual encounter at McGill also resulted in criticisms and even resistance. Some Muslims found McGill's academic culture alienating. From Rasjidi's hostile exchange with Schacht to Muslim faculty objections to Izutsu's method of analyzing the Qur'an, there were moments of conflict over what constituted the proper approach to studying Islam. On the other side of the spectrum, established Orientalists dismissed fusionist Muslim thinkers as insufficiently objective to be legitimate academics.

Although it lacked the stature to alter the norms of objectivity for Islamic studies as a field, the institute did open the doors of academia to a generation of Muslim intellectuals. It served as a significant intellectual space for Islamic thinkers who would eventually run national ministries, propose Islamic legal reforms, and rewrite education curricula. The institute was thus a critical stopping point for many Muslim professors and graduate students on their roads to larger interventions in modern Islamic thought. Consequently, the institute's greatest legacy lies beyond the Canadian campus and even outside academia. It is located, rather, in Muslim-majority countries such as Indonesia.

3 A FUSIONIST TRANSFORMATION AT THE MINISTRY OF RELIGIOUS AFFAIRS

IN THE EARLY DAYS OF SEPTEMBER 1971, Mukti Ali boarded a train from Yogyakarta to Jakarta. A well-respected professor of comparative religion at the time, Ali had been called to the capital by several of Suharto's top generals turned political advisors. As the train passed through the small towns and rice paddies of rural Java, Ali must have taken occasional moments to reflect. Perhaps he wondered whether Suharto's inner circle would judge him capable. If they did, then in how many ways would his life change? When the train, at last, pulled into Jakarta's chaotic station, Ali headed straight to the home of Kafrawi Ridwan, an old friend and fellow McGill alumnus. Over the next several days, Ali stayed in Ridwan's home and let the younger, albeit more politically adept, man guide him through a series of high-stakes meetings. The interviews progressed well, but Ali remained anxious. Unable to sleep, he passed one night lost in thought as he smoked his way through three entire packs of cigarettes. And then there was the matter of his wardrobe. Ali had carried his favorite suit—purchased in the United States during a trip down from Montreal years ago—on the train from Yogyakarta, but Ridwan had disapproved of its fit and out-of-date style. With less than a day to spare, Ridwan contacted a tailor and arranged for the delivery of a new shirt and jacket late that night.[1] The next morning, September 11, 1971, Ali met with President Suharto and, having received the final blessing, was sworn in as Indonesia's new minister of religious affairs.

Ali's appointment as minister represented a dramatic reorientation in Suharto's policy toward the Indonesian Muslim community. For nearly two decades, the traditionalist Nahdlatul Ulama (NU) had dominated the ministry, including its vast financial resources and its authority to administer the country's Islamic schools. Yet as Suharto's military government consolidated control in the late 1960s, its relationship with NU began to sour. In 1968, NU campaigned for a larger role for shariʿa in the Indonesian constitution, a demand that the army quashed outright. Many NU leaders were also reluctant to embrace Suharto's vision for national development. From the army's perspective, NU's extensive grassroots network of kyai and pesantren began to look less like a useful partner in governance and more like a formidable opponent.[2] Suharto took decisive action and ended NU's long reign over the state religious bureaucracy.

Suharto also restrained NU's long-time rivals: former Masyumi modernists. As chapter 1 discussed, Masyumi had a toxic relationship with Sukarno that culminated in the 1960 banning of the party and the imprisonment of many of its leaders. The downfall of Sukarno and the subsequent rise of Suharto thus gave modernists reason for optimism. The new military government released former party stalwarts such as Mohammad Natsir from prison in 1966. There were rumors that it might next grant permission to reconstitute Masyumi. Yet Suharto quickly dashed these hopes when he refused to lift the ban. Soon thereafter, Masyumi leaders began to speak out against governmental policies. They decried modernization as merely a guise for continued Western and even Christian domination over Indonesia. They also remained steadfast in their support for a more Islamic state. Lacking a party through which to pursue their grievances, many opted to withdraw from organized politics altogether and express their dissent through overtly nonpolitical organizations such as Muhammadiyah or Natsir's new Indonesian Dawah Council (Dewan Dakwah Islamiyah Indonesia [DDII]). Unable to counter Suharto politically, former Masyumi leaders dug in their heels outside the official party structure.

Emphasizing these stories of confrontation, historians have offered in-depth analyses of Suharto's fraught relationships with both NU and former Masyumi modernists.[3] In contrast, this chapter tells an equally important and yet often forgotten tale of cooperation and collaboration. In the early 1970s, a small but influential group of Western-educated Muslim intellectuals—led by

Kafrawi Ridwan, Mukti Ali, and Harun Nasution—chose to partner with Suharto's regime. From their positions of bureaucratic power, they worked to translate fusionist thinking into concrete programs of Islamic reform. They redesigned the IAIN curriculum and expanded policy research at the Ministry of Religious Affairs. In the process, they encountered fierce opposition from other Indonesian Muslims—foremost among them, fellow McGill alumnus Mohamad Rasjidi—who attacked academic methods as no more than foreign imports, which, contaminated by their inauthenticity, distorted Islam. The result was a battle over the very nature of Islamic knowledge and Muslim religious authority. Although the intellectual disagreements remained unresolved, Suharto's political support tipped the scales in Ali and Nasution's favor, enabling them to institutionalize fusionism as a viable alternative to both traditionalist and Masyumi-style modernist approaches to Islam.

Whereas chapter 2 examined the position of fusionist thinkers in Western academia, this chapter chronicles fusionism's fortunes in Indonesia through the careers of prominent McGill alumni. In part one, I investigate Muslim intellectual cooperation with Suharto's authoritarian state. Looking beyond the frequent explanations of political co-optation and opportunism, I argue that Muslim intellectuals shared many core values with Suharto's government and therefore forged a mutually beneficial partnership with the regime. In turn, part two examines how Ali, Ridwan, and other top ministry officials used their newly realized political influence to develop and spread fusionist epistemologies. They cultivated expertise in Western academic research methods and created a powerful new religious network that tied Indonesian Islamic intellectuals to Western academia. Part three explores the ways in which academic methods, especially Nasution's use of the discipline of history, altered how some Muslims understood and taught the Islamic tradition. In the final section, I analyze Rasjidi's forceful criticisms of Nasution. By attacking academic methods and the very ideal of objectivity, Rasjidi raised difficult questions about the limits of both academic scholarship and fusionist approaches to Islam.

SUHARTO AND THE RELIGIOUS TECHNOCRATS

Suharto seized power during a period of national turmoil and mass political violence. On the night of September 30, 1965, several disaffected army units under the command of Lieutenant Colonel Untung Syamsuri rose up in rebellion against their superiors. They kidnapped and killed six generals and then dumped their bodies in an abandoned well near Halim Air Force Base in East Jakarta. Calling themselves the September 30 Movement (Gerakan 30 September), the insurgents declared their loyalty to Sukarno and occupied the streets near the presidential palace. It was a remarkably short-lived movement. Within hours, surviving army commanders organized a counterattack that cleared Jakarta's streets and quashed the rebellion. While historians continue to debate the exact motives behind the ill-fated September 30 Movement, it is undeniable that the army moved swiftly to cast the PKI as the prime culprit. Under General Suharto's leadership, the army used the mass media to vilify all communists as bloodthirsty traitors and mobilized Muslim militias, nationalist paramilitary forces, and vengeful neighbors into a national campaign to annihilate the PKI. During the next six months, the army and their civilian allies executed between five hundred thousand and one million Indonesians and imprisoned many thousands more without trial.[4] Sukarno, for the most part, watched powerlessly from the sidelines. His feeble attempts to moderate the army's violence only spawned mass student protests that further marginalized him. Seizing on this weakness, the army strong-armed Sukarno into signing over full political authority to Suharto on March 11, 1966. That date marks the birth of what became known as the New Order (Orde Baru). For the next thirty years, Suharto and top New Order officials used the murderous events of September 30 and the latent threat of communism to justify their authoritarian rule over the country.

In addition to his rabid anticommunism, Suharto built his regime on a second pillar of Cold War–era global politics: development. New Order officials supervised a radical shift in Indonesia's economic and foreign policies. They lamented that for years, Sukarno had been too preoccupied with fighting the ghosts of colonialism and rousing the masses through his masterful revolutionary rhetoric to concentrate on sound economic policy-making. They were similarly appalled with Sukarno's costly foreign-policy ventures—including his military confrontation with Malaysia, refusal of Western development aid, and withdrawal from the United Nations—on grounds that they drained essential resources from the country.[5] New Order officials quickly reversed course. They ended the conflict with Malaysia and rejoined the UN in order to mend political relations with the West. They also welcomed Western economic assistance with open arms, courting development organizations for loan packages and drafting laws to facilitate direct foreign investment. To strengthen these initiatives, Suharto appointed a cadre of Western-educated economists and policy experts to cabinet-level posts. Widely known as technocrats, many of these men had won Ford Foundation scholarships to study at American universities, such as the University of California, Berkeley, and then returned to faculty positions at the University of Indonesia. They were devout adherents of developmental economics and believed in their abilities to use statistical indicators and macroeconomic models to engineer economic growth.[6] Ultimately, Suharto's technocrats aspired to transform Indonesia into a model for Western-style development.

Like many modernizing Cold War regimes, the New Order approached development as a neutral, empirical science rather than a pro-Western political ideology. The technocrats were supposed to be experts, not politicians. Economist Radius Prawiro (1928–2005) summarized this powerful self-image:

> One of the most dramatic shifts in philosophy and style between the New Order and the Old Order was the relinquishing of the extreme, emotion-charged focus on ideology for a more detached, analytical, and flexible pragmatism. This was particularly true in the formulation of economic policy.... The pendulum of economic policy swung in varying degrees between left and right. Yet, ultimately, these labels were inconsequential and were of no interest to Indonesia's New Order policymakers. Their concern was for what worked.... For the first time since independence, the country tried to formulate economic policy based on the best understanding of macro- and microeconomics, rather than political ideology.[7]

This devotion to pragmatic policy-making translated into a culture of perpetual planning.[8] By May 1966, New Order technocrats had already crafted a detailed economic stabilization plan for monetary policy, the national budget, and foreign-debt management.[9] During the next decade, they transformed the National Development Planning Agency (Badan Perencanaan Pembangunan Nasional [Bappenas]) into one of the country's most powerful political forces and rolled out a series of Five-Year Development Plans (Rencana Pembangunan Lima Tahun) that set government policy on everything from anti-inflationary measures to mosque construction. Indonesia began to experience substantial economic growth. At the same time, this technocratic conception of development as a science also served as a convenient political shield for the New Order. If the technocrats pursued unpopular economic and social policies, then Suharto and his advisors could simply present them as scientific necessities rather than ideological choices. They used such language to justify the painful austerity measures of the late 1960s.[10] According to this logic, New Order development was simply "what worked."

The New Order's antipathy for Sukarno-era "ideologies" also inspired a bid to redesign the country's political infrastructure. General Ali Murtopo (1924–84) spearheaded the effort to build Golkar (Golongan Karya [Functional Groups]) into Suharto's new governing machine. Drawing from Western academic literature on modernization, Murtopo articulated what historian Brad Simpson calls an "anti-politics doctrine" for Golkar.[11] He argued that because political parties inculcated a narrow ideological fanaticism among Indonesians that stalled development, Golkar would not act as a political party at all. It would serve instead as a nonpolitical think tank dedicated to the collective mission of modernization. Murtopo therefore designed Golkar as an umbrella organization under which "functional" groups such as the military, steel workers, farmers, and university students would come together to represent their particular interests, discuss shared social problems, and devise rational policy solutions. It would be cooperative and efficient.[12] Murtopo took an additional step to save the Indonesian people from political gridlock. He proposed that rather than join political parties, the general population remain a politically unaffiliated "floating mass." Only at designated election times would citizens align themselves temporarily with the political party that they deemed most effective, cast a vote, and then return to work. The "floating mass" concept enabled the New Order to prohibit regular political parties—but not Golkar—from staffing permanent local offices and organizing at the grassroots level of society.[13] These steps would supposedly eliminate overly emotional ideologies from the political arena and put Indonesia on a more rational and accelerated path toward modernization.[14]

In the late 1960s, a loose coalition of young Muslim modernists embraced the New Order's developmentalist vision. Pushing back against the Muslim mainstream, they called for an Islamic renewal (*pembaharuan*) that would foreground human reason and social ethics. Scholars often label these intellectuals "neo-modernists" or "liberal Muslims" and, in turn, debate their motives for cooperating with Suharto's illiberal authoritarian regime.[15] Some suggest that Suharto co-opted the young modernists as part of a broader effort first to divert support from Muslim rivals in the traditionalist NU and former Masyumi camps and then to cultivate a more regime-friendly version of Islam. This approach tends to paint Muslim intellectuals more as pawns in the hands of a manipulative state than as scholarly actors with their own agency.[16] Others characterize the young modernists as political accommodationists who willingly compromised some of their own values to get a foot in the regime's door rather than be locked out altogether. Proponents of this approach sometimes argue that because modernists lack a popular support base, they turn to authoritarian leaders as the most efficient option to realize their aims.[17] While these two explanations have their merits, they both assume that the decision to cooperate with Suharto was somehow anomalous or at least contrary to modernist principles. Few consider the alternative—that this alliance rested on a foundation that ran deeper than mere political convenience.[18]

In contrast, I argue that young Muslim modernists shared the New Order's disdain for "ideologies" and its reverence for reason-based pragmatism. Indeed, they often spoke—and acted—like religious technocrats. These positions were not concessions to the New Order regime but rather outgrowths of Muslim modernist thought itself. As chapter 1 discussed, Indonesian modernists had long argued that Islam was an innately modern and rational religion and that Muslims must practice ijtihad (reason-based interpretation of Islamic source texts) to keep the faith vibrant. Ijtihad was, after all, at the heart of the Kaum Muda and Muhammadiyah movements as well as Masyumi's old political platform. Yet, beginning in the late 1960s, young Muslim activists set their sights on wrestling the modernist mantle from their predecessors and claiming it for themselves. They attacked Masyumi's political vision as too rigid and accused their elders of abandoning ijtihad in favor of their own brand of taqlid (strict adherence) to party ideologies. This loose coalition found its initial footing at IAIN Yogyakarta and IAIN Jakarta.

As a comparative-religion professor at IAIN Yogyakarta, Mukti Ali played a critical role in mentoring Muslim student-activists in the city. Beginning in 1967, he hosted a study circle known as the Limited Group in his home every Friday afternoon to discuss Islam, politics, and social ethics. The group's most active members included Dawam Rahardjo (1942–2018), Djohan Effendi (1939–2017), Ahmad Wahib (1942–73), and other members of the Yogyakarta branch of the Muslim College Student Association (Himpunan Mahasiswa Islam [HMI]). Ali also extended occasional invitations to more established scholars such as Indonesian intellectual Deliar Noer, Dutch historian B. J. Boland, and American anthropologist James Peacock. With Ali's encouragement, they adopted an ethos of free thought. He wanted the young Muslim activists to reflect critically on contemporary issues without feeling constrained by religious or political taboos.[19] This open environment fostered forceful challenges to the Muslim political mainstream in Indonesia.

Seeking to reimagine Muslim modernist politics in particular for the Suharto era, the Limited Group took aim at the former Masyumi platform that had been written, in large part, by Mohammad Natsir. Natsir was, despite his long imprisonment under Sukarno, still an influential figure among Muslim students in the late 1960s. His essay "Islam as an Ideology"—the widely circulated pamphlet that we examined in chapter 1—remained fundamental for the modernist vision of an Islamic state. The Limited Group hence wasted little time in addressing Natsir's ideas. After months of personal reflection and intense conversation, Ali and core student members Effendi, Rahardjo, and Wahib reached a consensus in early 1968 that "Islam was not an ideology" and that "the ideologization of Islam signaled a lowering of Islam" because it rendered the rich spiritual and ethical teachings of Islam into little more than a rigid set of rules.[20] They suggested that defining Islam as an ideology constituted its own form of taqlid because it curtailed free thinking and the dynamic reinterpretation of Islamic source texts for the sake of party loyalty. This daring rejection of established Islamic politics placed Ali's students in direct conflict with the Masyumi-influenced HMI. Effendi and Wahib tried to persuade other Yogyakarta HMI members to alter their views but eventually lost a public debate over the future of the local branch. Both students resigned from the organization. While it was a temporary defeat, their statements of resignation circulated widely in Yogyakarta, bringing more attention to their movement for an Islamic renewal.[21]

Frustrations were also brewing among Muslim intellectuals in Jakarta. In 1969, Kafrawi Ridwan and Harun Nasution completed their degrees at McGill University and returned to Indonesia to work as faculty members at IAIN Jakarta. There they found a higher-education system that was struggling both financially and intellectually. Campus facilities were in disrepair. Ridwan recalled that in 1969–70 IAIN Jakarta bled into the surrounding street and farmland to such an extent that water buffalo, goats, and chickens often wandered into lecture rooms. As the assistant rector, he dedicated most of his time to basic infrastructural needs, such as building a fence around the campus and constructing a nearby dormitory so that students could attend class even when roads turned into muddy quagmires during the rainy season.[22] The intellectual climate was not much better. Nasution complained that political interests routinely overshadowed academic concerns on campus and that fiqh dominated the curriculum to the near exclusion of other subjects. He decried what he saw as a culture of "narrow thinking" and advocated for greater curricular attention to reason-based disciplines and modernist texts, such as the writings of Muhammad Abduh.[23] The young professors refused to remain quiet in the face of this dispiriting situation. Taking the lead, Ridwan gathered Nasution and other Western-educated professors into an informal discussion group where they voiced criticisms of the NU-dominated IAIN leadership and shared ideas regarding Islamic educational and political reform.

While IAIN faculty were organizing behind the scenes, Jakarta-based student-activist Nurcholish Madjid (1939–2005) brought the simmering Muslim intellectual discontent to the national stage. Born in East Java, Madjid attended Javanese pesantrens as a youth and then enrolled at IAIN Jakarta in 1961. He served as the national chairman of HMI for two consecutive terms from 1967 to 1971 and earned the nickname "young Natsir" because he appeared to have a strong devotion to the former Masyumi leader's ideals. Yet, on January 2, 1970, he delivered a controversial address that proved otherwise.[24] In this career-defining speech, he rejected Masyumi's authority with the unequivocal declaration: "Islam, Yes! Islamic Parties, No!"[25] He argued that Masyumi and Muhammadiyah were little more than hollow remnants from a bygone era. While their messages had once resonated powerfully with the Muslim masses, they had lost their "psychological striking force" somewhere along the way.[26] Madjid concluded that they were no longer capable of presenting Islam in a positive and sympathetic light. Consequently, he urged his fellow young Muslims to break away from the stagnant ideologies of their forefathers and advance fresh ideas even if they might "sound weird to the ears."[27]

Madjid followed his own advice and advanced the counterintuitive claim that secularization (*sekularisasi*) was necessary to revitalize Indonesian Islam. Seemingly drawing from the work of American theologian Harvey Cox, Madjid defined secularization as the process of disentangling eternal Islamic truths from man-made religious concepts and institutions. He took pains to distinguish secularism and his conception of secularization. Whereas the former entailed banishing religion from the public sphere, secularization—according to Madjid—would rescue religion from the accumulation of contingent customs and particular political policies. He argued that Indonesian Muslims needed secularization because, over the years, they had often confused Islam with man-made symbols. For instance, they mistook the virtue of modesty for donning traditional styles of dress. They equated immutable Qur'anic teachings on good governance and social justice with Masyumi's man-made political platform. In Madjid's assessment, secularization would enable Indonesian Muslims to relearn how to honor Islamic truths without being constrained by outdated Muslim traditions.[28] Like Ali's Limited Group, Madjid challenged the image of Islam as a static, ideological religion.

Instead of blindly following what they saw as antiquated Islamic ideologies, young modernists insisted that Muslims must exercise their God-given capacity to reason in order to achieve social progress. In the months following his influential 1970 address, Madjid refined his argument for a nonideological and rational Islam. Looking at Qur'an 33:72 in particular, he recounted that God had offered the capacity to reason to the sky, earth, and mountains, but they had all refused in fear that it was too heavy a burden. Man, in contrast, had accepted the gift of rationality as well as the risk that it might lead him astray. Consequently, Madjid named reason as God's mandate (*amanat*) for humanity. He explained:

> Humanity is the successor of God on Earth, meaning worldly affairs are transferred to the human community. Indeed, in order to manage the world, God provides the guidelines but only in broad strokes [*garis besar*]. God does not give detailed instructions nor does he give specific, detailed explanations about the world. But God does provide one prospective tool which enables humanity to understand and find solutions to problems in this world—reason or intellect.[29]

In other words, he urged Muslims to embrace the rationalization of society as an inherently Islamic process. While Madjid never declared himself a Muʿtazilite, his ideas about the place of reason in Islam closely resembled those of Nasution. The Yogyakarta Limited Group also agreed with Madjid's elevation of reason. In July 1969, Wahib mocked the idea that Islam limits the exercise of rational thinking in his journal. He wrote: "Strange. Why should thinking be limited? Is God afraid of reason, which was created by Himself? . . . One who believes in God, while refusing critical thinking, insults the rationality of God's existence."[30] Taking these ideas to heart, Wahib—along with Effendi and Rahardjo—began to experiment with fusing sociological research and Islamic principles to devise tangible social policies.[31] Like their technocratic counterparts at Bappenas, young modernists saw rational, anti-ideological thinking as the path forward for Islam and for Indonesia.

Given their similar intellectual frameworks, New Order officials and young Muslim modernists saw each other as natural allies in the new Indonesian political landscape. Ridwan made the first official moves. During a meeting of his informal discussion group, he suggested to his fellow Western-educated faculty members that they could most effectively counter NU's political power by aligning with Golkar. The men agreed. After reaching out to Ali Murtopo, Ridwan established an IAIN Jakarta Functional Group (Korp Karyawan Departemen Agama IAIN Jakarta) and then supervised the process of joining Golkar in 1970. The partnership quickly bore fruit. When Golkar triumphed in the 1971 election, the New Order won a popular mandate to enact further reforms, especially concerning religious matters. Murtopo honored his pact with Ridwan. He consulted the IAIN group over whom to appoint as minister of religious affairs and suggested four possibilities: Kafrawi Ridwan himself (McGill), A. Timur Djaelani (McGill), Bahrum Rangkuti (University of Indonesia), and Mukti Ali (McGill). After extensive discussion, they agreed that Ali's seniority and expertise in comparative religion made him the best choice for the post.[32] Soon thereafter, top New Order officials called him to Jakarta for those anxiety-producing interviews.

BUREAUCRATIC ISLAM IN ACTION

When Ali took over the reins of the Ministry of Religious Affairs in September 1971, Muslim resistance to Suharto's developmentalist agenda remained strong. Powerful voices in NU and former Masyumi circles criticized development as a thinly coded euphemism for Westernization. They also protested what they saw as the New Order's permissive posture toward Christian proselytization and overly friendly relations with heterodox mystical sects (*kebatinan*).[33] Ali's ministry worked to reconcile these skeptical Muslims with Suharto's state. In speech after speech, Ali challenged the image of Islam and development as antithetical forces. His oft-repeated motto was "Development is for humanity; humanity is not for development."[34] In other words, he argued that development was a holistic process devoted not only to economic growth but to cultural, intellectual, *and* spiritual progress. He assigned religion the crucial roles of providing motivation for development and ensuring that it served the broader interests of humanity. He therefore enjoined Muslim leaders to lend their expertise.[35] Ali delivered this same message to technocrats at Bappenas and to worshipping Muslims at the national mosque in Jakarta. His aim was to persuade all audiences that religion—especially Islam—and development were essential partners in building a prosperous Indonesia.

As an integral part of his mission, Ali worked to transform the ministry into a fusionist institution. In numerous public addresses, he stressed that thanks to modernization, Indonesian society was in a state of constant flux. Urban populations were exploding, economic relations were shifting, and educational needs were changing. Yet most religious scholars clung to their traditional ways of thinking, rendering them incapable of responding to the rapid social changes unfolding around them. Ali worried that without significant reform, Islamic education and maybe even Islam itself would become irrelevant. To prevent this harrowing potentiality, he urged Muslims to embrace academic research methods and new forms of knowledge. He advised Muslim intellectuals to study social change and consider the ways that new demographic and cultural norms can and should inspire new interpretations of Islamic texts.[36] Ali also championed an interdisciplinary approach to Islamic knowledge that recognized the degree to which religion was intertwined in other spheres of life, such as politics, economics, and health. He argued that Islamic texts could not be read in isolation from modern-day economic structures or medical advances. Instead, Muslims must study economics, medicine, and other disciplines in sufficient depth so that they can comprehend these subjects and then use their knowledge to ensure policies align with Islamic values. At its core, his was a fusionist vision that integrated knowledge of Qur'anic exegesis and Islamic jurisprudence with the study of Western academic natural and social sciences.

Ali knew that his vision required a new cadre of Muslim leaders. As a result, he quickly replaced the preponderance of NU kyai at the ministry with Muslim intellectuals trained in modern policy sciences and management. For example, Ali promoted fellow McGill alumni Kafrawi Ridwan and Timur Djaelani to new positions as the director general of the Islamic Division and the inspector general, respectively. He also appointed Mulyanto Sumardi (b. 1937), a former IAIN Jakarta professor and member of Ridwan's discussion group, as the director of Religious Higher Education. Sumardi held both a bachelor's and master's degree in linguistics from the University of Michigan and a doctorate in education from Columbia University.[37] These senior fusionists opened doors for young intellectuals such as Limited Group member

Djohan Effendi, who worked first as Ali's personal assistant and was then recruited to write speeches for Suharto himself. In addition to these high-level personnel changes, Ali had more expansive goals for altering ministry culture. He often mused about nurturing a "creative minority" that would lead Indonesian Muslims out of their current malaise. Ali explained to one Bandung university audience that

> in order to set the process in motion, a *creative minority* (if I may use [Arnold] Toynbee's term from his book, *The Study of History*) is needed. "Creative minority" is a small group that because of its power to create, intelligence, and faith, is able to blaze a trail and lead the passive masses to become active and energetic regarding development. This "creative minority" must be produced by the university. From the university, it is hoped that this creative minority, or what is now known as the technocrats, will arise.[38]

In similar public statements, Ali identified Muslim intellectuals as the engines driving national development.[39] He devoted much of his ministerial energy to growing their ranks through various initiatives.

Given his background as an IAIN professor, it is unsurprising that Ali directed the first of his two major fusionist initiatives toward reforming the State Islamic Institute system. Ali often heralded IAIN as the future of Indonesian Islam, but he also expressed major concerns about the system's quality. In March 1972, he outlined three systemic weaknesses.[40] At the top of his list was the dearth of methodological training. Ali argued that the widespread failure to train IAIN students in disciplinary theories and research methods produced weak, indiscriminate scholarship. Students graduated without the ability to speak knowledgeably about pressing social problems, leaving them ill-equipped to contribute to development planning. He also cited poor language instruction. According to Ali, IAIN students did not possess sufficient fluency in Arabic to approach essential Islamic texts in their original form, and they were likewise incapable of reading the latest Western scholarship on Islam, further isolating them from important innovations in academic methods. Finally, he lamented the poor academic culture within the IAIN system, noting that political and material concerns often took precedence over genuine intellectual curiosity. Ali urged his fellow Muslim intellectuals to engage in honest introspection and be open to constructive feedback.[41] Many former IAIN professors, including Ridwan and Sumardi, agreed with his critical assessment. Together, they drafted plans to "raise the quality" of IAIN.

To begin, Ali decided to reorganize the entire State Islamic Institute system.[42] In the early 1970s, the system was experiencing rapid growth. The student population multiplied at IAIN Yogyakarta nearly five times between 1960 and 1968.[43] The number of IAIN campuses also grew at an exponential rate. Whereas there were only 4 IAIN faculties in 1960, the number reached at least 104 just one decade later.[44] To further complicate administrative matters, the faculties were geographically dispersed with large campuses managing small-town faculties located hundreds of miles away. Determined to halt this proliferation, Ali moved to cluster IAIN faculties at "main campuses" in provincial capitals and eliminate "branch" faculties that had sprung up in smaller cities and towns. Ministry officials hoped that this plan would reduce administrative red tape and facilitate cooperation with nearby secular universities. It also enabled the ministry to phase out unqualified faculty in IAIN branches and concentrate qualified professors on the main campuses, thereby raising the overall level of scholarship and teaching.[45] As director of Religious Higher Education, Muljanto Sumardi supervised the reorganization. In October 1973, he consolidated several branch faculties, including those located in Singkawang (West Kalimantan) and Pasuruan (East Java) into the Pontianak and Surabaya main campuses, respectively.[46] Sumardi made consistent progress over the following year. By August 1974, the ministry reported that all branch faculties except two holdouts had been streamlined into their corresponding main campuses.[47] Thanks to this process, the ministry now had more centralized control over the IAIN curriculum and its faculty.

The ministry next made a concerted effort to integrate social sciences into IAIN intellectual culture. Ali invited Indonesian social scientists such as Taufik Abdullah (Cornell PhD, 1970) and Alfian (University of Wisconsin, Madison, PhD, 1969) to advise on educational policy and research. Ali also encouraged IAIN faculty to participate in the Ford Foundation–financed Social Science Research Training Program, in which experienced academics mentored junior scholars in crafting research questions and conducting fieldwork at a series of "field stations." Ali even gave his blessing to open the first field station on the IAIN campus in Banda Aceh in 1974 and ensured that IAIN faculty had opportunities to join the program.[48] He was determined to capitalize on these domestic opportunities for methodological training.

Ali's ministry also sponsored graduate study in the West as a way to raise the quality of IAIN faculty. The McGill Institute of Islamic Studies was again at the center of this endeavor. In July 1973, Wilfred Cantwell Smith—who was then a professor at Dalhousie University in Halifax—traveled to Indonesia as a consultant for CIDA. While only tasked with evaluating the possibility of an IAIN-McGill exchange program, he petitioned CIDA to sponsor a decidedly more ambitious project in which the institute would help develop Indonesian "expertise and capacity" to construct a modern Islamic education system.[49] He argued that McGill could "help launch (and not merely . . . provide theoretical data for) the modernizing process."[50] Although this additional funding never materialized, CIDA did sponsor a modest program that enabled nine IAIN lecturers to complete their master's degrees at the institute.[51] The ministry also pursued opportunities to work with American and Dutch universities. Top officials encouraged promising Muslim students to apply for Fulbright, Rockefeller, and other fellowships in order to study Islam at American universities. In 1977, Timur Djaelani traveled to the Netherlands to explore options for a formal partnership with Leiden.[52] These exchange programs facilitated a rising tide of Western academic influence in the IAIN system.

Ali's second major fusionist initiative was creating the Office of Religious Research and Development (Badan Penelitian dan Pengembangan Agama [Litbang Agama]) in 1975 as the ministry's own policy-oriented think tank. He appointed Mulyanto Sumardi as its first director. Under Sumardi's leadership, Litbang Agama's early projects included gathering quantitative and qualitative data on Indonesian religious life, researching religious education, and publishing bibliographies on important religious topics.[53] Sumardi also used Litbang Agama to train more Muslim scholars in data-driven research in order to fill the perceived lacuna at the ministry. Toward this end, he founded a twenty-week-long seminar known as the Religious Research Training Program in Jakarta. The program brochure explained its objectives:

> It is hoped that, after attending this program, participants will be able to conduct independent scholarly research concerning religious issues or other [subjects] related to religion in Indonesia. As a result, we will gradually overcome the lack of research capabilities in the field of religion in Indonesia. Religious research should be conducted according to the research methods of the social science and humanities disciplines.[54]

During the first ten weeks, the participants studied academic research methods under the supervision of senior professors, including Ali and Sumardi. Then, using these newly acquired methods, the junior scholars selected a contemporary "religious problem" on which to conduct independent research for six weeks. The program concluded with a four-week-long seminar during which participants presented their research to the group for criticisms and suggestions. In early 1978, Litbang Agama invited sixteen alumni from the Religious Research Training Program and four alumni from the Social Science Research Training Program to present at a national conference on "the Development of Religious Research." Sumardi hoped the conference would "push them to become more skilled in research" and intensify research efforts by other scholars on religious matters.[55] Ultimately, these types of training programs fulfilled two aims. They produced the data necessary to implement religious development programs and encouraged fusionist thinking among Indonesia's rising class of Muslim scholar-bureaucrats.[56]

As director of Litbang Agama, Sumardi also led the fusionist movement by example. In 1974, he submitted a grant proposal to the Ford Foundation seeking funds for an extensive research project on Indonesian Islamic education. He explained the choice of topic not only in terms of intellectual interest but as essential for policy-making:

> Without the empirical data that research can provide, we lack the necessary information for establishing priorities, formulating policies, and designing or evaluating programs. Yet, a genuine research orientation and the empirical data it could provide are almost invariably lacking in almost all fields, including the field of Islamic education. Consequently, most experimental ventures launched thus far have been based on hunches, traditional patterns, or personal whims.[57]

To fill this distressing gap in actionable information, Sumardi recruited and trained a team of IAIN Jakarta students. Over the next two years, Sumardi's team conducted archival research at a variety of Indonesian Islamic schools and at relevant libraries abroad. They also designed and distributed a national survey on Islamic school enrollments and curricular choices.[58] At the conclusion of the project, Sumardi published a detailed bibliography and a concise history of Indonesian Islamic education that argued for further reforms.[59]

Sumardi's project exemplified the alternative fusionist network that was beginning to flourish in the 1970s. A Western-trained Muslim intellectual himself, Sumardi obtained Ford Foundation support for an interdisciplinary research project. He then traveled extensively in the West, utilizing the libraries at McGill University, the University of Chicago, and Leiden University in the Netherlands. He also met with academic scholars to discuss the history of Indonesian Islamic education. In his final manuscript, Sumardi stressed the need to dismantle the dualist education system in favor of a fusionist one. It was a self-perpetuating cycle. Without a doubt, this emergent Western academic network did not displace the more traditional connections to Arab Islamic centers such as Egypt and Saudi Arabia. Even Ali's ministry continued efforts to procure scholarships for Indonesians to study at al-Azhar and to invite Arab scholars to the archipelago for brief periods as visiting lecturers.[60] However, the Western academic connections gained traction and enabled fusionism to become a viable alternative to more established modes of Islamic knowledge.

HARUN NASUTION AND HISTORICAL METHODS AT IAIN JAKARTA, 1973–84

Ali's transformation of the Ministry of Religious Affairs caused the winds to shift at IAIN Jakarta as well. In the early 1970s, two consecutive Egyptian-educated rectors, Bustami A. Gani (r. 1969–70) and Toha Yahya Omar (r. 1970–72), had focused on strengthening IAIN ties to al-Azhar. They invited Egyptian scholars to campus, improved Arabic instruction, and ensured that the degrees of IAIN students would be recognized if they chose to continue their educations in Egypt.[61] While these connections raised the status of the State Islamic Institute vis-à-vis its Middle Eastern counterparts, Ali and his top advisors wished to see IAIN Jakarta adopt a more Western academic orientation. Accordingly, when Omar fell ill and then passed away, Ali made his move. He appointed Harun Nasution as the new rector in 1973.[62] Nasution advocated a reason-based Islam that eschewed loyalty to what he saw as fatalist theologies, traditionalist schools of law, and ideological party politics. Equally important, he used historical research methods to underscore the contextual contingency and hence dynamism of Islamic teachings, thereby creating space for his students to adapt Islamic values and practices to modern Indonesian realities. Over the next eleven years, Nasution built IAIN Jakarta into the foremost center for fusionist thinking in Indonesia.

Nasution championed the unrestricted use of rational inquiry in Islamic thought during his tenure as rector. In a series of essays and public addresses from the 1970s, he explained that the Qur'an frequently enjoins humans to reflect on the world around them. Early Muslim scholars had understood this injunction to reason and shape their environment and, as a result, accomplished great feats in the fields of law, science, and philosophy. Unfortunately, political strife and traditionalist entrenchment in the medieval period had eroded this rational Islam and replaced it with intellectual stasis. Nasution yearned to recapture the rational spirit of the Qur'an and early ʿulama at IAIN Jakarta. Toward this end, he delivered lectures on the significance of reason in the Islamic tradition on campus.[63] He also called on fellow faculty members to encourage students to "have a rational attitude, an open view, and [pursue] knowledge that is not limited to religion but also includes general sciences."[64] Ultimately, he worked to teach IAIN students to think both normatively and empirically about Islam so that they would become agents for Islamic progress.[65]

Like his counterparts among New Order technocrats and young Muslim activists, this reverence for human reason led Nasution to embrace Suharto's developmentalist agenda. He never shied away from this intellectual alliance. In 1975, he wrote:

> We are currently living in an era of national development, development not only in the physical realms but also in religious ones. The success of development heavily depends upon mental attitudes. Accordingly, it is important to focus on changing traditional mental attitudes to rational mental attitudes in the religious realm. In other words, traditional philosophies of living that are still followed nowadays have to be replaced with liberal-leaning philosophies that were followed by the Muslim community in the early centuries.[66]

He also disparaged ideological politics, including Islamic political parties. In Nasution's assessment, the New Order was admittedly less "free" than Sukarno's government, but he also insisted that it was a necessary and beneficial trade-off because Suharto delivered stability and economic growth whereas Sukarno had produced neither.[67] Accordingly, Nasution supported the New Order's campaign to depoliticize university campuses in the mid-1970s. He maintained that "the duty of a college student is to study, not to play politics. . . . If [they] want to be active in politics, then their studies will surely be neglected."[68] As rector, he distanced IAIN Jakarta from the only remaining Islamic party (Partai Persatuan Pembangunan) and worked to ensure its reputation as a state-owned and government-friendly institution.

With the active support of Ali's ministry, Nasution spearheaded a movement to overhaul the IAIN curriculum so that it included more Western-style academic disciplines.[69] At a national meeting of IAIN rectors in August 1973, he proposed that all IAIN students be required to take certain foundational courses in languages (Arabic, English, and Indonesian), philosophy, sociology, and research methods before they delve into the courses offered by their specific faculty.[70] He saw the requirement as a way to broaden students' intellectual horizons and to raise the quality of an IAIN education. The older generation of IAIN rectors resisted the potential changes, but Nasution had the committed support of Muljanto Sumardi and other top ministry officials. After several days of discussion, the rectors reached a compromise. The new subjects would be taught, but traditional courses on fiqh, hadith, and Qur'anic exegesis would remain unaltered.[71] Nasution also managed to push through a major change to the first year experience: a mandatory "Introduction to the Study of Islam" course that examined Islam from multiple disciplinary perspectives. He even wrote its popular textbook, titled *Islam Viewed from Its Various Aspects*.

First published in 1974, *Islam Viewed from Its Various Aspects* introduced Nasution's fusionist commitments to his widest audience yet: all incoming IAIN students. As its title suggests, the book set out to do nothing less than transform how Indonesian Muslims viewed the Islamic tradition. Nasution believed that Muslim students all too often saw Islam as a limited religion because Islamic schools overemphasized—to the point of near exclusion of all else—fiqh, *ibadah* (religious ritual), and *tawhid* (the doctrine of God's oneness). He wrote with concern that "knowing Islam only from the three abovementioned aspects creates an incomplete understanding of Islam [that can] lead to narrow understanding and attitudes."[72] To correct this gross imbalance, the book provided chapter-length introductions to a more diverse collection of Islamic subjects, including theology, spirituality and morality, history, culture, politics, and philosophy. Nasution claimed that such a multifaceted approach captured "Islam in its genuine understanding."[73] Yet Nasution took his "genuine" understanding of Islam a step further. Drawing extensively from Western academic scholarship, he presented the various aspects of Islam historically, spelling out the gradual transformations of, the heated contestations over, and the undeniable plurality within Islamic thought. By thinking seriously about the historical nature of Islamic teachings, Nasution located space for adaptation and individual choice.

In chapter 8 of his widely read textbook, Nasution applied historical methods to the domain of Islamic theology. He examined the early splits among the Kharijites, the Murji'ah, and the Mu'tazilites over whether grave sinners remained Muslims or became infidels. He also addressed the debates over free will versus predestination and reason versus revelation as stories of ever-evolving Muslim outlooks.[74] As he explained the history of these theological schools, Nasution refrained from judging their respective claims to superiority or from seeking to identify any one transhistorical theological truth. Instead, Nasution's historicizing led him to adopt a decidedly plural approach to theology. He wrote:

> From the above analysis, it can be seen that . . . there are various schools (*madhhab*) or streams within Islamic theology. The existing and re-emergent streams are the Ash'ari, Maturidi, and Mu'tazilite. These three streams . . . are not outside the bounds of Islamic teachings. All of them are still within the Islamic sphere, and therefore, every Muslim has the freedom to choose whichever stream of theology or life philosophy which is suited to his soul.[75]

With these words, Nasution emphasized the importance of individual choice and hence contingency in Islamic theology. He nonetheless capitalized on his authorial prerogative to argue for the relative strengths of his own school, Mu'tazilism. Specifically, Nasution claimed that the Ash'ari orientation, which is the dominant theological school in Indonesia, "was ill-suited for the educated Muslim classes among whom many received Western education" because of its overly traditional characteristics.[76] Because of this fundamental incompatibility, educated Muslims should follow his lead and look toward Mu'tazilite theology. This suggestion did not violate Nasution's historical lens because he presented Mu'tazilism as only one possible theological orientation among many; he just happened to believe that it was the most viable school for the modern Indonesian context.

Whereas historicizing Islamic theology had radical implications for Muslim conceptions of God and humanity, Nasution's move to historicize Islamic political theory placed him at the center of the heated debate about the Islamic state. In his chapter on "the political aspects" of Islam, Nasution again examined contestation among Muslims over what Islamic politics should be. He recounted stories of conflict among the first four caliphs, leaders whom Sunni Muslims usually revere as collectively righteous.[77] He then outlined how Sunnis, Shi'a, Kharijites, and other Muslim sects understood proper political succession after the Prophet's death.[78] He wrote:

> Muhammad, as a prophet sent by God, brought teachings which not only encompassed spiritual life but also teachings regarding the worldly life of

humanity. Because of this, the Prophet had a status not only as the head of a religion but also as Head of State. In other words, the Prophet combined two types of authority: spiritual and secular. He became the Head of State not because of selection or because of inheritance rights [but because he was] a prophet.

Who had the right to become the Head of State as Muhammad's successor and how he should be chosen emerged as a point of difference in Islamic political affairs. As already discussed, the Kharijites were of the opinion that any Muslim had the right to become Head of State and that the method of selection was election. The Shiʿa, in contrast, believed that only the descendants of Ali had the right to become Head of State and that the right to rule was a matter of inheritance. The Sunnis maintained that the right belonged to the Quraish tribe (Muhammad's tribe) and that the method of selection was election. But among the Sunnis, there were also those who believed that selection was hereditary.[79]

According to Nasution, Islamic politics were riddled with unresolved and perhaps unresolvable differences. Because there was no agreed upon blueprint for an Islamic state, he believed that modern Muslims had ample room to explore their options and practice creative appropriation. He especially encouraged students to take a second look at the Kharijites. Although often denigrated by other Muslims as extremists and even terrorists, the Kharijites argued that any Muslim could become the head of state through election. Nasution suggested that because this position resonated with modern democratic sensibilities, Indonesian Muslims could use the Kharijites as an Islamic precedent for Western-style electoral democracy.[80]

By adopting historical methods, Nasution restored a sense of dynamism and relevance to Islamic theology and political theory. In his textbook, Islamic theology was no longer just a list of doctrinal precepts on the attributes of God or the necessity of revelation. It became a lively sphere for debate. Likewise, Nasution demonstrated that Islamic political theory was more than a dusty collection of medieval texts about the required credentials for a caliph; it could be an adaptable set of Islamic precedents for the modern world. While transformative, this historical approach also made Islamic theology and political theory appear contingent and even relative. Nasution did not shy away from these consequences. He embraced the power of the historical lens to contextualize and hence desacralize religious teachings. By assuming the perspective of an intellectual historian, he thus abandoned the notion that Islamic research should produce a single universal truth and instead championed the multivalent nature of the Islamic tradition.

Nasution's work to fuse the Western academic and Islamic traditions did not stop at the level of methodology. It also shaped his citation practices. At the conclusion of each textbook chapter, Nasution provided readers with a selected bibliography that integrated the writings of medieval Islamic figures, modern Arab and South Asian Muslim thinkers, and a wide selection of Western Orientalists. For example, in the chapter on Islamic theology, Nasution recommended books by both Muhammad Abduh and W. Montgomery Watt as further reading.[81] These bibliographies demonstrated Nasution's fusionist conviction that scholarship transcends cultural and religious boundaries.

While Nasution used historical methods to tackle Islam's crisis of relevance, he still had to convince fellow Muslims of the authenticity and authority of his approach. On the surface, this task seemed straightforward. Nasution relied, after all, on Islam's own past to emphasize its plurality and dynamism as a tradition. For example, the Muʿtazilite reverence for reason and the Kharijite struggle for a pseudodemocratic head of state arose from within the Islamic tradition instead of being imported concepts tainted by their foreign origins. As a result, Nasution did not marshal a defense of his methods. He merely presented intellectual history as a tool to help Muslims dive deeper into the Islamic tradition in order to uncover its nuances, points of contestation, and genuine diversity. He likewise framed his textbook as a means to acquaint Muslim students with the greatest Islamic thinkers and thus widen young Muslims' view of their own religion. As we will see shortly, other Muslims intellectuals strongly disagreed, but Nasution never wavered in his conviction that historical methods could help address Islam's intellectual crisis.

In addition to disseminating academic methods, Nasution was a key node in the emerging alternative network that connected Indonesian Muslims to Western academia. He was deeply involved in the abovementioned Ford Foundation–sponsored projects at the ministry.[82] As a McGill alumnus, Nasution helped coordinate the 1970s exchange program and even reassured Ford officials that despite Wilfred Cantwell Smith's departure, McGill's Institute of Islamic Studies remained strong and worthy of financial support.[83] He used his professorial authority to encourage students to pursue higher religious education in the West. In the popular Islamic magazine *Panji Masyarakat* (Banner of the Community), he underscored the benefits of sending IAIN lecturers to Western universities to strengthen their scholarly credentials. When the reporter questioned why Muslim scholars should go to Western rather than Muslim countries, he explained that "Al-Azharites themselves prefer to study in the West," implying that Indonesians should as well.[84] Privately, he also advised top students to apply for scholarships to continue their educations in Canada or the United States.[85] From his positions of influence, Nasution both capitalized on and worked to expand Muslim institutional connections to Western academia.

Nasution had a lasting impact at IAIN Jakarta and, through his textbook and curricular changes, at other IAIN campuses across the country. During the course of his career, he mentored a cohort of IAIN students that included his future successor as rector, Komaruddin Hidayat (b. 1953). In 1989, Hidayat cited reading Nasution's textbook and attending his "Introduction to Islamic Studies" lectures as experiences that fundamentally altered his way of thinking. He recalled, "Pak Harun [Nasution] not only focused on the content of Islamic teachings; rather, he prioritized introducing students to methods for understanding Islam."[86] Hidayat stressed Nasution's historical and sociological methods as particularly significant in challenging monolithic understandings of the religion. According to Hidayat, Nasution also encouraged young Muslims to question their inherited theological or sectarian affiliations and even suggested that as students they "had the right to establish a new school of thought [*madhhab*] within Islam."[87] For Hidayat and his activist friends, Nasution's introductory course and more advanced seminars taught them to think more liberally, to be courageous, and to develop their own opinions. They are not alone in owing an intellectual debt to Nasution. The Jakarta campus actively celebrates his legacy, and his textbook *Islam Viewed from Its Various Aspects*, which has seen at least five editions, continues to be published and assigned in the twenty-first century.

RESISTING HISTORY: MOHAMAD RASJIDI AND THE DDII OPPOSITION

Not everyone in Indonesia was pleased with Ali's and Nasution's reforms. The resistance was led by Natsir's DDII. Established in 1967, DDII served as an alternative to top-down Islamic political parties. Instead of working to Islamize the state as Masyumi had done, DDII adopted a bottom-up approach that aimed to Islamize society first. DDII members therefore built mosques, trained preachers, advocated for greater attention to religious education, and published popular Islamic magazines. While this focus on Islamic social activism resembles that of Muhammadiyah, Robert Hefner has rightly stressed DDII's distinctive vision, writing, "In choosing *not* to join forces with Muhammadiyah, Natsir and his colleagues signaled that their program was to be more boldly political than its modernist predecessors."[88] Put another way, DDII shifted away from Muhammadiyah-style modernism and toward Islamism. Three points underscore this Islamist orientation. First, DDII advocated for a literalist interpretation of shariʻa similar in style to Egypt's Muslim Brotherhood and Pakistan's Jaamat-i Islami. While continuing to endorse ijtihad in principle, Natsir and other DDII leaders distanced themselves from the detailed methodological conversations about how best to derive new legal rulings and embraced instead what Michael Feener calls an "intuitive" approach to shariʻa that rested on the contention that "Islam is Islam."[89] Second, DDII was particularly outspoken in challenging Muslim conversions to Christianity and Hinduism in the 1960s and 1970s. Its activists boldly and sometimes aggressively confronted non-Muslim groups in the name of defending Islam. Third, DDII adopted a decidedly global Islamic identity. It translated the writings of Arab and South Asian Islamists into Indonesian and used its popular *Media Dakwah* magazine to encourage Indonesian Muslims to sympathize with the plight of Palestinians and other victimized Muslim communities. It also forged close financial and educational ties with Saudi Arabia.[90] Within the span of several short years, DDII became the leading voice for Islamism in Indonesia.

DDII activists pushed back forcefully against fusionist thinking, and it was none other than Mohamad Rasjidi who led the charge. As we saw in chapter 2, Rasjidi had earned a doctorate from the Sorbonne and then spent five years as a professor at the McGill Institute of Islamic Studies. For Rasjidi, familiarity bred contempt for the Western academic study of Islam. He returned to Indonesia in the mid-1960s and built his career as a distinguished professor of Islamic law at the University of Indonesia, teaching courses at IAIN Jakarta and delivering public lectures on the side. He also joined Natsir's DDII as vice chairman. As a professor and DDII activist, Rasjidi became a well-known Islamic polemicist. He published a series of books in the 1960s that leveraged his knowledge of Western academic disciplines to defend Islam against perceived enemies such as Christianity, communism, and socialism.[91]

However, he saved his fiercest criticisms for Western academics and for Indonesian fusionists who looked to places such as McGill for Islamic knowledge.

Rasjidi's first fusionist target was Nurcholish Madjid. In 1972, Rasjidi published a multipronged, book-length critique of the young modernist's controversial speech on secularization. He derided Madjid's efforts to distinguish secularization from secularism and to rebrand the former as integral for revitalizing religion. To Rasjidi, this redefinition was simply nonsense. He argued that Madjid's attempt to detach the concept of secularization from its historical moorings willfully ignored how secularism had led to the gradual marginalization and eventual exclusion of religion from public life in Europe. Rasjidi warned that Madjid's call for secularization—if heeded by Muslims—would only enable Western vices such as gambling, alcohol, nightclubs, and a general disregard for religious values to seep into Indonesian society as well.[92] Rasjidi devoted another section of the book to "correcting" Madjid's misinterpretation of Qur'anic teachings on human reason.[93] Yet he saved his harshest words for what he saw as Madjid's naive fascination with all things Western, writing: "I feel as if I am face to face with a Western scholar who has no personal relationship whatsoever with Islam . . . I can only shake my head [and wonder] why Dr. Nurcholish's words are so similar to those of people who dislike Islam."[94] Despite his own Western academic credentials, Rasjidi warned that Madjid's Western-style ideas were foreign imports into the Islamic tradition and hence posed a real danger to Muslims.

Rasjidi also courted conflict with Harun Nasution. In 1977, Rasjidi published a 150-page refutation of Nasution's textbook, which he not so creatively titled *A Correction for Dr. Harun Nasution regarding Islam Viewed from Its Various Aspects*. Rasjidi claimed in the preface that he had not originally intended to air his differences with Nasution in public, but circumstances had forced his hand. Specifically, after reading the textbook, Rasjidi had become concerned that Nasution's approach to Islam would confuse students and potentially weaken their faith. He therefore submitted a secret report in 1975 to the Ministry of Religious Affairs that challenged the book's contents paragraph by paragraph. Rasjidi recalled that he waited in vain for over a year for a response from the ministry. The official silence compelled him to publish the report in hope of educating IAIN students and other readers about the grave problems with Nasution's work.[95] Although Rasjidi's book criticizes Nasution on multiple fronts, I argue that the crucial point of conflict between Nasution and Rasjidi concerned the place of Western academic methods in studying Islam. Whereas Nasution celebrated the potential of academic disciplines to reveal new facets of the Islamic tradition, Rasjidi read Nasution's use of academic methods as an effort to destabilize Islamic claims to universality and ultimate truth.

In his *Correction for Dr. Harun Nasution*, Rasjidi repeatedly criticized Nasution's willingness to translate between the Islamic and Western (primarily Christian) discourses on religion on grounds that the two traditions were incommensurable. For example, he challenged the textbook's gloss of *ilmu tawhid* and *kalam*, two terms indigenous to the Islamic tradition, as merely *teologi* (an Indonesian adaptation of "theology"). Rasjidi argued that the indigenous Islamic terms had specific meanings, whereas the Christian term *teologi* encompassed everything from systematic Christian theology to Jesus's teachings on social justice. It was simply too expansive and therefore ill-fitted for an examination of Islam.[96] Rasjidi disparaged other translation choices, including Nasution's move to ascribe what Rasjidi saw as exclusively Christian doctrines such as "God is love" and the sinfulness of the body to Islam.[97] By highlighting these relatively minor acts of translation, Rasjidi was able to paint a damning picture of Nasution as a scholar whose understanding of Islam was tainted by undue Christian influence.

Building on this damaging accusation, Rasjidi also denigrated Nasution's use of comparative religion in the textbook. Whereas Nasution offered students a universal definition of religion and outlined what he saw as the principles shared by all monotheistic religions, Rasjidi rejected this emphasis on interreligious comparison. He wrote, "The method of presentation in this book is the method of Western authors who in their mind hold the feeling that all religions are essentially the same and consist of social characteristics that can be discovered in every human group."[98] Rasjidi, in contrast, insisted that Islam was unique. He acknowledged that some would call his perspective fanatic or exclusivist, but he maintained that Muslims need not falsely equate Islam with other religions—as Nasution had—because it degraded God's final message to mankind as merely one religion among many.[99]

While the comparative study of religions troubled Rasjidi, his most sustained attack on Nasution revolved around the place of historical methods in the study of Islam. Interestingly, Rasjidi did not take issue with the chapter in which Nasution explicitly dealt with the "Historical and Cultural Aspects" of Islam. Rasjidi actually praised this chapter on history as Nasution's best.[100] It was when history seeped into the textbook's other chapters, especially those on Islamic theology and politics, that Rasjidi raised his vehement objection. Specifically, he characterized Nasution's use of historical methods to explicate the gradual development of, contestation over, and plurality within the Islamic tradition as highly problematic. Rasjidi took Nasution's chapter on theology to task for introducing IAIN students to marginal or even extinct schools of thought. He decried Nasution's explanation of minor Shi'i sects as irrelevant and his detailed discussion of Mu'tazilism as an underhanded attempt to inculcate his own fringe theological beliefs in impressionable IAIN students.[101] In Rasjidi's eyes, these theological schools were not legitimate alternatives to prevailing Islamic teachings in Indonesia but rather were relics from the past that had been rightfully relegated to the dustbin of history. By presenting them as viable Islamic traditions, Nasution was merely bringing uncertainty to and sowing division within the young generation of Indonesian Muslims.[102]

Rasjidi believed that Nasution's flawed historical method reached its most dangerous heights in regard to Islamic political theory. He castigated Nasution's chapter as a story of the ugliest moments in the Islamic past rather than an introduction to Islamic politics:

> What we receive in chapter five about political aspects is a dark and red page of history because it is mixed in blood and is completely at odds with the teachings of Islam. In every nation or community, there are evil people who only consider themselves important, but no space should be given to them when discussing the principles of the state. They are considered the exception, the disease within the normal body.
>
> Dr. Harun Nasution's method is exactly like the method used by Western Orientalists who are anti-Islam. They emphasize the deplorable things which have happened in Islam and which have been done by Muslims, but they never highlight the good Islamic teachings which are violated by such people.[103]

In Rasjidi's view Nasution had committed a fundamental error. He looked at Muslim history and saw a series of diverse, albeit legitimate, manifestations of Islam, but, in fact, he witnessed nothing more than the unfolding of man's inadequate obedience to God's will over time. History could teach Muslims very little about the transcendent ideal Islam because Islamic history was simply not Islam. To believe otherwise was, according to Rasjidi, to mistake practice for theory, flawed human execution for a perfect divine design. Rasjidi's Islam was transhistorical and hence universal. He worried that the discipline of history threatened to secularize the sacred.

In this same chapter on politics, Rasjidi drew a sharp distinction between how Orientalists and Muslims conceived of Islamic politics. Orientalists erroneously relied on history, but Muslims turned to the Qur'an and the Sunnah. Rasjidi drove this difference home by analyzing Qur'anic verses and hadith on equality, consultation, and justice in order to provide readers with a "properly Muslim" introduction to Islamic political ideals.[104] After all, in Rasjidi's words, "this approach was the way that a Muslim discovers the teachings of Islam."[105] Rasjidi's less-than-subtle implication was that Nasution, by choosing Orientalist methods, had left the Muslim fold. Rasjidi made the accusation explicit in the book's conclusion, writing:

> Dr. Harun Nasution's book demonstrates that there are now among us those who have been influenced by Western Orientalist methods to the extent that he considers Islam as one social element that must assimilate itself with Western civilization. With that, our Islamic identity will be lost along with the spiritual strength that we garner from the Qur'an.[106]

Ultimately, Rasjidi accused Nasution of writing less like a devout Muslim than as a Western Orientalist who was deeply critical of Islam.

In Rasjidi's eyes, academic methods posed a serious threat because they were anything but objective. At the most fundamental level, Rasjidi rejected the possibility that Western academic methods—from the terminology of comparative religion to the practice of intellectual history—provided scholars with a critical distance from which to see the expanse of the Islamic tradition. He chided Nasution in particular for this delusion of objectivity, at one point demanding that Nasution insert the word *we* into sentences describing the faith of Muslims. Rasjidi explained that "the problem is that Dr. Harun Nasution's book was written by a Muslim and will be read by the Islamic community of Indonesia," so why did the book not speak in the inclusive first person plural (*kita*)?[107] Rasjidi saw Nasution's imagined transcendence of his Muslim identity as ridiculous if not heretical. Neither Muslims nor Christians nor anyone else for that matter could be neutral over whether they were located inside or outside the Islamic tradition. As a result, Orientalist methods were, in Rasjidi's view, inherently foreign to the Islamic tradition and thus mired in anti-Islamic sentiments and Christian frameworks. By adopting these methods, Muslims did not gain a more expansive view of the Islamic tradition; they merely gained a Christian one. The existence of neutral or universal methods was a myth. The Western academic and Islamic perspectives and, by extension, the two traditions of knowledge were incommensurable.

After reading Nasution's textbook, Rasjidi grew increasingly disenchanted with Western academia. He worried that impressionable Muslim students would "not realize the fount of errors [*sumber kekeliruan*] that Western scholars [make] about Islam but instead swallow everything that they say without using their critical energies."[108] He clearly believed that both Madjid and Nasution had fallen into this regrettable pattern. By the 1980s, Rasjidi began to argue that young Muslims should deepen their religious knowledge first in Indonesia or the Middle East and only then go to the West. That way, they would not need to enroll in courses and learn Orientalist content from Western professors; they could simply conduct research and participate in conferences. He concluded, "If it is necessary to send faculty personnel to the West, then certainly we do not need [to send] very many."[109] As an alternative, he suggested that studying Islam in Egypt and Saudi Arabia was perhaps "good enough."[110] These were damning assessments from a man who himself had earned a doctorate in France and taught in Canada.

Rasjidi's attacks on Nasution and, to a lesser extent, on Madjid presaged many potent postcolonial critiques of Western academia from the late twentieth century. Following Michel Foucault, postcolonial scholars often argue that knowledge regimes were at the heart of colonial power. European colonial officials used science, Orientalist scholarship, and bureaucratic tools such as the census to restructure indigenous social organizations and forms of knowledge. Historians have shown that colonial discourse achieved such a degree of hegemony that even anticolonial resistance movements were dependent upon its logics. Rasjidi made a similar argument about Nasution. Even if he sought to revitalize Islam, Nasution relied on Western forms of knowledge to accomplish that goal. In Rasjidi's assessment, Nasution's work was thus not an endeavor to strengthen Islam in the face of Western modernity but rather the capitulation of Islam to Western modernity. More recently, postcolonial scholars of religion such as Talal Asad and Tomoko Masuzawa have used genealogical research to expose the Western and frequently Protestant roots of modern religious discourse. Rasjidi's attacks on Madjid and Nasution rested on a similar contention—that is, that the academic study of religion was entrenched in Christian as well as secular assumptions. In an ironic twist,

Rasjidi would likely have found himself at home in postcolonial circles within Western academia. However, his critical ideas came too early and were articulated in a language (Indonesian) and style (Islamism) that rendered him inaudible for the vast majority of academics.

Rasjidi raised some troubling questions about the viability of fusionism. Were academic methods and concepts inescapably Western? Were Western-educated Muslim intellectuals compromising the integrity of Islamic thought? Despite the seriousness of these criticisms, fusionist thinkers remained largely silent. Nasution did not muster a defense against Rasjidi's attack presumably because he could rest assured that Ali's ministry supported his vision for a more dynamic and flexible Islam. Likewise, ministry officials continued to endorse *Islam as Viewed from Its Various Aspects* as a core text in the IAIN curriculum because they had Suharto's blessing to administer the country's sprawling religious bureaucracy. Their proximity to political power granted them the luxury of ignoring their critics. Ultimately, fusionist thinking thrived in New Order Indonesia thanks not only to articulate intellectual advocates such as Ali and Nasution but also to powerful political patrons such as Murtopo and Suharto.

In 1978, Ali's term as minister ended, so the comparative religion professor returned to his academic post at IAIN Yogyakarta, where he continued to experiment with fusionist methods for religious research and mentor young Muslim intellectuals. The state religious bureaucracy, in turn, came under the control of long-time Suharto ally General Alamsjah Ratu Perwiranegara (1925–98). Despite his lack of Islamic scholarly credentials, Perwiranegara furthered the ministry's commitments to academic methods and scholarly connections with Western universities. He retained Ali's circle of advisors, including both Ridwan and Sumardi. He also continued the ministry's relationship with the Ford Foundation. One foundation officer noted with approval that "Alamsjah was surprisingly open, personable, thoughtful, and enthusiastic—surprisingly because his appointment was viewed with deep misgivings by many circles including the modernist Muslims within the [ministry], and we had no reason to believe that any of the above adjectives would apply."[111] As a result of this cooperative attitude, the ministry secured several new Ford grants aimed at Islamic educational reform during Perwiranegara's tenure. Although Ali was no longer at the ministry's helm, many of his fusionist policies continued into the 1980s.

4 ISLAM AND DEVELOPMENT, CHICAGO-STYLE

BY THE CLOSE OF 1972, Mukti Ali had already made considerable headway in his fusionist transformation of the Ministry of Religious Affairs. He had promoted Western-educated Muslim intellectuals such as Timur Djaelani (McGill MA, 1959), Kafrawi Ridwan (McGill MA, 1969), and Mulyanto Sumardi (Columbia EdD, 1970) to influential administrative posts. He had cajoled Islamic scholars about contributing their time and energy to national development and had announced plans to better integrate Western academic disciplines into the IAIN curriculum. It thus came as little surprise when Ali welcomed two University of Chicago professors into his office in late December. The two scholars, Leonard Binder and Fazlur Rahman, had traveled to Jakarta to explore prospects for Indonesian collaboration on a new research project titled "Islam and Social Change." They planned to recruit a diverse team of scholars to research Muslim responses to modernization in six different countries, including Indonesia. Ali responded to the proposal with enthusiasm. He hoped that the Chicago professors would assist in compiling much-needed data on Indonesian Muslim communities and in training several young Muslim scholars in academic research methods.[1] His ministry was, after all, on the frontlines of "Islam and Social Change" and in dire need of more fusionist resources.

Although Binder and Rahman only spent one week in Jakarta that winter, their visit helped establish the University of Chicago as a significant site for modern Islamic thought in Indonesia. They were, in many ways, an unlikely pair to build this transnational bridge to the archipelago nation. Binder, a Harvard-educated political scientist, was a specialist in Middle Eastern politics who had little knowledge of or direct experience with Indonesia. Rahman, the Oxford-educated scholar whom we last encountered at the McGill Institute of Islamic Studies, was a native of Pakistan with expertise in classical Islamic history and modern South Asia. Nonetheless, their careers soon became enmeshed with those of Indonesia's most prominent Muslim intellectuals. Several months after their exploratory meeting with Ali, Binder and Rahman secured an enormous $360,000 grant ($2.2 million in 2019 dollars) from the Ford Foundation to underwrite the "Islam and Social Change" project. It was, at that point, Ford's largest ever religion-related grant.[2] Binder and Rahman used some of their new funds to hire Nurcholish Madjid, the young Jakarta-based modernist who had made controversial calls for secularization, as their Indonesian research affiliate. They quickly agreed that "he [had] such important potential that we ought to bring him out to Chicago and try to give him a Ph.D. here."[3] The Indonesian presence at Chicago then expanded to include M. Amien Rais and Ahmad Syafii Maarif, two future chairman of Muhammadiyah. By the 1980s, the University of Chicago had emerged, alongside McGill, as a crucial academic incubator for Indonesian Islamic leadership.

While it shared much—including Rahman himself—with the McGill Institute model, Chicago fostered a distinct fusionist culture that was rooted in the social sciences. Social scientists were, at the time, relative newcomers to Islamic studies. It was only in the late 1950s that they introduced their disciplinary proclivities for universal theoretical models and quantitative research methods into the field, challenging what had hitherto been the nearly exclusive domain of Orientalists.[4] At McGill, Wilfred Cantwell Smith had fought against this rising tide of social scientific research on the basis that academic objectivity alone was insufficient to understand Islam. He even likened social scientists and other academic champions of objectivity to flies crawling on the outside of a goldfish bowl; they might be able to calculate the number of scales on the goldfish, but they would never know how it felt to *be* the goldfish. Smith imagined a more holistic approach to Islam that combined objective academic research and subjective, faith-based experience. In contrast, Binder and Rahman found a way to bring the social sciences into meaningful conversation with modern Islamic thought at Chicago. By focusing on the troubled relationship between Islam and development, they created new opportunities for fusionist experimentation. In the process, Binder and

Rahman blurred the lines between "empirical" social sciences and "normative" Islamic thought and between academic "outsiders" and Muslim "insiders" to the point of nearly erasing them altogether.

This chapter argues that the University of Chicago emerged as a site for Indonesian Islamic thought due, in large part, to the understudied and unexpected connections between academic development discourses and Islamic reform. Part one chronicles how Binder and Rahman pioneered a new fusionist alliance between the social sciences and modern Islamic thought in the 1970s and 1980s. As codirectors of the "Islam and Social Change" project, they devised an interdisciplinary approach to Islam and development that looked to Qur'anic hermeneutics, in particular, as a way to balance Islamic authenticity—that is, continuity with the Islamic discursive tradition—and the capacity to adapt to the modernizing world. In part two, I examine how, under Binder and Rahman's supervision, Indonesian scholars experimented with fusionist thinking at Chicago. Nurcholish Madjid, Amien Rais, and Ahmad Syafii Maarif drew from the social sciences, Islamic history, and their own Islamic convictions to craft new Islamic frameworks that resonated with contemporary Indonesian politics. Part three maps the many feedback loops between the Chicago professors and Indonesian Muslim intellectuals, suggesting that the border between these two spheres had all but collapsed by the late twentieth century.

SOCIAL SCIENTISTS AND THE ALLURE OF ISLAMIC REFORM

Modernization theory dominated the Western social sciences between the late 1950s and the early 1970s. Its proponents classified human societies into two ideal types—the traditional and the modern—and then sought to understand the multifaceted process by which traditional societies would and should evolve into modern ones. They envisioned this transition, in Zachary Lockman's words, as "both universal and unilinear. It was universal because every society on earth had to undergo more or less the same, often painful process of transition if it was to escape tradition and reach the promised land of modernity."[5] It was also unilinear because "each contemporary society could be located somewhere along the fixed trajectory of historical development."[6] Modernization theorists adopted an interdisciplinary and comparative ethos in their research. Economists, sociologists, political scientists, and anthropologists all brought their disciplinary perspectives to bear on the modernization process. Together, they examined a dizzying array of social variables, including industrialization, urbanization, national saving rates, educational attainment, individual attitudes toward science and religion, access to mass media, and so-called modern personality traits, in a range of African, Asian, and Latin American countries in the search of a totalizing, transcultural model of social change. As political development theorist Gabriel Almond put it, "I had nurtured Weberian aspirations—to know just about everything there was to know, and to write with apodictic confidence about its meaning."[7]

Modernization theorists justified their ambitious intellectual aims in the language of academic objectivity. They touted the superiority of their research methods and issued lofty declarations about realizing "the end of ideology" and "a value-free social science."[8] At Harvard, Talcott Parsons spearheaded an effort to transpose the "mathematical rigor" and "analytical power" of neoclassical economics to the study of all human social relations. He sought nothing less than to locate "a universal and general science of society and of human behavior."[9] At the University of Chicago, political scientist David Easton contrasted his generation of social scientists with what he criticized as their less scientific predecessors. He derided political theory in particular as "metaphysical palaver" and "stated outright that political science ought to conform to the methodological assumptions of the natural sciences."[10] This argument helped Easton and his contemporaries secure quantitative research methods' dominance in political science. Anthropologists and other area specialists did try to moderate their colleagues' universalist ambitions through detailed case studies. Yet even the most influential scholars among them—such as Clifford Geertz—framed their research as revealing particular cultural manifestations of the supposedly universal process of modernization.[11] Overall, modernization theorists trusted that their empirical methods could yield objective, scientific truths about human social change.

In recent decades, intellectual historians have exposed modernization theory as deeply normative and therefore as anything but "value-free."[12] Indeed, its roots lie in the Cold War. In the early 1950s, American policy-makers and scholars understood that communism was an attractive revolutionary ideology in Asia, Africa, and Latin America. It inspired formerly colonized populations with its calls for solidarity, redistribution, and justice, and it provided new states with a blueprint for rapid industrialization and economic growth. Desperate to counter these Soviet inroads, the US government partnered with American social scientists, such as MIT-based economist Walt Rostow (1916–2003), to craft its own model for development: modernization theory. Rostow even subtitled his influential book, *The Stages of Economic Growth* (1960), *A Non-communist Manifesto*.[13] He later served as a close foreign-policy advisor to John F. Kennedy and as the national security advisor under Lyndon B. Johnson. While Rostow was the most politically prominent modernization theorist, many of his social-scientific colleagues accepted governmental grants and consulted for various federal agencies. Modernization theory was thus never merely cutting-edge social science; it also constituted the backbone of American Cold War foreign policy.

Indonesia exemplified the role that modernization theory played in global Cold War politics. As the previous chapter discussed, New Order technocrats were outspoken about their disdain for "ideologies" and their trust in quantitative, scientific planning. This similarity with American social scientists was no intellectual coincidence. Suharto's most prominent technocrats had studied economics and other social sciences at the University of California, Berkeley. These "Berkeley Boys" had imbibed modernization theory's aspirations for an "end of ideology" and "value-free social science" as graduate students and then translated these ideals into their policy-making practices in Indonesia.[14] They even interspersed Rostow's terminology, such as "economic take-off," into speeches and planning documents. Modernization theory functioned, whether in the hands of American social scientists or Indonesian technocrats, as a thoroughly pro-American and anticommunist framework.

Modernization theory equally rested on Western cultural presuppositions about the very nature of modernity and progress. Its proponents adopted a universal and teleological reading of history that projected particular modern European and American experiences—such as industrialization, democratization, and secularization—as natural stages in the development of humanity writ large. They then used these Western societal characteristics as benchmarks for evaluating the transition process in Asian, African, and Latin American societies. It is not difficult to find evidence for such Western- and especially American-centric definitions of modernity. In 1959, University of Chicago sociologist Edward Shils declared to a conference of leading modernization theorists that "'modern' means being Western without the onus of following the West. It is the model of the West detached in some way from its geographical origins and locus."[15] Several years later, Berkeley sociologist Seymour Martin Lipset published *The First New Nation* (1963), a book that "argued that the United States could and should serve as a developmental model for the rest of the world."[16] Another colleague acknowledged that the word *modernization* itself served as a more politically palpable term for *Americanization*, or *Westernization*.[17]

While undoubtedly the brainchild of Cold War America, modernization theory also shaped how a generation of Western social scientists approached Islam. The religion was seen, quite simply, as a traditional obstacle impeding modernization. Daniel Lerner's influential book *The Passing of Traditional Society* (1958) helped establish this perception. On the basis of extensive oral interviews conducted in six countries, the book identified key personality traits that enabled individuals to transition from a traditional to a modern lifestyle. Lerner emphasized the importance of a "mobile sensibility," or an empathetic capacity both to imagine oneself living an alternative life and to cultivate personal opinions about the world. He connected this "mobile sensibility" directly to mass media consumption.[18] Although his research focused on the psychological aspects of modernization, Lerner also had much to say about Islam. He suggested that there was a fundamental tension between "Mecca and mechanization" and worried that the Middle East lacked the visionary leadership necessary to either make the difficult choice or resolve the conflict.[19] He also characterized modernity as a "secular enlightenment" that would, by implication, eventually displace traditional Islam.[20] Other social scientists agreed. In the early 1960s, Princeton political scientist Manfred Halpern declared that "the road to modernization for all societies involves a march without a final prophet, a final book, or even assurance of final success."[21] Overall, academics understood secularization as integral to modernization.

Despite these secularist assumptions, most modernization theorists realized that few Muslims would simply abandon their Islamic faith in favor of a purely secular worldview. American social scientists instead came to champion what they saw as the most viable alternative: Islamic reform. Given the prevailing Western-centric reading of history, many pointed to the Protestant Reformation as a model.[22] For example, Lerner hoped for the emergence of a Muslim "spokesman," who like Martin Luther, would define "new identities for changing persons."[23] In his study of "religious development" in Morocco and Indonesia, Clifford Geertz wrote:

> Stepping backward in order better to leap is an established principle in cultural change; our own Reformation was made that way. But in the Islamic case, the stepping backward seems often to have been taken for the leap itself,

and what began as a rediscovery of the scriptures ended as a kind of deification of them. . . . Islam, in this way, becomes a justification for modernity, without itself actually becoming modern.[24]

In other words, Geertz understood Islamic scripturalism as an unfinished Protestant Reformation. It had shorn the religion of archaic traditions and clerical hierarchies but failed to push beyond the literalism of "reincarnating the seventh century."[25] Even with the formal demise of modernization theory in the 1970s, social scientists continued to call for an "Islamic Reformation" on the assumption that it was a historical necessity for modern Muslim societies.

Leonard Binder (1927–2015) built his career as a political scientist during the heyday of modernization theory. He first developed his abiding interest in the Middle East as a Harvard undergraduate through an unexpected medium: military service. Binder volunteered for the Palmach-Haganah, a Jewish militia that was later incorporated into the Israel Defense Forces, and fought in the 1948 Israeli–Palestinian War. He even learned his first words of Arabic as a prisoner of war in Jordan.[26] Building on this firsthand encounter with Middle Eastern politics, Binder decided to pursue graduate study in both political science and Near Eastern studies at Harvard. He conducted extensive fieldwork in newly independent Pakistan and wrote his doctoral dissertation on "the conflicting theories of the nature of an Islamic state" in the country.[27] This research peaked his interest in Islam and modernization. In 1961, Binder joined the Political Science Department at the University of Chicago, where he worked alongside notable modernization theorists such as Edward Shils and Clifford Geertz as a junior member of the Committee for the Comparative Study of New Nations. He shared with his colleagues a keen interest in "the problem of the reform of Islam."[28]

Over the course of the 1960s, Binder built a reputation as a prominent modernization theorist. In *Iran: Political Development in a Changing Society* (1962), he used Gabriel Almond's theory of "mixed political cultures" to evaluate Iranian political progress.[29] Drawing on extensive field research, Binder identified five distinct political cultures circulating in Iran: the three traditional systems of monarchy, aristocracy, and Islam as well as the two modern systems of nationalism and constitutionalism. He then argued that this multiplicity of often contradictory political cultures weakened many Iranian institutions, including the regime of Shah Mohammad Reza Pahlavi, because they lacked clear and consistent sources of legitimacy.[30] He concluded that Iran's political landscape was fundamentally unstable. Although he was rightly cautious about making definitive predictions about the country's future, Binder suggested that Iran's precarious attempt to balance modern and traditional political cultures either required substantial reform to survive or would simply collapse in on itself.[31] The argument implied that Islam could not easily coexist with modern nationalism or constitutionalism. Binder continued to study what he saw as the fraught relationship between Islam and political development in his next book *The Ideological Revolution in the Middle East* (1964).[32] By the late 1960s, he had assumed disciplinary leadership roles both at Chicago and on the national level.

Then, at the start of the 1970s, Binder forged an unexpected intellectual partnership with Fazlur Rahman that would last for over a decade. Rahman had joined the Chicago faculty as a professor in the Near Eastern Languages and Civilizations Department in October 1969 after a tumultuous political experience in his native Pakistan. In 1961, he had decided to leave the McGill Institute for an appointment at the Islamic Research Institute in Karachi. Rahman's fusionist vision for Islamic reform quickly won him the trust of then Pakistani President, General Ayub Khan (r. 1958–69), as well as a promotion to director of the institute. He used his new position to publish widely, train junior scholars in academic research methods, and advise Khan on Islamic policy matters. These efforts to institutionalize fusionist thinking made Rahman into a lightning rod for criticism from the traditionalist ʿulama. Rahman faced a series of public controversies and mass protests, which eventually forced him to resign his position and leave Pakistan altogether.[33] Rahman arrived at Chicago frustrated but eager to formulate a new approach to Islam and development. He found an academic ally in Binder. Soon after the two men first met to discuss their mutual interest in Pakistani politics over tea, they began to imagine the possibility of a collaborative research endeavor.[34] The result was the Ford-sponsored "Islam and Social Change" project.

In their proposal to Ford, Binder and Rahman articulated two principles that ungirded their long partnership. They first agreed that prevailing economic, political, and moral circumstances required Muslim societies to modernize but *not* to secularize. This view was particularly important to Rahman, who was deeply critical of secularizing academic attitudes toward Islam. He lamented that Western social scientists too often equated development with economic growth and institutional rationalization alone, thereby ignoring the moral and intellectual dimensions of human flourishing. He had especially harsh words for modernization theorists such as Manfred Halpern, who suggested that in order to implement effective economic and political reforms, Muslim leaders should sidestep discussion of Islamic principles altogether and instead restructure policies quietly without reference to controversial religious rationales. Rahman castigated this strategy as "the total displacement in time of not only traditional Islam but Islam itself."[35] Fortunately, Binder was more amenable to an Islamic alternative to secular modernization. Their proposal stated:

> In this new process, Islam has continued to be a powerful factor, interacting with the forces of social change. It has sometimes operated as an instrument of change, often a legitimizer of change, and is not infrequently conceived even as the purpose of modernization. In cases of explicit secularization, where secularism displaced Islam in the realm of policy, the former has sought to justify itself by the latter.[36]

In other words, Binder and Rahman agreed that Muslim societies would—and, for Rahman, should—only adopt modernizing reforms if they aligned with Islamic values.

Binder and Rahman agreed on a second point—that Muslim modernists, compared to their traditionalist and Islamist counterparts, faced an authenticity deficit. While the two heralded modernists as the heirs of a rich and dynamic "liberalizing legacy," they also worried that modernists were too dependent on the West for their values and methods.[37] This dependency made them vulnerable to attacks on their Islamic authenticity. According to Binder and Rahman, the traditionalist ʿulama were particularly adept at mobilizing the masses "in the name of historical Islam."[38] Both scholars had witnessed these dynamics firsthand. Binder had conducted extensive field research on traditionalist impediments to political development in Iran and Egypt, and Rahman had been forced to resign because of powerful traditionalist protests against his modernist policies at the Islamic Research Institute. Consequently, the two Chicago professors proposed to investigate the educational roots of this opposition and the prospects for internal adaptation within the Islamic tradition.

Building on these two principles, Binder and Rahman constructed what they termed a "bimodal" approach to research. Their proposal explained:

> We seek to learn the consequences *for Islam* and *for development* of the modernization of society, economy, polity, and culture. Certainly, religious

phenomena must be studied in their own terms. Evaluation from within does not, however, mean that a system of religious institutions and attitudes cannot be evaluated in terms of its consequences for development.[39]

This "bimodal" approach thus traversed two divides. The first was disciplinary. While Binder as a political scientist sought to understand how religion impacted the development process, Rahman as a humanistic scholar of religion wanted to examine the effects of modernization on religious practices and institutions. Their priorities were different, but they were also sufficiently intertwined to enable collaboration. The project also tackled the long-contentious insider–outsider divide. Binder and Rahman exhibited an acute awareness of their own personal commitments and the broader tensions in the field. They wrote:

> We wish to understand in a sense meaningful both to ourselves as well as in a sense or senses meaningful to Muslims in a number of countries. In doing this we will be guided by the most sophisticated Social Science considerations of the possibilities and limits of objectivity, but we would prefer not to sacrifice cultural sensitivity to methodological arbitrariness. We feel that the greatest danger to objectivity in a study of this sort is not biased reporting nor even biased sampling, but cultural parochialism.[40]

To reduce "cultural parochialism," Binder and Rahman made the conscious choice to recruit a diverse team of Western academic and indigenous Muslim researchers. As a result, the project constituted nothing less than an effort to build bridges between the social sciences and religious studies and between Western academic outsider and Muslim insider perspectives.

After securing Ford's final approval in late 1973, the Chicago professors embarked on the initial phase of the project: recruiting researchers. Binder complained that this process was "enormously time-consuming, with hundreds of letters and dozens of phone calls and numerous interviews all with the required waiting period for answers devouring weeks of [our] time."[41] Locating indigenous Muslim researchers proved especially challenging because it required Binder and Rahman to navigate bureaucratic and political mazes in multiple Muslim countries. They inevitably ran into walls. In Egypt, Binder's Israeli military service cast a shadow of suspicion over the entire project. One Ford representative reported that "questions about Professor Binder's background have been raised privately with us by Middle Eastern scholars, and we fear that if this project goes forward, there may be repercussions involving our program more broadly."⁴² Binder tried to assuage these concerns. After regaling another Ford official with "lots of . . . personal history designed to show the absurd sensitivity of donors over the last twenty years," Binder eventually agreed to minimize his own presence in Egypt and delegate in-country research to other team members.⁴³ In Pakistan, it was Rahman's personal history that acted as a double-edged sword. His tenure at the Islamic Research Institute had helped him cultivate relationships with prominent scholars and government officials across the country, but his forced resignation had shrouded his name in controversy. Pakistani colleagues who were eager to meet him in private were therefore wary about any public associations.⁴⁴ With institutional connections off the table, Binder and Rahman focused on recruiting independent Muslim scholars from Egypt and Pakistan.

Indonesia, in turn, produced a mixture of institutional frustrations and individual successes. While Mukti Ali continued to express support for the project, Binder and Rahman still encountered a series of bureaucratic delays and communication breakdowns in the country. First, their two carefully selected American scholars were denied research visas.⁴⁵ Then, they found the parallel Indonesian team funded by Ford and led by Taufik Abdullah (Cornell PhD, 1970) to be "relatively reticent" about sharing research.⁴⁶ Nevertheless, Binder and Rahman established rewarding relationships with their indigenous researcher, Nurcholish Madjid, and project affiliate, Amien Rais. Binder later reported that "there is no doubt that we have influenced more indigenous scholars in Indonesia than anywhere else."⁴⁷

After fifteen months of phone calls and letter writing, Binder and Rahman had recruited over a dozen diverse researchers to their team.⁴⁸ It was time for the project's second phase: conducting fieldwork. In 1975, team members dispersed to field sites in Morocco, Turkey, Iran, Egypt, Pakistan, and Indonesia and conducted a mixture of ethnographic, archival, and quantitative research. Binder and Rahman called the scholars back to Chicago the following year for the third and final phase: collaborative research seminars. The inaugural winter 1976 seminar attracted over twenty participants, including team members and Chicago graduate students, and featured a "quite lively" atmosphere and "animated" discussion.⁴⁹ The spring 1976 and summer 1977 sessions, in turn, functioned as smaller writing workshops where researchers presented drafts and received feedback from colleagues. At the end of the four-year project, the team had produced seven dissertations, over a dozen journal articles, and multiple book manuscripts.⁵⁰

Binder and Rahman submitted their final report to the Ford Foundation in 1980. It was comprehensive and reflective in tone. Regarding their "bimodal" approach in particular, they wrote, "Obviously, in designing the project, [we] were very much aware of the problems of academic imperialism, of the issues of cultural authenticity, and the difficulties of studying and understanding another culture."[51] They enumerated some successes on this front. The diverse team had produced academic research that was markedly more sympathetic to indigenous Muslim perspectives. Several Muslim research associates completed or would soon complete doctoral degrees at Chicago. Yet Binder and Rahman also acknowledged that it was easier to address the entrenched problems of academic imperialism and cultural authenticity "in symbolic form" than in intellectual or institutional practice.[52] They particularly regretted that the project had not yet achieved their highest aim—to produce an "original and authentic paradigm" for understanding Islam and development.[53] Binder and Rahman would have to tackle this monumental task in their own postgrant books.

Rahman offered his synthetic reflections on the project in *Islam and Modernity: Transformation of an Intellectual Tradition* (1982). The book was a scathing critique of modern Islamic thought that castigated secular Muslim officials, traditionalists, Islamists, and Muslim modernists alike for failing to balance core Islamic values with rapid social modernization. According to Rahman, the majority of Muslim politicians were "self-styled brokers" who sold a foreign conception of development that alienated their "conservative masses," and they refused to make meaningful investments in public education to change the masses' minds.[54] He characterized traditionalist 'ulama as overly isolated and defensive and dismissed Islamists as irredeemably anti-intellectual. He argued that Muslim modernists, in contrast, possessed promising ideas but lacked the necessary Islamic credentials to persuade their traditionalist and Islamist opponents to listen to their reformist ideas.[55] Having surveyed this dismal landscape, Rahman called for an intellectual transformation. He implored Muslims to return first and foremost to the Qur'an as the source for Islamic authenticity and dynamism in the modern world.

Rahman devoted a significant portion of *Islam and Modernity* to outlining a new hermeneutic for the Qur'an designed to balance Islam's universality with social change. He called it the "double movement" theory. Rahman's first movement involved translating specific Qur'anic injunctions into universal principles. He explained the need for this step:

> The Qur'an and the genesis of the Islamic community occurred in the light of history and against a social-historical background. The Qur'an is a response to that situation, and for the most part, it consists of moral, religious, and social pronouncements that respond to specific problems confronted in concrete historical situations.[56]

In other words, Rahman argued that the universality of the Qur'anic message was buried in contextual particularities. Scholars were to conduct careful historical research into Muhammad's life and his sociocultural environment so that they could understand the personal and social situations to which the Qur'anic revelation was responding. It was only with this crucial historical knowledge that they could then "generalize those specific answers and enunciate them as statements of general moral-social objectives."[57] Once Muslims understood the principles underlying the Qur'anic message, they could perform the second movement: translating those universal precepts into the particular circumstances of the present. This step required detailed knowledge of the modern world. Muslims needed to unravel the complexities of modern social, political, and economic systems before they could imagine how Islamic principles such as modesty and economic justice could best fit into that landscape. Rahman stressed that "the instrumentality of the social scientist is obviously indispensable" for this policy-oriented work.[58] Overall, Rahman hoped that his double-movement hermeneutic could recapture "the original thrust" of the Qur'an *and* enable modern Muslims to adapt, as the early Muslim exemplars had done, to their evolving social circumstances.[59]

Rahman's double-movement theory was "bimodal" in both senses of the term. It was interdisciplinary in its embrace of literary, historical, and social-scientific methods to interpret the Qur'an. It also troubled the Muslim insider–versus–academic outsider distinction. Rahman acknowledged that Muslims had a special relationship with Qur'anic interpretation because they were committed to living the faith, but he also created space for non-Muslim academics. He encouraged those who possessed "the necessary sympathy and sincerity" to conduct historical research into the Qur'anic milieu and contribute to the hermeneutical process.[60] Rahman thus granted non-Muslim academics, such as Binder, a liminal and yet important role in Islamic thought.

For his part, Binder devoted several years to reflecting on the "Islam and Social Change" project before publishing *Islamic Liberalism: A Critique of Development Ideologies* (1988). It was a book that—despite its wide-ranging and even eclectic collection of interlocutors—bore some remarkable similarities to Rahman's work. Like Rahman, Binder opened with a bleak assessment of Middle Eastern politics and especially the region's prospects for political liberalism. He wrote:

> The outstanding characteristic of the Islamic political revival of the 1980s is its rejection of Western liberal pretensions and practices and its sense of a heady freedom in reaching back into the history of Islam for authentic political and cultural inspiration that may have nothing to do whatsoever with the West. The outstanding characteristic of the contemporary Islamic political revival is that it points towards the end of a dialogue [with the West].[61]

Recognizing the powerful allure of Islamic authenticity, he stressed the need for Western social scientists to look beyond knee-jerk calls for secularism, which was so clearly "declining in acceptability" in the Middle East.[62] In contrast, Binder pinned his hopes on cultivating a robust Islamic liberalism that was capable of balancing Western-style development and Islamic claims to authenticity.

Binder structured his book as an extended, cross-discursive conversation with Muslim intellectuals in the hope that "engaging in rational discourse with those whose consciousness has been shaped by Islamic culture ... [can] enhance the prospects for political liberalism in [the] region."[63] He practiced critical and yet constructive close readings. In a chapter on Sayyid Qutb, Binder challenged the dominant image of the Muslim Brother as a scriptural literalist whose interpretation of the Qur'an produced an idealist politico-legal theory. He instead highlighted the Egyptian's later writings on Qur'anic aesthetics and individual religious consciousness, arguing that Qutb valued lived experience over grand theories about political revolution.[64] This "pragmatic, existentialist ... preference for practice over theory" could, in Binder's optimistic estimation, open a path for political cooperation without individual religious compromise in Egypt.[65] In another chapter titled "The Hermeneutic of Authenticity," Binder argued that modern Muslim intellectuals faced a fundamental problem: how "to distinguish between inauthentic or unacceptable historical manifestations of Islam and authentic manifestations, between the inauthenticity of the 'decline' and the authenticity of the period of the *salaf* [Companions]."[66] He examined the writings of Zaki Naguib Mahmud and Abdallah Laroui in search of potential strategies for and pitfalls in confronting this dilemma. Through such careful textual analysis, Binder sought to extract existing intellectual resources from the Islamic tradition and then meld them together into a more liberal approach to the Qur'an. In this sense, the book served as a piecemeal guide for how to reinvigorate Islamic liberalism in the Middle East and the wider Islamic world.

Binder made no attempt to minimize the normative implications of his arguments. On the contrary, his engagement with postmodernist and postcolonial theory over the preceding decade had led him to abandon earlier social-scientific claims to objectivity in favor of a more reflexive and forthright mode of scholarship. He laid his cards on the table for readers to see. The book's first pages declared Binder's own commitment to political liberalism and described the entire project as "tied together by my personal quest for an understanding of great events and by my own role as a professional scholar who is called upon to explain these events."[67] He pushed himself and his readers to abandon academic pretensions about being "outsiders" and to accept instead their situated roles in a cross-cultural dialogue. He wrote: "I believe that the further strengthening of Islamic liberalism and the possibility for the emergence of liberal regimes in the Middle East is directly linked to the invigoration and wider diffusion of this dialogue. This belief defines the purpose of this book."[68] Ultimately, Binder overturned the conventional insider–outsider dynamics that underpinned the academic study of Islam and replaced them with a dialogic model where every participant spoke from within some intellectual or political tradition.

By the conclusion of the "Islam and Social Change" project, Binder and Rahman had located common ground between the social sciences and modern Islamic thought. Both men sought to reform Islam for the modern context, and both proposed a Qur'anic hermeneutic—or, in Binder's case, at least a series of alluring partial methods—to underpin any such reform. The political scientist and the Islamic modernist no longer seemed so different. This social science–inspired space for fusionist thinking extended beyond Chicago and into other corridors of the academy. In contrast to the criticisms his earlier work had garnered, Rahman's two project-related books, *Major Themes of the Qur'an* (1980) and *Islam and Modernity* (1982), were well-received by reviewers who cited his deft navigation of faith and academic arguments as an accomplishment rather than a limitation.[69] In 1983, he even received the prestigious Giorgio Levi Della Vida Award for his contributions to the field of Islamic Studies. After Rahman's untimely death in 1988, fusionist thinking continued to spread. Binder's *Islamic Liberalism* was among the first of a wave of books that examined indigenous Muslim precedents for democracy and liberalism in the wake of the Iranian Revolution.[70] Academics such as Dale Eickelman and journalists such as Robin Wright continued to celebrate the prospect of an Islamic reformation, even identifying Muhammad Shahrur and Abdolkarim Souroush as possible "Muslim Luthers."[71] This scholarly interest in Islamic reform made Western academia increasingly hospitable to fusionist thinkers.

A FUSIONIST MADRASA IN HYDE PARK

During the 1970s and early 1980s, Binder and Rahman fostered a rich fusionist culture at the University of Chicago. Rahman especially encouraged Muslim intellectuals to integrate their academic and faith commitments. In *Islam and Modernity*, he outlined this vision:

> There has been a constant flow of those scholars who have earned their Ph.D.'s from Western universities—but in the process have become 'orientalists.' That is to say, they know enough of what sound scholarship is like, but their work is not Islamically purposeful or creative. They might write good enough works on Islamic history or literature, philosophy, or art, but to think Islamically and to rethink Islam has not been one of their concerns. Obviously, in order to carry out Islamic purposes on the plane of thought, a purposeful, creative-interpretative study is a sine qua non, and this is precisely what is lacking. There is little doubt that this . . . class of scholars wanted to avoid becoming controversial, and they much preferred a cozy corner in a university with a smug and secure career, but the question must be raised whether what they are doing was Islamic studies at all.[72]

In other words, Rahman believed that many so-called Muslim Orientalists lacked the necessary Islamic values that could give their scholarship significance for the Muslim world. If these Muslim academics could combine their objective methods with an Islamic inspiration, then Rahman believed that they, following his own example, could help transform the Islamic intellectual tradition. He modeled this integration not only in print but also through his life as a Chicago professor. Specifically, he played an active role in the university Muslim community. Although he usually commuted to Hyde Park from his suburban home in Naperville only twice a week, Rahman was routinely on campus for Friday prayers. He walked with students from his office to the prayer location at the International House, the Chicago Seminary, or in Bond Chapel, discussing a variety of Islamic issues on the way.[73] He then served as the imam (prayer leader) and delivered *khutbahs* (sermons) for the campus congregation. He even invited Muslim advisees to his home one year to read the Qur'an during Ramadan.[74] Rahman consistently refuted any need to erect barriers between one's Muslim faith and one's academic research.

Although Rahman may have been the driving force behind Chicago's fusionist culture, Binder played a significant role in encouraging interdisciplinary inquiry and in mentoring graduate students. Together, the two scholars advised a number of highly influential Muslim intellectuals, including one-time President of the International Islamic University of Islamabad Mumtaz Ahmad (1940–2016), the former Grand Mufti of Bosnia-Herzegovina Mustafa Ceric (b. 1952), and the prolific Malaysian Islamic scholar Wan Mohd Nor Wan Daud (b. 1955).[75] Yet as Binder had reported to the Ford Foundation, they had the most substantial impact on their Indonesian students, primarily Nurcholish Madjid, Amien Rais, and Ahmad Syafii Maarif. At Chicago, the three Indonesians learned to use academic methods from history and the social sciences to balance the twin demands of Islamic authenticity and development. They wrote dissertations that—like Rahman and Binder's books—challenged the empirical-versus-normative and the academic outsider–versus–Muslim insider binaries. Their fusionist visions resonated not only with Chicago academics but with Muslim intellectuals back in Indonesia.

Nurcholish Madjid

Madjid had already made his mark on Indonesian Islam as an outspoken young modernist by the time he arrived at the University of Chicago.[76] He first traveled to Chicago in spring 1976 to attend the "Islam and Social Change" project seminar where he presented preliminary research on Javanese pesantrens. He then enrolled in the political-science doctoral program in 1978. Yet, shortly thereafter, Madjid began to have second thoughts. He worried that because he did not have a master's degree in political science, his estimated eight years to degree would put great emotional and financial strain on his young family, who had accompanied him to Chicago. He also had concerns about Binder's pro-Israeli past. Madjid heeded these nagging doubts and decided to transfer to the Near Eastern Languages and Civilizations Department to work with Rahman.[77] It was a decision that shaped the rest of his intellectual career. Building on Carool Kersten's analysis, I argue that Madjid's experiences at Chicago helped establish his expertise in the Islamic intellectual tradition.⁷⁸ He immersed himself in the study of classical Islamic philosophy, theology, and jurisprudence under Rahman's guidance. Studying Islam at the University of Chicago therefore increased Madjid's authority and authenticity as a *Muslim* thinker—an unexpected and perhaps even ironic result of his Western academic encounter.

As a graduate student, Madjid learned to value intellectual continuity with the Islamic discursive tradition. In the late 1970s, he wrote a conference paper, "The Issue of Modernization among Muslims in Indonesia," that dovetailed with Binder and Rahman's contemporaneous work on the modernist authenticity deficit. Specifically, the paper offered a self-critical reflection on his controversial secularization speech. Madjid recalled how he had mistakenly expected the speech to be a closed, private affair and recounted his subsequent regrets over the very public and largely hostile response that it produced. He admitted: "It was socially too expensive, and we suffered almost irreparable damage to our reputation within the Muslim community. If I were to go back in time, I would follow my previous methods, i.e. *penetration pacifique*, the 'smuggling method' of introducing new ideas."⁷⁹ While it is impossible to pinpoint Madjid's exact motivations for writing this paper, the timing and content suggest some form of collaboration with Binder and Rahman. Indeed, Rahman repeatedly urged Madjid to ground his modernist reforms firmly in the Islamic tradition. In 1983, Madjid recounted his advisor's frequent frustrations with Muslim modernists who carelessly rejected aspects of the Islamic intellectual tradition without possessing sufficient knowledge of its contents.⁸⁰ Years later, he relayed how Rahman "regarded any development in Islamic thought that did not have roots in the riches of classical Islamic thought or that slipped from the ability to locate the threads of continuity with that past as inauthentic."⁸¹ Madjid learned the lesson well, devoting his graduate studies to mastering classical and medieval Islamic scholarship.

This growing respect for Islamic intellectual history also inspired Madjid's selection of a dissertation topic. Like Harun Nasution before him, Madjid took an interest in the age-old theological debate over reason and revelation and how it delineated the scope for ijtihad in the modern world. He chose to examine these issues through an unlikely source: Ibn Taymiyya (1263–1328), the medieval Hanbali scholar whom Islamists often cite as their intellectual forefather. According to Madjid, Ibn Taymiyya acknowledged humanity's God-given capacity to reason but believed that its power was severely limited by the fallibility of human perception. This position led Ibn

Taymiyya to reject both *kalam* (Islamic theology) and *falsafa* (philosophy) as feeble human efforts to derive truth through Greek-inspired rational methods and to insist instead that Muslims could only access truth via the Qur'an and the Sunnah.[82] At first glance, this argument seems to foreclose on the possibility of ijtihad in favor of a literalist adherence to the Qur'an and Sunnah. Islamists celebrate Ibn Taymiyya for this very position, among others. Madjid, however, disagreed with this reading. His dissertation argued that Ibn Taymiyya actually preferred ijtihad because its alternative, taqlid, encouraged Muslims to revere man-made and hence fallible interpretations as absolute laws. Ijtihad, in contrast, emphasized the tentative nature of all human knowledge. Admittedly, Ibn Taymiyya only endorsed a limited ijtihad that avoided borrowing from any man-made philosophies, but Madjid presented it as an endorsement nevertheless.[83] The dissertation thus "established an alternative *silsila* [genealogy] of renewalist Muslim intellectualism connecting his own reformist ideas to this alternative interpretation of Ibn Taymiyya."[84] Put another way, Madjid could now marshal Ibn Taymiyya's authenticity and authority as a conservative medieval scholar to augment his own calls for ijtihad.

Madjid used the conclusion of his dissertation to draw contemporary lessons from his research. He praised Ibn Taymiyya's rejection of overly complicated theological and philosophical concepts as progressive, writing:

> Followed consistently, Ibn Taymiyya's principles might result in the purification and revitalization of religion. We can see his vigorous refutation of *kalam* and *falsafa* was meant to clean out the religious thought-system, to return Islam to its original, simple, pristine nobility.... If they want to participate successfully in this complicated world, contemporary Muslims need the simple but sensibly principled understanding of their religion.[85]

While inspired by this "return ... to pristine nobility," Madjid also cast Ibn Taymiyya's embrace of the hadith cannon as highly problematic. He argued that Ibn Taymiyya overlooked crucial questions, such as those Rahman had frequently raised, about the historical authenticity of hadith. This blind trust had troubling consequences. According to Madjid, it bound Muslims to the "doctrinal minutiae" of hadiths instead of facilitating a dynamic reinterpretation of the Prophet's legacy. He concluded that Ibn Taymiyya's "strong and even fanatical adherence to [hadiths] can only be worrisome to Muslims concerned with modernity."[86] By refuting this conservative approach to hadiths,

Madjid sought to recuperate Ibn Taymiyya as a progressive scholar who simply fell short in one aspect of his thought.

As Madjid delved into the depths of the Islamic intellectual tradition at Chicago, he also worked to share his new knowledge with fellow Muslims in Indonesia. He took pains to translate important passages from Ibn Taymiyya, Abu al-Hasan al-Ashʿari (873–935), Abu Hamid al-Ghazali (1058–1111), and Ibn Rushd (1126–98) into Indonesian so that a broader audience could access the medieval texts. He then compiled the translations into a book titled *Intellectual Treasures of Islam* (1983) and wrote its extended introduction. It stressed the historical importance of ijtihad for his readers.[87] Specifically, Madjid celebrated the second caliph Umar as the most creative intellectual among Muhammad's companions, highlighting his "courage to propose ideas and undertake innovative actions that had not been enacted by the Prophet" and his profound respect for and knowledge of the Qurʾan.[88] He praised Ibn Taymiyya as a "radical egalitarian" who rejected all religious authorities except the Qurʾan and Sunnah.[89] He concluded that although ijtihad would never be perfect, "there was no path forward other than it."[90] The volume enabled Madjid, whether consciously or not, to position himself as the Indonesian translator and hence heir of the classical Islamic tradition. That tradition, by extension, supported his own reformist ambitions.

Taken together, Madjid's dissertation research and his translated volume helped cement his expertise in classical Islamic scholarship against those Muslim critics—such as Mohamad Rasjidi—who doubted his commitment to the Islamic tradition. Admittedly, Madjid continued to see the Islamic tradition through a distinctly fusionist lens. He borrowed from Rahman to present Umar as an early and exemplary practitioner of ijtihad and to depict Ibn Taymiyya as a protomodernist.[91] He relied on Ernest Gellner and Marshall Hodgson to frame the history of Islamic encounters with modernity. While Muslim critics would continue to attack him for these Western academic inspirations, his graduate studies at Chicago endowed Madjid with a new aura of Islamic authenticity, or what Rahman had called "roots" in history.

Amien Rais

As Madjid's classmate at Chicago, Amien Rais (b. 1944) took advantage of the fusionist climate to examine the relationship between Islam and development and, in the process, to reconsider his own position on the Islamic state. Born and raised in the Central Javanese city of Solo, Rais attended Muhammadiyah schools until he completed high school in 1962.[92] He then faced a difficult choice: continue his education at a Muhammadiyah university as his mother, who was a Muhammadiyah activist herself, had always hoped or follow his own interest in diplomacy to Indonesia's premier university, Universitas Gadjah Mada (UGM). Rais did some soul searching and eventually won his parents' blessing to matriculate at UGM. To compensate for the choice, he decided to enroll simultaneously at IAIN Yogyakarta where he studied Qur'anic exegesis, Islamic philosophy, and even comparative religion under Mukti Ali.[93] Rais described his undergraduate years as divided between two worlds: "The difference in lifestyles at IAIN and Gadjah Mada was no small matter. At IAIN, all the female students wore *hijab* whereas at Gadjah Mada, many wore 'you can see' clothing, among them some even wore miniskirts."[94] Yet he gradually found ways to navigate the two spaces. He joined HMI and gave Friday sermons at various Yogyakarta mosques, earning a reputation as "a Muslim activist in the Masyumi mold."[95] After graduation, Rais secured a lectureship at Gadjah Mada and, then, several years later, earned his master's degree in politics and international relations at the University of Notre Dame.[96] He had chosen the life of an activist academic.

In 1976, Rais won a Rockefeller Foundation scholarship to study political science at the University of Chicago. Although he was not an official member of the "Islam and Social Change" team, he participated in the summer 1977 seminar and became a regular in Binder and Rahman's circle.[97] For Rais, Chicago was an unwelcoming and even alienating place. His relationship with Binder, his advisor, was complicated and at times even strained. They sparred over the site of his dissertation research. Rais had originally hoped to study Islamic politics in Indonesia and therefore capitalize on his extensive ties back home, but Binder had insisted that the doctoral student broaden his perspective beyond the archipelago.[98] He also grew frustrated with prevailing academic attitudes about Islam.[99] Rais did find companionship in frequent late-night chats over coffee with fellow Indonesian and Malaysian students in the basement of Regenstein Library, but the friendships never managed to alleviate this sense of isolation altogether.[100] Indeed, Rais recalled decades later: "After more than three years in Chicago, my wife and I still felt like foreigners. In reality, we never felt *at home*."[101]

After enduring several years of coursework, Rais relocated to Egypt for dissertation research on the Muslim Brotherhood. He was relieved to be away from Chicago and live in a Muslim-majority society once again. Egypt even came to feel like his "second country."¹⁰² In his research, Rais framed the Muslim Brotherhood's recent "resurgence" as a direct challenge to the secularist assumptions underpinning Western academic theories of modernization and development. He agreed with and frequently cited Binder on this issue.¹⁰³ He also stressed the importance of Islamic authenticity, writing:

> Almost every Muslim country now is trying to reconcile between the authentic tradition which is deep-rooted in Islam and the requirements of modernization. The reaction of the fundamentalist in this case is predictable. He insisted that the emphasis be on authenticity and, avoiding a compromise, he sought to move society in the direction of rejection of foreign elements. It is true that the fundamentalist also accepted some new elements, but their main effort showed the opposite direction [i.e., away from diversity and openness].¹⁰⁴

Like Binder, Rais neither challenged nor problematized the Muslim Brotherhood's claims to Islamic authenticity. Rather, he argued that the Brotherhood's recourse to authenticity made it an alluring alternative to Western liberalism and Marxist socialism in the Islamic world.¹⁰⁵ He thus insisted that Western academics and Muslim modernists needed to take the power of these Islamic appeals more seriously.

Although Islamic fundamentalism may have been an attractive alternative to Western-style modernity, Rais argued that the Muslim Brotherhood, at least, was not a viable one. Taking the pragmatic perspective of a political scientist, Rais criticized the Brotherhood for its vague definition of an Islamic state. He wondered how the sovereignty of God would work in practice: "If God is the sovereign, how does He delegate His sovereignty to the people? Who is to interpret the sovereign? An elected legislative assembly or the ʿulama who have traditionally interpreted the body of Islamic teachings?"¹⁰⁶ Rais looked again to his professors for support:

> That to make a workable concept of [the] Islamic state is not an easy matter has been indicated by Professor Binder and Rahman in their observation of the development of Pakistan as an Islamic state. After nearly a year reading and talking about the idea of an Islamic constitution, Professor Binder described it as an idea "which so many Pakistanis seemed to hold dear, and which seemed so consistently to elude them." Professor Rahman even showed the contradictory nature of the three Pakistani constitutions . . . with the true

Islam. . . . If the Ikhwan ideologists and leaders are aware of the problems which the Pakistanis have been facing in constructing an Islamic constitution, probably they would reduce their rhetoric about [the] Islamic state and think more seriously over the delicate problems.[107]

In addition to these glaring weaknesses in the Brotherhood's political message, Rais noted the organization's failure to explain how "the economic organization of an Islamic society would be different from that of other states in the modern world."[108] He also criticized the Brotherhood's conception of pan-Islamism as "based on very shaky foundations" and "rather illusionary."[109] Rais concluded that the Brotherhood propagated a pure rather than a practical ideology and therefore "lacked a guide of action to solve the sociopolitical and economic problems confronted by Muslim communities in the modern time."[110] It was a scathing and important critique. In Rais's assessment, Islamic authenticity alone was insufficient; Muslims also needed the wisdom and flexibility to adapt to their particular circumstances.

Rais carried his critique back to Indonesia in 1981 at the height of an Islamic political crisis. Beginning in the late 1970s, top New Order officials had taken decisive actions to strengthen the multireligious national ideology of Pancasila and further marginalize Muslim demands for an Islamic state. Suharto requested that the Indonesian parliament introduce "Guidelines for Understanding and Enacting Pancasila" (Pedoman Penghayatan dan Pengalaman Pancasila [P4]), in 1978. The P4 guidelines instructed Indonesian citizens on how to live according to Pancasila and mandated two-week Pancasila indoctrination courses for all members of the military, civil servants, and students at the middle school, senior high, and university levels. Many Muslim leaders objected to the measure, and the entire delegation of the Islamic coalition party (Partai Persatuan Pembangunan) even walked out of parliament in protest, refusing to participate in the vote. The P4 guidelines still passed. Continuing his push for ideological homogeneity, Suharto announced plans to require all political parties and mass organizations, including Islamic ones such as Muhammadiyah and NU, to declare Pancasila as their "sole foundation" (asas tunggal) in 1982. The stipulation forced all organizations to choose between endorsing Pancasila as their official ideology or dissolving altogether.[111]

In this tense political climate, Rais declared that "there is no [such thing as an] Islamic state" in an interview with *Panji Masyarakat*.[112] He insisted that neither the Qur'an nor the Sunnah even mentioned the term *Islamic state*, absolving Muslims of the responsibility to build any specific political system. He stressed instead the obligation to enact Islamic principles such as socioeconomic justice and equality and even questioned the validity of some states, such as Saudi Arabia, that proclaimed Islam as their basis and yet violated these Islamic principles in practice. It was an implicit nod toward his recently completed dissertation that rejected both secularism and Islamism as seriously flawed ideologies.

The interview became a media phenomenon. The magazine sold out across country, and numerous Indonesians wrote letters to the editor in response.[113] In early December, *Panji Masyarakat* published a polite but stinging reply from a self-identified "average man" named Agus Fadjar. Fadjar commented that Rais's interview left him "feeling dissatisfied and full of questions in his heart" and asked about prophetic Medina and contemporary Saudi Arabia as examples of the Islamic state ideal. He concluded with the question "Is it not true that the ultimate aim of an Islamic state, besides justice and social prosperity, is to become a state blessed by Allah?"[114] Fadjar's attack elicited more responses. In February 1983, no less of an Islamic politician than Mohammad Roem, former JIB and Masyumi leader, came to Rais's defense. Roem stated unequivocally that "if Dr. Amien Rais says there is no Islamic State in the Sunnah, then I believe he is right."[115] He argued that the Prophet Muhammad never felt compelled to name his polity an "Islamic state," even though it surely qualified as one in substance. According to Roem, the lesson was clear. The Prophet demonstrated that the name was meaningless, whereas striving to fulfill Islamic political ethics was absolutely imperative.[116] With the public support of a former Masyumi luminary, Rais regained his political footing in the Indonesian Muslim community and emerged as a young, albeit influential, voice in persuading Muhammadiyah to cooperate with the New Order's "Pancasila as sole foundation" policy. He defended his position by declaring that Pancasila was merely the ticket required to ride "the bus of Indonesia."[117]

Although still toiling on his dissertation thousands of miles away in Chicago, Madjid soon obtained copies of Rais's interview and Roem's response. He wrote to the former Masyumi leader with gratitude for denouncing the Islamic state and thus lending his authoritative voice to the young modernist cause. Madjid also regaled the elder statesman with details about his research on Ibn Taymiyya and his belief that Indonesian Muslims must become better acquainted with the Islamic intellectual tradition.[118] They continued to exchange letters until Roem's passing six months later. By refusing to recognize any wall between their academic and activist pursuits, Rais and Madjid traversed the geographic and discursive space between Chicago and Jakarta to remain active participants in both worlds. Their fusionist ideas knew no boundaries.

Ahmad Syafii Maarif

Like Rais, Ahmad Syafii Maarif (b. 1935) changed his views on the Islamic state while at Chicago, but his transformation was even more pronounced, thanks to his close relationship with Rahman. Born into a polygamous family of merchants in West Sumatra, Maarif lost his mother before his second birthday and was raised primarily by his father's extended family. He attended a public elementary school in the mornings and then learned to memorize the Qur'an at a Muhammadiyah madrasa in the afternoons.[119] Hungry for more education, Maarif moved first to a nearby West Sumatran town and then to Yogyakarta where he studied at the prestigious Madrasah Muʿallimin Muhammadiyah. He graduated in 1956 and spent the next fifteen years in constant motion, shifting jobs and residences with great frequency. He served as a Muhammadiyah teacher in Lombok, married and had his first children, and graduated with his bachelor's degree in history in 1968.[120] With so many aspects of his life changing, only his loyalty to Muhammadiyah held firm. In the mid-1960s for example, Maarif worked as a magazine editor for *Suara Muhammadiyah* (Voice of Muhammadiyah). He also believed wholeheartedly in the cause of an Islamic state. He wrote in his memoirs that "in those years, I was indeed a follower of [Pakistani Islamist] Abul Aʿla Mawdudi."[121]

In 1972, Maarif had his first encounter with Western academia when he won a Fulbright scholarship to study history at Northern Illinois University. He was impressed with the university but was compelled to cut his studies short after only two semesters because of the failing health of his young son.[122] When he managed to secure a second Fulbright grant in 1976, he decided to complete his MA at Ohio University. Maarif later described this time at Ohio as "a status quo" period in philosophy.[123] He lived with fellow Muslim students, delivered Friday sermons, and found friends with similar Islamist sympathies.[124] He decided to write his master's thesis on Muslim demands for an Islamic state in Indonesia. Then, Rais—an old friend from Muhammadiyah circles in Yogyakarta—altered his plans. Rais introduced Maarif to Rahman and inquired on his friend's behalf about how to gain admission to

Chicago.¹²⁵ The back channels worked. In late 1978, Maarif obtained permission from Ohio University to complete his thesis in absentia and relocated to Chicago to begin doctoral study with Rahman.

Soon after his arrival at Chicago, Maarif underwent nothing short of a religio-political conversion. He abandoned his long-held beliefs in what he called the Islamic fundamentalism of Masyumi and Mawdudi in exchange for the Islamic modernism of Rahman.¹²⁶ In his memoirs, Maarif wrote:

> This complete change in heart has been in effect since about 1979 and has continued into my old age. I have already explained that during the [Ohio University] years there was not much change in the direction of my Islamic thought. Freshly arrived in Chicago, that essential change occurred. I felt as if I was experiencing a rebirth in philosophy.... My struggles with Rahman's courses over four years have influenced my attitude towards life in an absolutely fundamental way.¹²⁷

Maarif was awestruck by Rahman's wide-ranging knowledge. He attended courses with a renewed sense of purpose, invigorated by the freedom that Rahman gave students to debate history, interpretation, and methodologies. Maarif's most memorable experience was a one-on-one reading course with Rahman on Muhammad Iqbal's writings. Despite struggling through Iqbal's Persian poetry with the aid of a dictionary, Maarif developed a deep appreciation of Iqbal's philosophical ideas and earned his only A+ in the course, a success that was even more meaningful because it came from Rahman.¹²⁸ By the end of coursework, Maarif was not only Rahman's graduate student but one of his intellectual disciples.

Rahman's profound influence is most evident in Maarif's doctoral dissertation. The Indonesian scholar framed his entire project around Rahman's exhortation in *Islam and Modernity* "to distinguish clearly between normative Islam and historical Islam" and use the former to judge the "conformities and deformities" of the latter.¹²⁹ Accordingly, Maarif first worked to extract universal political principles from the contextual particulars of the Qur'an and Sunnah. He drew extensively from Rahman's writings on the Qur'an for this step, concluding that the Qur'an prioritized justice, equality, brotherhood, and democratic consultation as the foundations for political life. Maarif then used this "normative Islam" anchor to assess the extent to which Indonesian Islamic organizations (i.e., "historical Islam") embodied these Qur'anic ideals. He took his own Muhammadiyah to task for falling short of its modernist commitment to ijtihad. Maarif argued that although Muhammadiyah leaders proclaimed the necessity for continual reinterpretation of the Islamic source texts, they had only ever ventured the most "peripheral kind of ijtihad."[130] Consequently, he recommended that Muhammadiyah members increase their knowledge of the Islamic tradition so that they could truly embrace "the dynamic, radical, and future-oriented character of the Qur'anic imperatives."[131]

In addition to criticizing Muhammadiyah, Maarif used Rahman's method to refute Indonesian conceptions of the Islamic state. He addressed the issue in unequivocal terms:

> In retrospect, the Qur'an does not appear interested in any specific theory of state to be followed by the Muslim *umma*. The primary concern of the Qur'an is that the society be based on justice and morality. It is on Qur'anic ethical values that the Islamic political edifice should be based. Since the Qur'an does not lay down any specific form of state, the model and structure of Islamic polity is [sic] not immutable; it is always subject to change, modification, and improvement according to the requirements of the time and the need of Muslims.[132]

Like Rais before him, Maarif maintained that the Qur'an emphasized ethics over institutional forms. He therefore denigrated efforts by Indonesian Muslims to locate a Qur'anic blueprint for Islamic politics as acts of intellectual "laziness."[133] He had particularly harsh words for Masyumi's campaign in the 1950s—led by Mohammad Natsir—to revise the constitution so that Islam was the basis of the state:

> By repeating the confession that the Qur'an is the last Word of God but without trying seriously to comprehend its message intelligently and formulate it in a unity of logic is not, in effect, different from ignoring the Holy Book and putting it in the limbo of history. This is exactly what happened in historical Islam for centuries. If the Muslim really grasps what we mean, he will be definitely circumspect in using the term "an Islamic state" or "a state based on Islam" as proposed by the Muslim leaders in the Constituent Assembly of Indonesia.[134]

Until Muslims truly understood the unity and universality of the Qur'anic message, Maarif castigated any attempts to build an Islamic state as "premature" and "unrealistic."[135]

After defending his dissertation in 1983, Maarif returned to Yogyakarta to teach Islamic history at a variety of local colleges, including IAIN Yogyakarta. He also continued his Muhammadiyah activism and worked to spread his new ideas about ijtihad and the Islamic state. He delivered public lectures and wrote short articles about recapturing the unity of the Qur'anic message.[136] He translated his dissertation into Indonesian and published it as a book in 1985.[137] In all these post-Chicago activities, Maarif drew inspiration from Rahman's fusionist approach to the Qur'an and Islamic history.

Despite their similar backgrounds as Indonesian Muslim activists and graduate students at the University of Chicago, the intellectual journeys of Madjid, Rais, and Maarif were ultimately personal and contingent. Madjid spent his years at Chicago discovering the classics of the Islamic intellectual tradition and deepening his knowledge of medieval Arab thinkers such as Ibn Taymiyya under Rahman's guidance. Rais felt alienated by many aspects of Western academia but nonetheless emerged from his doctoral studies skeptical about the viability and even desirability of an Islamic state. Maarif became a devoted convert to Rahman's fusionist brand of Islamic modernism, echoing many of his advisor's arguments in his own writing on Indonesian Islamic politics. While their intellectual encounters at Chicago differed, each returned to Indonesia better equipped to balance the competing imperatives of Islamic authenticity and development. Chicago proved to be an ideal training ground for Suharto-era Islamic politics.

FEEDBACK LOOPS AND ENTANGLED TRADITIONS

The story of Chicago's fusionist madrasa exemplified the collapsing distinctions both between "empirical" social sciences and "normative" Islamic thought and between academic "outsiders" and Muslim "insiders" in the 1970s and 1980s. It also produced a series of feedback loops that increased cross-discursive, transnational entanglements. These feedback loops arguably began with Binder and Rahman's collaborative partnership. Together, the two professors traveled to Indonesia to meet with Mukti Ali, who, of course, had studied at the McGill Institute, and to recruit indigenous scholars to their research team. They eventually wrote two books, *Islam and Modernity* and *Islamic Liberalism*, which served simultaneously as academic publications and blueprints for Islamic reform. The connections only multiplied from there. Several Indonesian Muslim intellectuals relocated to Chicago to study Islam with Binder and Rahman. They utilized Western academic disciplines and research methods—not to mention financial and institutional resources—to write dissertations on Islamic reform and to intervene in Indonesian Islamic politics. The feedback loops continued to grow. In the 1980s, Rahman consulted for the Ministry of Religious Affairs, and more Indonesian students came to the United States to study Islam under his and Binder's supervision. Rahman and Binder became so enmeshed in Indonesian Islamic politics and vice versa that the two worlds almost blended into one.

In March 1983, Suharto named Munawir Sjadzali (1925–2004) as the new minister of religious affairs, ushering in a second era of fusionist transformation that cemented Ali's earlier achievements. Sjadzali was a career diplomat with a master's degree in international politics from Georgetown University and extensive foreign-service experience in both the United States and Arab Gulf countries. While not a Muslim intellectual by profession, he had long nurtured an interest in Islamic political theory. Specifically, he wrote his master's thesis on Muslim approaches to governance and occasionally advised New Order officials on Islamic policies.[138] Like Ali before him, Sjadzali used his ten-year tenure as minister to strengthen IAIN's fusionist culture. He often encouraged IAIN students and faculty to embrace relevant secular knowledge, such as empirical approaches from the social sciences, so that Islamic scholarship could overcome its isolation and make a concrete impact on national development.[139] In one 1983 speech, he declared that IAIN should become "not only a factory for producing religious teachers and Ministry bureaucrats but a birthplace for new Islamic ideas needed for development and society at large."[140] He sought, in other words, to build IAIN into a center for development-oriented ijtihad. To realize his ambitious aim, Sjadzali embarked on another round of assessment and reforms of the undergraduate program. He also expanded IAIN's fledging graduate programs and entrusted Harun Nasution to lead the flagship center at IAIN Jakarta.

Thanks to the Ford Foundation's financial support, Sjadzali invited Rahman and the Turkish sociologist Serif Mardin (1927–2017) to visit Indonesia and offer their expert recommendations on the IAIN reforms. It was another feedback loop. Rahman, who was in such poor health that he required his wife's physical support, spent the month of August 1985 traveling with ministry official Murni Djamal (McGill MA, 1975) around Indonesia.[141] Rahman toured five IAIN campuses and met with leading Muslim intellectuals and religious bureaucrats to discuss the state of Islamic higher education in the country. At the conclusion of his visit, he recommended a series of reforms, including better incorporation of the natural and social sciences into the curriculum, improving English- and Arabic-language instruction, and reducing student course loads in order to facilitate deeper understanding of the material.[142] He also advised teaching undergraduates "a critical religious history of Islam" so that students would better understand "the historical development" of Islamic disciplines such as fiqh and hadith.[143] Echoing his statements in *Islam and Modernity*, Rahman encouraged IAIN scholars "to research and publish not like Western Orientalists but in terms of purposefully Islamic scholarship but not like preachers either as is usually the case with traditional scholarship—but on the basis of scientific and sound scholarship."[144] Mardin issued similar advice. Overall, Rahman hoped for a complete "integration of knowledge" at IAIN.[145]

Rahman made one final recommendation: send the most promising IAIN scholars to the West for higher Islamic education. The ministry already shared this ambition. In October 1985, Sjadzali undertook a three-week tour of North American and European universities to facilitate more opportunities for Indonesians to study Islam in the West. His small entourage of ministry officials visited the University of Chicago, UCLA, Columbia University, New York University, and Georgetown University and then flew to Europe to see the School for Oriental and African Studies in London and the Sorbonne in Paris.[146] Sjadzali was especially impressed with his visits to the various American universities and soon thereafter requested a meeting with then US ambassador to Indonesia Paul Wolfowitz to discuss possible exchange programs. These conversations spurred an increase in the Fulbright scholarships available for Indonesians and the creation of a special Islamic Studies Fulbright program that enabled select IAIN lecturers to study Islam at American universities. In 1990, USAID expanded the program to include financial support for doctoral degrees as well.[147] It was a major success for Sjadzali's ministry.

Sjadzali's efforts provided another cohort of young Indonesian Muslims the opportunity to study under Rahman at Chicago and Binder, who since 1985 had relocated, at UCLA. In fall 1986, three Indonesians entered the Near Eastern Languages and Civilizations graduate program at Chicago. R. Mulyadhi Kartanegara, Qodri Azizy, and Abdul Muis Naharong all took courses with Rahman and completed their master's degrees under his guidance. When Rahman passed away in 1988, he left a palpable absence at

Chicago. Kartanegara recalled in his memoirs: "Professor Rahman's death reduced not only my own enthusiasm for philosophical discovery but moreover had the same effect on my friends who were studying at the University of Chicago, especially my Indonesian and Malaysian friends. The two [Malaysians] returned immediately to Malaysia whereas my Indonesian friends and I persevered."[148] All three Indonesians managed to finish their doctorates at Chicago and carried Rahman's teachings with them back to the archipelago. Fall 1986 also saw three Indonesians—Din Syamsuddin, Atho Mudzhar, and Toha Hamim—embark on their study of Islam halfway across the country at UCLA. Binder advised Syamsuddin's dissertation on Muhammadiyah and religious politics during the New Order. Syamsuddin, yet another future chairman of Muhammadiyah, thanked Binder for his "brilliant teaching" and wrote that he considered himself "fortunate . . . to be his protégé."[149] These later students constitute another significant part of Rahman and Binder's Indonesian legacy.

The feedback loops continued to reverberate in Indonesia as well. In the early 1980s, the Bandung-based Pustaka Press published Indonesian translations of Rahman's *Islamic Methodology in History* (1965), *Major Themes of the Qur'an* (1980), and *Islam and Modernity* (1982). Other translations and commentaries followed closely on their heels. Then, in December 1988, Limited Group alumnus Dawam Rahardjo hosted a major conference on Rahman's life and work in Jakarta. Ali, Maarif, Madjid, and other prominent fusionist thinkers presented papers and reflected on Rahman's many intellectual contributions, especially to Qur'anic hermeneutics. Madjid closed the conference with a tribute to his recently deceased mentor.[150] In many ways, the conference served as a public recognition of the profound impact Rahman had left on Indonesian Islamic thought. Binder's scholarship also gained a foothold among the country's Muslim intellectuals. His *Islamic Liberalism* (1988) was translated into Indonesian in 2001 and, like Rahman's writings, became a source for discussion and debate.[151] These translations and conferences helped spread the Chicago professors' ideas to Indonesian Muslims who would never have the opportunity to meet them in person or visit an American university.

While Binder and Rahman were likely more enmeshed in the Indonesian Islamic sphere than most of their colleagues were, these feedback loops still signal a more general trend toward intellectual entanglement. For example, Sjadzali also signed an agreement with Leiden University in 1988 that established the Indonesian-Netherlands Islamic Studies (INIS) program. INIS sought to "contribute substantially to Indonesia's development in the field of Islamic Studies and [provide] Indonesia with a core of highly qualified Islamic scholars."[152] The ministry also reached out to Turkish and Australian universities to create study opportunities for Indonesian Muslims. These programs fostered their own multifaceted transnational connections.

It is perhaps unsurprising that the McGill Institute of Islamic Studies reemerged as one of the most significant Western university partners for Indonesian Muslims in the late twentieth century. Sjadzali had visited McGill during his whirlwind university tour in 1985 and then worked to persuade Canadian officials to formalize the long-standing relationship. He even invited two institute professors, Charles Adams and Donald Little, to Indonesia so that they could tour several IAIN campuses and meet their Indonesian counterparts in person. The visit produced a signed memorandum of understanding and laid the foundations for an $8 million grant from CIDA in 1989.[153] Sjadzali celebrated the grant as a victory for Suharto and his Pancasila policies. He wrote a glowing letter to Suharto's vice president detailing its benefits: scholarships for five doctoral candidates, fifteen master's students, and numerous short-term researchers. McGill also agreed to send institute faculty to IAIN campuses as visiting professors.[154] Other ministry officials described the program as a way to "produce Muslim scholars who will function within the context of the national philosophy of Pancasila."[155] This CIDA grant marked a new and more intensive phase of the McGill-IAIN relationship. Between 1989 and 1996 alone, over eighty IAIN lecturers pursued graduate-level study of Islam at the McGill Institute.[156] The ranks of the so-called McGill mafia started to grow exponentially.

The exchange program also altered internal dynamics at the institute. Within two years of the CIDA grant, approximately one-third of its student body was Indonesian.[157] Indonesian scholars also joined the institute's faculty. During the 1990s, McGill invited prominent Muslim intellectuals such as Madjid (1991–92), Maarif (1993–94), and Sjadzali (spring 1994) to teach at the institute as visiting professors. They offered graduate courses on Southeast Asian Islam and also used their experiences at McGill to reflect upon and refine their own Islamic reformist agendas. In his autobiography, Maarif noted that he used his time at McGill to read vivaciously and "further develop [his] Chicago model" of Qur'anic hermeneutics.[158] He also described his engagement with students in primarily theological terms, recalling heated discussions over Sunni–Shiʻi differences and his personal insistence on rising above these historically contingent identities to embody a more universal and ideal Islam. Madjid, in turn, wrote what is sometimes referred to as his magnum opus, the over one-hundred-page-long introduction to *Islam: Doctrine and Civilization* (1992), during his year at the institute. By the 1990s, the institute not only trained Indonesian Muslims in the academic study of Islam but also served as a site for the production of Indonesian Islamic thought.

Ultimately, the stories of Chicago and, to a lesser extent, the McGill Institute demonstrate that it was nearly impossible and certainly artificial to untangle Western academia from modern Islamic thought by the 1980s. The border had largely collapsed, but fusionist thinkers continued to face some lingering constraints on their mobility. For the most part, they did not—and here Rahman is an exception—secure permanent academic employment. Madjid, Rais, and Maarif all returned to Indonesia after completing their doctorates. Other Chicago Muslims, including Mustafa Ceric and Wan Mohd Nor Wan Daud, also decided to forgo careers in Western academia to work in Bosnia, Malaysia, and other Muslim-majority countries. Perhaps each of these cases came down to personal preferences or the results of fellowship regulations, but the pattern stands in stark contrast to the career trajectories of Binder and Rahman's non-Muslim students, many of whom earned tenure at well-respected Western universities. Instead of enjoying undiluted identities as academic scholars of Islam, this second generation of fusionist thinkers seemed to hold only temporary memberships to the academic guild.

5 THE SPECTER OF ACADEMIC IMPERIALISM

DURING HIS FINAL YEAR in graduate school, Amien Rais published some ruminations on the Western academic study of Islam in the popular Islamic magazine *Panji Masyarakat*. It was one of the first translations of Edward Said's critique into Indonesian. Rais wrote: "As Muslims, every time we read books written by Orientalists, we certainly feel that many things are not quite right . . . The scholarly pillars of Orientalism, which have long been considered valid, are in reality false and incredibly weak."[1] He condemned Orientalists for mischaracterizing the Qur'an as the word of Muhammad rather than the Word of God and for maliciously misrepresenting its message.[2] He also drew explicitly from Said to argue that Orientalism was a means to control and colonize the East. Rais even refuted the claim popular among educated Indonesians that some Orientalists, such as H. A. R. Gibb and Wilfred Cantwell Smith, had been sympathetic to Islam, arguing instead that both men had denigrated Muslim thinkers and offered unsolicited advice about how to secularize Muslim societies.[3] Rais refrained from mentioning any of his Chicago professors by name, but the article gestured at his profound discontent with Western academia.

Although *Orientalism* (1978) was still making its initial waves when Rais penned his piece in 1980, Said's critique was not entirely new to Indonesian Muslims. On the contrary, the book's arguments mirrored long-time Islamic concerns about the Western academic study of Islam. Mohamad Rasjidi, for example, had denounced Orientalist scholarship in his responses to Nurcholish Madjid and Harun Nasution throughout the 1970s. Yet Western academics had seen Rasjidi as an angry Muslim on the very margins of the academy, if they had seen him at all. Said managed to bring the critique into the academic mainstream. Postcolonial theory gave Muslim intellectuals like Rasjidi and Rais an "appropriately academic" voice with which to express their frustrations with Islamic studies. It enabled them to talk—and to push—back against the Orientalist establishment that had long maligned their religious tradition.

At first glance, the rise of postcolonial theory seems like a positive development for fusionist thinkers. It challenged the Orientalist status quo and amplified calls for greater diversity in the academy, thereby opening space for more Muslim scholars. Many Indonesian Muslim intellectuals read these signs as progress. On closer examination, however, postcolonial theory destabilized the entire fusionist endeavor. Inspired by Michel Foucault, Said seized on the concept of discourse to challenge the myth of a disinterested production of knowledge. He argued, in painstaking detail, that Orientalism rested on a set of Western presuppositions about the absolute difference and inferiority of the East, especially Muslim societies. He also exposed how Orientalists put their knowledge in the service of Western imperialism. For Said, all knowledge—but especially knowledge about the "Other"—was political in nature. He therefore cautioned Muslims to be wary about the Western academic study of Islam:

> The predictable result of all this is that Oriental students (and Oriental professors) still want to come and sit at the feet of American Orientalists, and later to repeat to their local audiences the clichés I have been characterizing as Orientalist dogmas. Such a system of reproduction makes it inevitable that the Oriental scholar will use his American training to feel superior to his own people because he is able to "manage" the Orientalist system; in his relations with his superiors, the European or American Orientalists, he will remain only a "native informant."[4]

With these words, Said issued a provocation to Western-educated Muslim intellectuals (not to mention, to non-Muslim Arabs such as himself): Why should they engage with the imperial Western academy at all? Indonesian intellectuals recognized the challenge that postcolonial theory posed to fusionism and set to work on meeting it.

This chapter examines the state of fusionist epistemologies and networks in the age of postcolonial theory. I argue that by the 1990s, fusionists had reached a crossroads. On the one hand, part one demonstrates that Western-educated Muslim intellectuals possessed more political power and religious authority than ever before. After completing their doctorates at the University of Chicago, Amien Rais, Ahmad Syafii Maarif, and Nurcholish Madjid all ascended into the highest echelons of Indonesian Islamic leadership, and their meteoric rises were just the beginning. Dozens of Western-educated Muslims followed in their footsteps during the 1980s and 1990s, normalizing academic credentials as a new source of Islamic religious authority. On the other hand, postmodernism and postcolonial theory posed serious challenges to fusionist thinking. Part two explores how Rais, Madjid, and a third prominent Indonesian intellectual, Amin Abdullah, articulated new fusionist frameworks that pushed beyond the largely discredited language of objectivity to justify their cross-discursive projects. Finally, part three focuses on the ongoing and increasingly fierce Muslim opposition to Western academic entanglement in modern Islamic thought. Uninterested in or unimpressed by new postmodern and postcolonial sensibilities, Muslim critics raised uncomfortable and yet important questions about academic complicity with state power.

ACADEMIC CREDENTIALS AS THE NEW NORMAL

Late twentieth-century Indonesia experienced a series of interrelated demographic changes that, in turn, had profound consequences for modern Islamic thought in the country. Thanks to the New Order's developmentalist policies, more people were trading rural subsistence farming for urban-based salaried employment. Average incomes were improving, and literacy rates were also on the rise. M. C. Ricklefs observed that "in 1930, it would have been nearly impossible to find a literate woman in many parts of Java; by the 1990s, it was becoming difficult to find anyone who was not literate."[5] At the intersection of these societal trends was the urban, educated middle class.[6] This new middle class was, like the Indonesian population as a whole, predominantly Muslim and becoming more visibly pious. In the 1980s and 1990s, mosque construction skyrocketed, the call to prayer began to saturate the urban soundscape across the country, and increasing numbers of women chose to wear the popular Indonesian style of head-covering, the *jilbab*. This new religiosity broke with several Indonesian Islamic precedents. Instead of supporting Islamic political parties, middle-class Muslims tended to vote for and even join Suharto's Golkar. Muslim educational trends were also changing. Indonesian Muslims graduated from high school and college at unprecedented rates in the 1980s and 1990s, but very few could read or write Arabic.[7] They studied instead a mixture of Western-style and Islamic subjects mainly in Indonesian. These changing political and educational dynamics produced a new type of Muslim scholar that, as Yudi Latif argues, required a new name:

> The distinction between the category of *ulama* and *intelektuil* [secular intellectual] . . . blurred. Many *intelektuil* emerged as leading religious figures, while many *ulama* emerged as leading spokesmen on secular issues. Moreover, with the proliferation of religious universities, there were more and more *ulama* with academic degrees . . . In sharing a wide commonality in their knowledge base and exposure to modernity and higher education, the terms *ulama* and *intelektuil,* as far as they related to the groups of degree holders, were no longer mutually exclusive. . . . A new code was needed to mark the fusion of the two categories. . . . The meeting ground was . . . the neutral Indonesian neologism, *cendekiawan*.[8]

The term *cendekiawan* thus signaled a significant shift in the nature of Islamic religious authority. The three Chicago alumni embodied this change.

Rais was the first to return home from Chicago. In 1981, he rejoined the political-science faculty at his alma mater, UGM in Yogyakarta, and became an activist professor. He delivered public lectures on Islamic social ethics and mentored Muslim student leaders. He also became a well-known Muslim intellectual beyond the UGM campus. As we saw in chapter 4, Rais garnered national attention in 1982 when he renounced the Islamic state ideal and encouraged Muhammadiyah to accept Pancasila as its sole foundation. He continued to publish articles on Islam, democracy, and Indonesian politics in major newspapers and magazines and to comment on global Islamic politics especially, including the Israeli–Palestinian conflict, the Soviet invasion of Afghanistan, and American foreign policy.[9] Rais forsook the comfort of the "ivory tower" in favor of the life of a scholar-activist.

His status as an emerging public intellectual enabled Rais to ascend the ranks within Muhammadiyah. Positioning himself as a loyal internal critic, he argued that Muhammadiyah was suffering from an endemic leadership crisis in which senior members refused to cede power and younger members were disinclined to step forward into the limelight. In one essay, Rais wrote,

"Muhammadiyah's leadership, I believe, needs an injection of fresh thinking with a broad perspective so that it can become a 'future-oriented' Islamic dawah movement."[10] Rais was part of his envisioned vanguard. In 1985, he became the head of the Preachers Council (*Majelis Tabligh*) and spearheaded an effort to reimagine Muhammadayih's approach to dawah.[11] The position also secured him a voice on Muhammadiyah's powerful executive board for the first time. After leading the Preachers Council for five years, Rais was elected the national vice chairman of Muhammadiyah in 1990. He served under Azhar Basyir (1928–94), but when the elder Islamic scholar passed away in 1994, Rais assumed temporary responsibility for the organization. He won the election the following year to become the official twelfth national chairman of Muhammadiyah.

Rais helped normalize Western academic credentials as a source of Islamic authority within Muhammadiyah circles. In his memoirs, he described his election as chairman as a "water shed" moment because, instead of having been educated at a pesantren or Egypt's al-Azhar, he was educated at and received a doctorate in political science from an American university. Nonetheless, he stated:

> I never felt weighed down, except for one or two times when thoughts crossed my mind about my capability and also my educational background. However, over time, there was actually not much of a reaction from Muhammadiyah and, the more I developed relationships with various regions, branches, and various districts in this country, the more stable [my leadership was]. Muhammadiyah members were not confused about whether a member of the ʿulama or an intellectual led Muhammadiyah. That dualism no longer exists.[12]

Seeing this openness toward new leadership styles, Rais encouraged others to step forward to help spark an intellectual revitalization within Muhammadiyah. In one interview, he explained that the experience of studying in the West often increased Muslim piety and then invited Western-educated Muslims to bring their creative ideas into the Muhammadiyah fold.[13] He moreover argued that Muhammadiyah needed to expand its conception of the ʿulama to encompass Muslim economists, sociologists, and other academic scholars. To implement these ideas, Rais used his authority as chairman to host more seminars and research symposiums and to reach out with an inclusive ethos to non-Muhammadiyah Muslims who possessed the knowledge and skills to help administer the organization's sprawling network of schools and hospitals.¹⁴ He even took the time to praise those Muhammadiyah members who did adopt "academic" approaches to Indonesian social problems.¹⁵ These policies and statements produced little discernible backlash. This lack of response signaled that millions of Muhammadiyah members were amenable to the new academic model of leadership.

While Rais blazed the trail within Muhammadiyah, Ahmad Syafii Maarif was not far behind. Maarif spent most of the 1980s teaching college students in Yogyakarta and championing Rahman-inspired fusionism in print. He also traveled overseas to take up visiting professorships in the United States, Canada, and Malaysia.¹⁶ Despite his itinerant scholarly lifestyle, Maarif found time for Muhammadiyah. He served for two years as the editor for *Suara Muhammadiyah* (Voice of Muhammadiyah). He next earned his seat on Muhammadiyah's national executive board in 1990 and then, five years later, won election to become Rais's vice chairman. When his Chicago classmate resigned the chairmanship so that he could run for president in 1998, Maarif assumed leadership of Muhammadiyah and thus became a household name across the country.

Although Rais and Maarif were the most visible examples of Muhammadiyah's changing leadership profile, the last decade of the twentieth century saw other Western-educated intellectuals rise through the organization's ranks as well. One official Muhammadiyah publication noted that after the 1990 convention, "intellectuals dominated the leadership structure."¹⁷ Rais observed that 85 percent of the members of the Preachers Council possessed doctorates in academic disciplines in 1995.¹⁸ Among these academic activists was Amin Abdullah (b. 1953). Born in Central Java, Abdullah attended the modernized pesantren at Gontor and then completed his undergraduate degree in comparative religion at IAIN Yogyakarta. In the mid-1980s, he caught Minister of Religious Affairs Munawir Sjadzali's attention and won a scholarship to study Islamic philosophy in Turkey. He wrote his doctoral dissertation on the similarities between the ethical philosophies of Abu Hamid al-Ghazali (1058–1111) and Immanuel Kant (1724–1804) and later accepted a postgraduate fellowship at the McGill Institute of Islamic Studies. In 1995, Abdullah became the head of Muhammadiyah's Majelis Tarjih, the influential council that issues fatwas and other forms of religious guidance for the organization's millions of members. This position made his an important voice among the third generation of Indonesian fusionists. Maarif, Abdullah, and other fusionist intellectuals did face stiff opposition from within Muhammadiyah in the early 2000s. While these events lie beyond the scope of this book, it is important to note that the so-called conservative faction that unseated them was led by none other than Leonard Binder's former graduate student, Din Syamsuddin (UCLA PhD, 1991).[19] In 2005, Syamsuddin thus became the third consecutive chairman of Muhammadiyah who had studied Islam in a Western university.

Whereas Rais and Maarif made their careers within the organizational structure of Muhammadiyah, Nurcholish Madjid struck a more independent course. Madjid returned from his American educational sojourn on July 4, 1984, and soon thereafter accepted a professorial position at IAIN Jakarta.[20] In many ways, Madjid's activities as an outspoken Muslim reformer in the 1980s were a natural extension of both his student activism in the early 1970s and his graduate studies at Chicago. He continued to urge Indonesian Muslims to see reason as an integral, albeit imperfect, aspect of Islam and to exercise a contextual and dynamic approach to ijtihad. However, he cultivated new interests as well. He began to reflect on the relationship between Islam and Indonesian cultures and ultimately rejected the common assumption that indigenous cultural practices posed a threat to the purity of the faith.[21] He also wrote extensively about interreligious tolerance, pluralism, and democracy.

Madjid collaborated with other modernist intellectuals such as Limited Group alumni Dawam Rahardjo and Djohan Effendi to found an independent Islamic think tank called Paramadina in 1986. Together, these men hoped to spur an Islamic intellectual renaissance, especially among educated, middle-class Muslims in Jakarta and other major cities. They characterized their work as "rational, scientific, and academic dawah."[22] Paramadina hosted occasional courses on Islam, organized public lectures, and published books on pressing religious issues such as socioeconomic justice, gender equity, and religion-state relations. One of its most popular programs was the Religious Studies Club (Klub Kajian Agama). The club was held at a Jakarta hotel on the third Friday of every month and featured a thematic lecture by Madjid and one or two guest speakers. The lectures were then followed by a robust question-and-answer session with the two hundred to four hundred people in attendance. Club events often garnered national press coverage or spawned follow-up articles in Islamic magazines. For example, when Munawir Sjadzali appeared as the special guest at the inaugural session in 1986, he discussed his vision to "reactualize" Islamic inheritance law. Whereas the Qur'an outlined an explicit 2:1 ratio as the inheritance rate for sons versus daughters, Sjadzali argued that children should receive equal shares of their parents' wealth regardless of gender. The proposal sparked a national debate over whether Qur'anic injunctions were eternal or should be adapted, as Sjadzali proposed, to align with contemporary social dynamics.[23] Other frequent guests included Madjid's close associates at Paramadina, such as Effendi and Rahardjo, and his colleagues at IAIN Jakarta, such as Harun Nasution and Quraish Shihab (b. 1944).[24] Madjid used Paramadina as an important platform for bringing reformist ideas to the public's attention and for sparking sustained discussion and deliberation.

As Madjid's stature as a scholar and media personality grew, he continued to teach at IAIN Jakarta and eventually attracted a substantial following among some of the institution's brightest young scholars. This circle of students became known as the Mazhab Ciputat, or the Ciputat School, in reference to the southern Jakarta neighborhood where the IAIN campus is located. Members included Bahtiar Effendy (Ohio State PhD, 1994), Fuad Jabali (McGill PhD, 1999), Saiful Mujani (Ohio State PhD, 2004), Yudi Latif (ANU PhD, 2004), and Ali Munhanif (McGill PhD, 2010).[25] One of the Mazhab Ciputat's most prominent members was Azyumardi Azra (b. 1955). Born and raised in West Sumatra, Azra moved to Jakarta in 1976 to study Arabic at the flagship IAIN campus. He took courses with both Nasution and Madjid and participated in discussion groups with other members of the Mazhab Ciputat. Then, in 1986, he won one of the special Islamic Studies Fulbright scholarships that Sjadzali had negotiated the previous year. Azra attended Columbia University, receiving his master's degree in Middle Eastern studies in 1988 and his doctorate in history in 1992. Upon returning to Indonesia, he accepted a professorial post at IAIN Jakarta and was named its new rector in 1998, a post he would hold for eight years.[26] Inspired by but never bound to the ideas of their mentors, Azra and other members of the Mazhab Ciputat have made their own names, like Amin Abdullah, as the next generation of fusionist thinkers in Indonesia.

The establishment of the Indonesian Association of Muslim Intellectuals (Ikatan Cendekiawan Muslim Indonesia [ICMI]) solidified the changing face of Islamic religious authority in the country. ICMI began with a modest request from Muslim students at Brawijaya University in Malang, East Java. The Brawijaya students had attended several Islamic lectures on campus and "were forcefully struck by the ongoing cleavages among the Muslim intelligentsia."[27] They discussed ways to address this troubling polarization and, in February 1990, proposed to two Muslim leaders, Dawam Rahardjo and Muhammad Imaduddin Abdulrahim (1931–2008), the convening of a broad-based Islamic conference. Despite their ideological differences, Rahardjo and Abdulrahim recognized the proposal as an opportunity to establish a formal Muslim intellectual organization. They secured the support of Suharto confidant B. J. Habibie and collected signatures from prominent Muslim scholars, including both Rais and Madjid. By the end of September, they had the signatures of forty-nine Muslim intellectuals, forty-five of whom held doctoral degrees. Suharto approved the proposal, and ICMI officially opened its doors in December 1990. Within seven years, it boasted over ten thousand members.[28]

While this origin story appears straightforward, the birth of ICMI became "one of the most consequential political events" of the late New Order period.[29] Debates raged over Suharto's true motivations for supporting the new Muslim association. Some worried that ICMI was little more than the latest New Order ploy to co-opt Muslim leaders into the regime. For example, Nahdlatul Ulama chairman Abdurrahman Wahid (1940–2009) was vocal in his opposition to ICMI. He refused to join the organization on the twofold basis that it was merely a puppet of Suharto and that it represented a dangerous drift toward religious sectarianism. Other Muslim intellectuals argued that ICMI was a positive development because its creation formalized their growing influence in national politics. In addition to the controversies that shrouded its birth, ICMI endured numerous internal leadership fights as Habibie's loyal Muslim bureaucrats and independent Muslim intellectuals jostled for authority.[30] Rais, moreover, used ICMI as a springboard from which to criticize Suharto. In the mid-1990s, Rais broached the taboo topic of succession and began to speak publicly against the Suharto family's corruption. He was forced to resign from his high-profile ICMI post in 1997.[31] While this series of political conflicts attracted the most attention, Yudi Latif persuasively argues that ICMI's real significance was to make Muslim intellectuals a national media phenomenon. Indonesian newspapers published countless articles on the various ICMI controversies and provided column inches for members to opine about the organization's objectives.[32] This media attention helped to popularize the hybridized cendekiawan as a source for Islamic religious authority.

FUSIONIST THINKING IN A POSTCOLONIAL AGE

The ranks and stature of Indonesian fusionist thinkers undoubtedly grew during the 1980s and 1990s, but the same period also saw a groundswell in internal critiques of Western academic knowledge. Postmodernists attacked the stability and universality of all knowledge, even the natural sciences. Even more damaging to the fusionist enterprise were postcolonial works that linked academic disciplines to Western imperialism and especially the domination of Muslim-majority societies. Indonesian fusionists were not impervious to these escalating criticisms of Western academia. On the contrary, many were familiar with postmodernist attacks on objectivity and had read, often with avid approval, postcolonial works such as those by Edward Said. These forceful critiques of academic knowledge raised troubling questions about whether, why, and under what conditions Muslim intellectuals should interact with the Western academy.

Whereas fusionist pioneers such as Mukti Ali and Harun Nasution were generally reluctant to acknowledge the limitations of academic knowledge, younger scholars openly wrestled with the issue of epistemological imperialism. They knew that they could no longer appeal to "sound methodologies" or "objective research" to defend fusionism from Muslim detractors. Some even published books, such as Atho Mudzhar's *Studying Islam in America* (1991) and Yudian Asmin's edited volume *The Experience of Studying Islam in Canada* (1997), to explain the graduate school process and to dispel popular misconceptions about Western Islamic studies.[33] Interestingly, many Muslim intellectuals cited postcolonial theory as a reason *to* engage with Western academia. They noted that Western scholarship had long been marred by Christian, Jewish, and even outright anti-Islamic biases but also insisted that not all academics fell into this hostile camp. Instead, they drew distinctions between "good" and "bad" Orientalists and suggested that anti-Islamic bias was largely a problem of the past. For example, Faisal Ismail (McGill PhD, 1995) argued that the current generation of Western scholars engaged in "purely academic" research and were thus eager to identify each other's weaknesses in order to produce better work.[34] Azyumardi Azra stressed that the "new Orientalism" viewed the Islamic world as dynamic and was more open to interreligious cooperation.[35] Such statements positioned postcolonial theory as part of an academic progress narrative. After critics exposed the ethnocentric limitations of Western knowledge, academics worked hard to improve, thereby making the Western university a safe space for Muslims seeking to study Islam.

Indonesian Muslims also pointed to their intellectual independence as graduate students to refute charges that studying Islam in the West contaminated their Muslim faith. Fuad Jabali (McGill PhD, 1999) emphasized that the

McGill Institute never made any books or questions off limits. Rather, he described his graduate school experience as an open-minded and self-driven exploration of the Islamic tradition in which he selected his own dissertation topic and advisors. He therefore challenged critics that "if they [Western academics] have a mission like brainwashing or indoctrination, then surely they would forbid such free discussions."[36] In this manner, Jabali and like-minded colleagues foregrounded their agency as scholars and their ability to navigate the political currents in Islamic studies.

Although optimistic, these initial answers were too quick to sidestep postcolonial critiques about entrenched Western presuppositions and imperial epistemologies. These concerns lingered, compelling several fusionists to reflect more deeply and to craft more detailed responses. This section focuses on three such Muslim intellectuals: Rais, Madjid, and Amin Abdullah. While Ahmad Syafii Maarif certainly exerted a profound influence on Indonesian Islamic thought in the late twentieth century, he generally followed Fazlur Rahman's ideas about academic methods and Qur'anic hermeneutics, which we have already explored in some depth. Consequently, I analyze Abdullah's writings in order to shine more light on the third generation of Indonesian fusionist thinkers.

Amien Rais and a Pragmatic Fusionism

Rais had what can only be called a complex relationship with Western academia. He had felt alienated by the academic culture at Chicago and published that scathing article about Orientalism in *Panji Masyarakat*. Yet he also chose to participate in two postdoctoral programs in the United States, the first at George Washington University in 1986 and the second at UCLA in 1988. He then championed an academic revitalization of Muhammadiyah and worked to open the organization's doors to other Western-educated Muslims. Given Rais's reputation as a strategic politician, it is tempting to attribute his seeming inconsistency to pandering, opportunism, or sheer political expediency. While I do not deny these possibilities altogether, I argue that Rais's ambivalence toward Western academia reflects a more fundamental tension between postcolonial skepticism and policy-oriented practicality. On the one hand, Rais assailed academics for imposing Western frameworks on Muslim societies and exposed the long-term damage they wrought. On the other hand, he saw Western-style social sciences as useful and even indispensable tools for implementing Islamic values in the contemporary world.

These two views led Rais to adopt a pragmatic and even utilitarian posture vis-à-vis Western academia.

While he graduated at a time when postcolonial theory was still in its infancy, Rais became an early and vocal critic of academic imperialism. He fortified his critiques with insights from diverse sources. In addition to Said, Rais credited Leonard Binder—despite their strained relationship—with opening his eyes to the limitations of the Western social sciences. Binder had cautioned Rais early in his graduate career that the social sciences served the interests of the Western bourgeois; those words raised Rais's doubts about academic claims to objectivity.[37] He also drew inspiration from Iranian sociologist and revolutionary Ali Shariati (1933–77), echoing his warnings about Westoxification and his appeals for intellectual emancipation.[38] In one essay, Rais argued that Western colonialism had driven a deliberate wedge between Muslims and their religious tradition so that "the Muslim community at last became mere consumers of Western ideology and could no longer see Islam's own rich treasures."[39] Because nationalist struggles had done little to reduce Westoxification among Muslims, he called for a "mental and intellectual revolution to rediscover Islamic teachings in a comprehensive manner."[40] Said, Binder, and Shariati constituted an eclectic patchwork of mentors, but they all shaped Rais's postcolonial skepticism toward the academy.

Applying his postcolonial perspective to the social sciences, Rais came to see many of the models he had studied at Chicago as inadequate for or even downright incompatible with Indonesian realities. He articulated this position most clearly in a 1984 essay titled "Illuminating the Crisis of the Social Sciences." The article took particular aim at Gabriel Almond's early work on political systems. Rais noted that Indonesian students memorized Almond's specialized vocabulary and then, when attempting to apply it to Indonesia, discovered that it was inapplicable. Many social scientists attributed such misfits to insufficiently modern systems in developing countries, but Rais argued instead that the framework itself was deeply ethnocentric. He wrote in frustration: "Every theory that is claimed as universal—valid for all places and for all times—is, in reality, rather poorly done or simply trivial. Therefore, the seven functional categories from Almond and his friends cannot be made the basic guide for empirical research."[41] Rais also charged that the modern–traditional dichotomy, which positioned the West as rational and progressive in contrast to an irrational and backward East, merely reproduced Western neocolonial dominance through an academic language.[42]

In his assessment, many social scientific paradigms served elite Western interests. Rais clearly possessed serious reservations about the universality of academic modes of knowledge and aimed to expose its Western and often anti-Islamic roots.

Although he sharply criticized the ethnocentric presuppositions undergirding Western social science, Rais was also a pragmatist. He acknowledged the unfortunate reality that Indonesia still depended on more developed nations for economic and technological aid as well as for social-scientific paradigms and research methods. In the long run, Rais hoped that Indonesian social scientists would create their own theories grounded in Indonesian realities and values, but, in the meantime, he embraced a certain intellectual realism regarding the Western social sciences. Rais elaborated on this stance:

> In order to create theories more relevant to our own society, perhaps we still require much time. Because of that, we have to adopt a genuinely critical attitude in using theories that come from abroad. Or, borrowing the concept from Iranian thinker Ali Shariati, Third World scholars must undertake selective and progressive borrowing in relation to what is taken from either the Western or Communist worlds.[43]

In other words, Rais advised his fellow Indonesian academics to first expose the severe limitations of Western social science but then assume an "open-minded attitude" toward ideas that might serve Indonesian interests. It was a largely utilitarian approach to Western academia. In light of the geopolitical realities that governed the postcolonial world, Rais conceded that certain Western theories and methods were essential to living and thriving in the here and now.

These principles, in turn, inspired Rais's vision of "social monotheism" (*tawhid sosial*).[44] He chose this particular phrase to denote that God's oneness was not merely a theological truth but also a social imperative that required Muslims to build a more united and equal world. Social monotheism had significant fusionist elements. Fauzan Saleh noted that Rais "used scientific and empirical approaches to reinterpret the universal message of Islam."[45] His interpretations, in many ways, resembled Fazlur Rahman's "double movement" theory. Like Rahman, Rais approached the Qur'an as a source of universal ethical principles, foremost among them justice, democracy, and equality.[46] He then strived to translate those universal Qur'anic precepts into concrete social policies. Rais even urged fellow Muslims to familiarize themselves with economics, sociology, and political science just as Rahman had encouraged. Although he rarely acknowledged Rahman in his writings, it is hard to believe that Rais did not build on some of Rahman's ideas, especially given their extensive interactions at Chicago. Regardless, Rais applied his conception of social monotheism to democratic politics, international affairs, and capitalist economics throughout the 1990s. He was, at heart, a pragmatic fusionist and maintained that Islamic research should produce "action-oriented knowledge" and "knowledgeable action."[47]

Rais used his social science–infused approach to Islam to reconceptualize the obligatory Muslim charity tax (*zakat*) for the modern Indonesian context.[48] His argument began with a simple observation: the Qur'an mandated zakat as a means to achieve socioeconomic justice but did not specify an exact rate. According to Rais, the widely accepted 2.5 percent rate was not even based on hadith but was instead the product of ijtihad by early members of the ʿulama. It was only after considering the requirements for economic subsistence and the existing gaps between rich and poor in their societies that early Islamic scholars had concluded that a just zakat rate was one-fortieth of yearly surplus income. However, Rais argued that economic circumstances had so radically changed that this previous effort at ijtihad was no longer valid. The early jurists had never dreamed of the diversity of the modern workforce nor witnessed the rise of professions, such as banking and medical specialties, that enabled individuals to amass fortunes with relative ease. As a result of these economic transformations, Rais called for a renewed ijtihad that would push the zakat rate up (perhaps even to 20 percent) for white-collar professionals.[49] By applying economic and sociological modes of analysis to evolving Indonesian income structures, Rais highlighted how Muslims could harness social scientific inquiry in order to practice an empirically based version of ijtihad.

The 1980s and 1990s were busy decades, to say the least, for Rais. In addition to his full-time job as a professor of political science at UGM, he assumed increasing responsibilities for running Muhammadiyah and then ICMI. Rais nonetheless managed to carve out time to consider postcolonial challenges to fusionist thinking. He rejected social-scientific claims to both objectivity and universality and denounced Muslim overreliance on Western academic frameworks. On these important points, he differed from fusionist predecessors, such as Rahman, Ali, and Nasution, who believed that academic methods could reveal new truths about Islam. For his part, Rais preferred the postcolonial skepticisms of Edward Said and Ali Shariati and warned his fellow Muslims to resist becoming enchanted with the West. However, Rais never went as far as rejecting any and all engagement with Western academia. He adopted a utilitarian posture instead. While the social sciences were not avenues to truth, they did offer indispensable tools with which Muslims could implement Islamic principles in the complex and ever-changing modern world.

Nurcholish Madjid and a Radical Universalism
During the 1980s and 1990s, Nurcholish Madjid spoke and wrote prolifically about his vision of Islamic reform, and scholars in turn have produced a rich secondary literature that analyses his work. Several have noted his proclivity to draw from Western scholars such as Harvey Cox, Robert Bellah, and Marshall Hodgson.[50] For example, Carool Kersten highlights how reading Hodgson's *The Venture of Islam* inspired Madjid to reconsider the relationship between religion and culture and to work toward legitimizing a specifically Indonesian Islam.[51] This section does not attempt an exhaustive study of Madjid's post-Chicago writing but instead seeks to answer a more specific question: how did he justify cross-discursive borrowing in the age of postcolonial theory? In stark contrast to Rais's pragmatism, Madjid responded to postcolonial challenges to academic objectivity with an idealistic and even radical universalism. He reasoned that if Islam was indeed a universal religion that conveyed timeless truths, then those truths could not be confined to any one society or intellectual tradition. Rather, genuinely universal truths must—by their very nature—cross discursive boundaries and live in multiple cultural and religious contexts. This definition of universality necessitated exploring widely and learning from others in the search for truth. As a result, Madjid untethered universality from objectivity, believing instead that truth could be and often was located in the subjective and contextual but was not confined to them.

Although Madjid shared a commitment to contextual ijtihad and an ethical exegesis of the Qur'an with his doctoral supervisor, he nevertheless departed from Rahman's fusionist vision in significant ways. Rahman repeatedly stressed the need for objective and sound methods in Islamic studies. He believed there was an accessible historical truth about the origins of hadith and maintained that one could and should approach the Qur'an on its own terms. In contrast, Madjid took only sporadic interest in research methods.

This disinterest shined through in Madjid's frequent and yet eclectic use of Western academic sources. Despite referencing a wildly diverse range of Western scholars from phenomenologists Rudolph Otto and Joseph Campbell to futurologists John Naisbatt and Patricia Auberdene, Madjid rarely discussed the basis for their knowledge or credibility. For example, he cited the work of German social psychologist Erich Fromm multiple times in a major lecture from 1992 but only provided a three-word description, "a well-known psychoanalyst [seorang psikoanalis terkenal]," to orient his Indonesian audience to the German thinker.[52] Even when drawing from Western scholarship on Islam, Madjid paid little heed to scholars' credentials or methods. One of Madjid's favorite interlocutors was sociologist Robert Bellah. In several pieces from the 1980s and 1990s, he borrowed Bellah's insights into early Islamic history and the nature of Muhammad's state. These were sensitive subjects for Muslims, but Madjid did not examine Bellah's evidentiary base, nor did he even mention the fact that Bellah was, by his own admission, no expert on Islam and actually only ever wrote two pieces on Muslim societies.[53] Whereas his fusionist predecessors staked their cross-discursive borrowing on the methodological authority of select Western scholars (such as Rahman with Joseph Schacht), Madjid appeared to shrug off such concerns as peripheral and perhaps even immaterial.

On the one hand, Madjid's inattention to academic methods and scholarly authority might merely render him a less meticulous and erudite scholar than Rahman was. Madjid never explicated a detailed theory of Qur'anic interpretation nor conducted his own historical research into the evolution of Islamic legal terminology as Rahman did. Instead, Madjid often borrowed research from others and stitched the ideas together into grand-scale theological statements. On the other hand, Madjid's disinterest in methodological matters may signal more than poor attention to detail. It seems to reflect a deeper ambivalence regarding the potential of human reason. Madjid certainly encouraged Muslims to use their God-given capacity to reason so that they could devise solutions for the problems plaguing humanity. Yet, following Ibn Taymiyya, Madjid also acknowledged the limits of the human intellect, arguing that knowledge was never absolute but always relative in nature.[54] In an essay from the early 1990s, Madjid emphasized the fallibility of the social sciences in particular. He suggested that, in contrast to their colleagues in the natural sciences, social scientists could not generalize with any certainty because human beings, unlike electric currents, are unpredictable and cannot be observed in a controlled laboratory setting. The closest alternative was to study human history and to learn its lessons about human nature as the Qur'an advised.⁵⁵ In these ways, Madjid understood reason as indispensable and yet imperfect. He even classified knowledge as secondary to faith—a position reflected in his frequent reliance on the Qur'an to encourage human reason—rather than the reverse.⁵⁶ It was on this point that Madjid diverged from Rahman. While Rahman, too, upheld faith as an absolute necessity, he built his brand of fusionist thinking on the belief that academic research and Islamic faith were nearly equal paths to the same truth. Madjid seemed to imply that when in doubt, faith trumped reason.

Instead of investing his energy in methodological discussions, Madjid focused on the concept of Islamic universalism. This subject had long aroused his curiosity. As a student at IAIN Jakarta in 1968, he completed a thesis on "The Qur'an: Arab in Its Wording, Universal in Its Meaning."⁵⁷ He reprised this interest with full force in the early 1990s. Specifically, Madjid rejected the common definition of Islamic universalism as a teleological process of Islamization through which all Muslim societies were to adopt Arab linguistic and cultural practices and hence become replicas of the Prophet's Medina. For Madjid, this conception of universality was actually particularistic because it required Muslims to conform to a narrow and homogenous definition of Islam. In contrast, he argued that Islam's universality required flexibility. In 1994, he wrote: "The Qur'an indicates that the Islamic message, because of its universality, is adaptable to any cultural environment, as it has been adapted to the imperatives of the Arabian Peninsula cultures. Therefore, it must also be adaptable to the environment of any culture of its adherents, anywhere and at any time."⁵⁸ By extension, he suggested that the universal applicability of Islamic teachings enabled Muslims to engage freely with key features of modernity, including scientific research, technological advancements, and even political ideals such as democracy and human rights. For example, he wrote an essay titled "The Possibility of Using Modern Resources for Re-interpreting the Islamic Message," in which he asserted that Islam's very universality suggested that modern thinkers, endowed with their own cultural and temporal frameworks, should be able to understand the Qur'an and may even possess a clearer perspective on some verses than their medieval predecessors did.⁵⁹ Ultimately, Madjid maintained that Islamic universalism guaranteed that humans could approach the Qur'an and other Islamic teachings *with* their cultural and temporal baggage intact and then infuse Islamic values into their own unique social fabrics. He endorsed subjectivity, not objectivity, as the path to Islamic truth.

While Madjid championed pluralism within Muslim societies, he also used his conception of universality to challenge—as Wilfred Cantwell Smith had in the 1960s—the reification of Islam into a bounded religious tradition.[60] In *Islam: Doctrine and Civilization*, Madjid began to reinterpret the Qur'anic meaning of *al-islam*. Translating the term as "self-surrender to God," Madjid noted that the Qur'an used *al-islam* and its personal noun, *muslim*, to denote all revealed religions, beginning with the prophecies of Noah and Abraham through those of Moses and Jesus. He wrote that "al-islam is the universal foundation for human life, valid for all people in every place and time."[61] Of course, the teachings of the Prophet Muhammad held a special status because they represented the most recent and final revelation, but Madjid maintained that the Qur'an was still only one part of a long line of revealed teachings about al-islam.[62] Madjid argued that because this message of self-surrender to God was bound by neither space nor time, other religions must contain parts of that universal truth as well. He made this argument not only for Abrahamic religions but for any religions with scriptures.[63] In this manner, Madjid sought to tear down the walls between Islam and other religious traditions and to establish knowledge and truth as the shared possessions of humanity.

Building on this radical conception of Islamic universalism, Madjid delivered a controversial speech in 1992 in which he urged Indonesian Muslims to reject their reified religious identities and instead embrace an inclusive and individualist mode of spirituality. He first encouraged Muslims to pursue the pieces of truth contained in other religions and cultures, stating, "It is decidedly good for Muslims to study and take wisdom from other revelations."[64] Madjid then took the argument a step further. He suggested that the exclusivist claims of sectarian and communal identities actually impeded this pursuit of universal truth. To make his case, he pointed to Abraham as a "pure truth seeker" who was never tied to any organized religion. The Qur'an held up Abraham's individual piety as a model for Muhammad and, by extension, for all humankind.[65] Madjid portrayed man's search for truth as profoundly personal rather than communal. He concluded that in order to be genuine followers of the Qur'an and Muhammad, Muslims must loosen their communal bonds and recognize that Islamic universalism enjoined them to search beyond the restrictive limits of the "Islamic tradition." He even condemned religious fundamentalism as a dangerous social addiction. Madjid's speech was a radical religious and political statement. Throughout the 1990s, he continued to insist upon the existence of multiple "doors towards God" and the imperative that Muslims avail themselves of these diverse entry points.[66]

Admittedly, Madjid did not explicitly connect his call for cross-religious exploration to his frequent engagement with Western academic scholarship, but I argue that the two rest on the same foundation of Islamic universalism. If other religious traditions contained elements of Islam's universal truth, then presumably so did other nonreligious ways of knowing. Consequently, academic epistemologies need not be objective or free from cultural influences because Madjid believed that subjectivity led to truth. Islam's very universality also erased any concerns that academic knowledge was alien to Muslim teachings. Put another way, Madjid's move to expand the boundaries of al-islam legitimized all forms of knowledge. This reconceptualization enabled him to engage in prolific borrowing from Western academics without fearing contamination or subjugation by other systems of knowledge. It was a daring solution to the fusionist dilemma.

Yet Madjid's preference for big theological ideas over methodological treatises meant that his radical universalism left several significant questions unanswered. He had devoted substantial attention to the existence of truth across religious traditions but neglected to address the issue of falsehoods. How were Muslims to distinguish falsehoods from truths when studying and "taking wisdom" from other traditions? If the Qur'an was to serve as that guide, then how exactly should Muslims derive universal principles from this one specific, albeit final, piece of revelation? For the most part, Madjid relied on arguments about the innate human orientation toward truth (*fitrah*) to justify his exhortations to search without inhibition.[67] It was, he implied, a matter of trust and individual spirituality. Still, not all individuals possessed the piety and moral compass of Abraham. Madjid did not provide a clear measure to evaluate the results of exploration, nor did he provide guidelines on what could be included within al-islam's expansive umbrella and what fell beyond it. Without answering these questions, Madjid left himself vulnerable to misunderstandings and rampant criticisms from other Muslims.[68]

Amin Abdullah and a Postmodern Islam

Whereas Rais and Madjid encountered critiques of objectivity in the middle of their careers, the next generation of Indonesian Muslim intellectuals was raised on a steady diet of postmodernism and postcolonial theory. In the early 1990s, Dawam Rahardjo devoted an entire issue of his journal *Ulumul Qur'an* (Qur'anic Studies) to examining the intersection of postmodernism and Islamic thought.[69] Later in the decade, the Mazhab Ciputat published a volume titled *Dekonstruksi Islam* (1999) with a decidedly postmodernist bent. Michael Feener noted that the bookstalls surrounding IAIN Jakarta began to stock translations of Michel Foucault and Antonio Gramsci's writings alongside copies of the Qur'an, hadith collections, and classical Arabic texts.[70] While based in Yogyakarta rather than Jakarta, Amin Abdullah emerged as one of the most dynamic fusionist thinkers of this postmodernist generation.[71] He embraced postmodernist and postcolonial theories as crucial tools not only for criticizing Western scholarship but also for reimagining long-established Muslim interpretations of Islam.

Like Rais before him, Abdullah was deeply concerned with the problem of academic imperialism. He stressed that European colonization of the Islamic world rested not only on the physical occupation that defined the lives of previous generations but on the intellectual subjugation that persisted into the present. He referred to Muslim economic and technological dependence on the West as merely "the newest form of colonialism."[72] Abdullah extended this critique into the social and religious realms. Citing Edward Said, he denied the possibility of a "value-free knowledge" and argued that Western scholars of Islam continued to possess "motives to protect the Western cultural status quo that dominates the world."[73] He predicted that this intellectual imperialism would likely continue until Muslims managed to offer a persuasive alternative. Overall, Abdullah viewed Muslim intellectual capitulation to the West as a much greater threat than Rahman, Nasution, and Ali had ever acknowledged.

While Abdullah expressed concerns about epistemological imperialism, he also insisted that every generation approaches their religious tradition in different ways than their predecessors did. He therefore defended Muslim "acculturation" to Suharto's developmentalist agenda as necessary and natural. To exemplify such generational changes in religious thinking, Abdullah highlighted the common Indonesian use of *theology* over the more traditional concepts of *kalam* or *falsafa Islam*. In chapter 3, we saw Mohamad Rasjidi attack Nasution's textbook on this exact issue, arguing that *theology* was a Christian term that was ill-suited for the Islamic tradition. Abdullah took a different position. He suggested that Indonesian Muslims were simply uninterested in the term's Western origins; they wanted to use *theology* as part of their larger efforts to reinterpret and revitalize stagnant aspects of the Islamic tradition. Abdullah saw such acts of reinterpretation as common, largely unavoidable, and yet significant because they were "automatically changing the ways religious people think."[74] He was attuned to the power of discursive change but sought to erase its stigma by pointing to historical comparisons for legitimation. For example, he argued that what Muslims considered as "pure" kalam was itself produced in interaction with Greek philosophy. If classical kalam relied on Greek knowledge, then it was only natural that modern kalam would adopt certain ideas and terms from contemporary Western thought.[75] Abdullah was still vigilant about which Western frameworks might be borrowed, but he urged Indonesian Muslims to see cross-discursive encounters as a *part* of the Islamic tradition rather than an inherent threat to it.

Abdullah wrote several essays in the mid-1990s that explored these ideas about discursive change through the lens of historian of science Thomas Kuhn.[76] To begin, he classified Islamic studies as a field of human-produced knowledge rather than a divine doctrine, making it akin to the natural sciences.[77] Drawing this parallel with the natural sciences enabled Abdullah to apply the Kuhnian categories of "normal" and "revolutionary science" to Islamic disciplines, especially kalam. He argued that kalam had been stuck in the "normal science" phase since the early medieval period. In other words, Muslim theologians had, for many centuries, accepted the core ideas of the Muʿtazilite, Ashʿari, and Maturidi schools and restricted their own intellectual endeavors to investigating small-scale questions and writing commentaries on classical texts. Despite the persistence of "normal kalam," Abdullah acknowledged that a handful of Muslim theologians such as al-Ghazali, Muhammad Abduh, and Muhammad Iqbal had identified inconsistencies and unanswered questions in the prevailing schools of theology. Following Kuhn, Abdullah called these lingering issues "anomalies" and optimistically suggested that their accumulation in the late twentieth century would ignite a revolutionary phase for kalam.[78] He believed in the benefits of such a theological revolution, but he also reassured his Muslim audience that the new kalam would not altogether erase earlier theological teachings, just as Einsteinian physics did not render Newton irrelevant. Instead, revolutionary kalam would simply "foreground new interpretations that are in accordance with contemporary developments in knowledge."[79] Abdullah pointed to integrating empirical sciences and eliminating "exclusivist" religious identities as two examples. Ultimately, Abdullah used Kuhn to justify calling for an Islamic theological revolution.

In addition to appropriating Kuhn's work, Abdullah found inspiration in the postmodernist assault on stable and monolithic categories. In one essay, he argued that both Muslim and Western institutions had focused for too long on the text-based "high tradition" to the near exclusion of local practices or so-called "low traditions," which actually represented the religious experiences of the vast majority of Muslims. He derided this approach as both elitist and myopic. To correct the imbalance, he proposed that the IAIN system invest in an alternative area-studies model that would funnel resources into researching the local beliefs and practices prevalent in various corners of the Islamic world.[80] Abdullah envisioned postmodernist Muslims challenging other simplistic claims to universality as well. For example, he encouraged non-Western scholars to use postmodernist and postcolonial analysis to question dominant Western constructs such as human rights so that they could eventually combat entrenched systems of power.[81] He also hoped that the postmodernist distaste for universals would defuse aggressive missionary activity, whether it was done in the name of science, Christianity, or Islam. In contrast to Madjid, Abdullah saw the postmodernist collapse of universalism as a cause for celebration and a catalyst for cross-cultural cooperation.[82]

Abdullah derived valuable insights from postmodernist ideas, but embracing postmodernism produced its own troubling contradictions. While Western theorists such as Foucault and Kuhn helped dismantle the myth of objectivity, Indonesian scholars often deployed postmodernist frameworks as authoritative models in their own right. For example, Abdullah adopted Kuhn's ideas about normal versus revolutionary science and the accumulation of anomalies wholesale without interrogating whether and why Kuhn's history of Western science could be transposed onto the Islamic tradition. Azyumardi Azra hinted at this tension when he wrote: "Postmodernist tendencies within the Muslim community are actually ahistorical and asociological in character. This is similar to the ahistorical and asociological project of modernism in the Muslim community."[83] In other words, Azra highlighted that postmodernism was a distinctly Western response to the failures of Western-style modernity. Consequently, Muslim thinkers had to prove postmodernism's applicability for Islamic thought if they were to avoid simply reedifying Western academic authority in a postmodernist rather than a modernist guise.

These three Indonesian Muslim scholars adopted diverse approaches to the postmodernist and postcolonial impasse. Persuaded by postcolonial critiques of Western academia, Rais cautioned Muslim intellectuals to engage with academic scholarship only on the basis of a discerning pragmatism. Madjid endeavored to break down walls between intellectual traditions entirely in the name of Islamic universalism. Abdullah theorized about a postmodern Islam. He turned Kuhn's critical gaze on authoritative Islamic doctrines to build an alternative Islamic theology. Despite these differences, they all shared one fundamental assumption—that Western academic imperialism was primarily an intellectual problem that should and could be surmounted through emancipatory thinking.

RESISTING ACADEMIC IMPERIALISM

The new generation of Western-educated Muslim intellectuals was acutely aware of the shortcomings of Western academia. They read Edward Said and other postcolonial theorists, and they devoted substantial energy to determining how to engage with academic scholarship on Islam without unwittingly adopting Western cultural and religious presuppositions. They generally believed that their creativity and agency as intellectuals would enable them to navigate the knowledge-power nexus. In contrast, other Indonesian Muslims foreclosed on the very possibility of meaningful cooperation with Western academia. These opponents built on established lines of criticism to attack academic claims to objectivity and to accuse Western and Western-educated scholars of harboring malicious political agendas. Yet slamming the door on Western academics was no longer so straightforward by the 1990s. Decades of fusionist curricular reforms and exchange programs had made Western academic ideas staples in the country's Islamic sphere. Resistance, by necessity, took on increasingly hostile forms. In this final section, I present a magazine-mediated conflict in late twentieth-century Indonesia as a parable about the often unexpected consequences of Western academic ideas and networks.

A curious episode involving Ohio State University professor William Liddle (b. 1938) exemplifies both Indonesian Muslim entanglement with Western academia *and* the vigorous opposition to that very entanglement. In the early 1990s, Liddle wrote an essay on DDII's major magazine, *Media Dakwah*, which analyzed the competition between DDII "scripturalists" (i.e., Islamists) and Muslim modernists. Liddle's language and framing made it readily apparent where his sympathies lay. He characterized the ascent of modernists such as Nurcholish Madjid as a reason for "optimism" and declared that "the new thinkers' ideas unquestionably hold out considerable promise for the revitalization of the *umma*."[84] In contrast to this praise for Madjid and his colleagues, Liddle described the so-called DDII scripturalists as an "openly hostile," "defensive," and "closed, sharply bounded group" with a "long list of enemies."[85] He questioned the scripturalists' intellectual acumen, arguing that they concerned themselves only with the implementation of Islamic law instead of devoting time to the real intellectual work of deriving Islamic values and knowledge from source texts.[86] He called them "naïve" and argued that their conspiracy theories "betray[ed] a shallow and unsophisticated understanding of the way in which the world in fact works."[87] Overall, Liddle presented *Media Dakwah* as an extremist publication whose content represented little more than "shallow" Islamist propaganda.

Initially, Liddle's essay appears like a rather typical academic assessment of Islamist writings, but it soon developed a life of its own.[88] As a long-time professor of Southeast Asian politics at Ohio State, Liddle was well-connected. He consulted for various US governmental agencies such as USAID and lectured regularly at the State Department's Foreign Service Institute.[89] He also had close relationships with several Indonesian intellectuals, including his former graduate students and Mazhab Ciputat members, Bahtiar Effendy and Saiful Mujani. Thanks to these latter connections, his paper was soon translated into Indonesian and published in *Ulumul Qur'an*. Indonesian Muslims could then read Liddle's assessment of Madjid and DDII in their own Islamic magazine.

As Western academics such as Liddle became increasingly visible in the Indonesian Islamic sphere, Muslim opponents—including the so-called DDII scripturalists—did not fail to take notice. In fact, *Media Dakwah* editors dedicated their August 1993 issue to "answering Liddle." Contributors criticized Liddle's work on multiple fronts. They questioned his knowledge of Islam, castigated what they saw as his underhanded political agenda, and raised doubts about his personal religious motivations. In the process, *Media Dakwah* deployed blatantly anti-Semitic imagery and language. The August 1993 issue featured several photos of Liddle superimposed on the Star of David. The cover story opened with a quote—"I do not understand how William Liddle, a rotten [*tengik*] Jew, was given so many pages in *Ulumul Qur'an*"—from

Amien Rais, a sometime ally of DDII, that left no doubt about the magazine's anti-Jewish sentiments.[90] The Liddle issue was not the magazine's only case of flagrant anti-Semitism. *Media Dakwah*'s pages were often littered with anti-Semitic language and stories about international Jewish conspiracies, making the magazine a catalyst for the spike in Indonesian anti-Semitism in the late twentieth century.[91]

Yet there is more to the story. Without diminishing the magazine's offensive anti-Semitic content, I argue that *Media Dakwah*'s response to Liddle should not be reduced solely to a case of religious intolerance, for two reasons. First, as political theorist Wendy Brown argues, the language of tolerance and intolerance obscures underlying power dynamics. She writes: "At the collective and individual levels, the strong and secure can afford to be tolerant; the marginal and insecure cannot. A polity or culture certain of itself and its hegemony, one that does not feel vulnerable, can relax its borders and absorb otherness without fear."[92] DDII certainly did not possess the necessary power at either the national or global level—let alone hegemony in either sphere—to feel "certain of itself." On the contrary, the magazine's response to Liddle foregrounded its contributors' fears of foreign interference and domination. Second, an exclusive focus on the anti-Semitic statements misses the fact that *Media Dakwah*'s attacks were directed at Western academia as a whole. Magazine contributors did not see Liddle as an isolated case but rather as only one particularly flagrant example of unwelcome Western academic penetration into the Indonesian Islamic sphere.

The August 1993 issue of *Media Dakwah* provides a rare opportunity to reverse the looking glass and see academic scholars of Islam through hostile Islamist eyes. It can be an uncomfortable and even unsettling experience. *Media Dakwah* contributors sought to rob Liddle and others of their scholarly authority. They ripped off the veils of neutrality and expertise in order to expose Western academics and their Western-educated Muslim colleagues as situated actors with political and religious agendas. They reduced scholars to sets of institutional connections, financial interests, and personal identities. These were grossly oversimplified depictions of academic scholarship that depended on essentialist explanations and conspiratorial theories. However, simplification may very well have been part of *Media Dakwah*'s strategy. The magazine contributors dismissed the nuances of academic analysis and argumentation as secondary to the material interests underpinning the production of knowledge. As a result, they cast Western academia as a dangerous manifestation of American soft power and issued forceful demands for intellectual autonomy.

Media Dakwah writers attacked Western academic authority on grounds that scholars failed to measure up to their own standards of objectivity. Daud Rasyid (b. 1962) emerged as a particularly outspoken proponent of this position. Rasyid was a graduate of IAIN North Sumatra and alumnus of both Cairo University and al-Azhar, who returned from Egypt in the early 1990s and soon thereafter became a major opponent of fusionist epistemologies and networks. In a series of essays, he drew on the writings of Mohamad Rasjidi and Ismail al-Faruqi to articulate his own critique of Islamic studies and rail against the various exchange programs with North American and European universities. He condemned Western academics for their obsessions with Islamic philosophy and their preference for Muslims scholars who had been rejected by the Muslim mainstream, such as Fazlur Rahman.[93] Yet Rasyid saved his most damning criticisms for the ways that personal religious affiliations and values seeped into academic writing about Islam. He explained:

> Exactly what I emphasize is the confusion of Western methodologies in studying Islam. Orientalist methodologies depart from the certainty that the Qur'an is not God's revelation but the work of Muhammad, Muhammad is not the final prophet sent by God, and Islam is not a religion that comes from God.
>
> As a consequence, for them, the truth of the Qur'an still needs to be examined and, if necessary, critiqued. Muhammad is only a normal human being rather than being free from all faults/sins. And because of this, the Prophet's character and life need to be studied in the critical way to which they are predisposed. The "lens" that they use to evaluate the Prophet's character is a Western lens that is "value-neutral." For example, they imagine that Muhammad was similar to Western men who "need" sex, cannot differentiate between right and wrong [*halal haram*], and are materialistic.
>
> As a result, in their perspective, Islam is not God's religion and therefore must be turned into an object of research. Its position is equated with other objects. What is not fair is that their method is still closely tied, even dictated by, their own religious doctrine.[94]

In this manner, Rasyid emphasized the significance of scholars' underlying metaphysical assumptions about the existence of God, the divinity of the

Qur'an, and the prophetic identity of Muhammad. He maintained that there was no neutral ground on these essential questions. Either an individual believed or did not. These core metaphysical commitments then shaped historical, literary, and social-scientific methods in fundamental ways. For example, Western academics often posed questions about the historical origins of the Qur'an or the nature of Muhammad's motivations that practicing Muslims would never need to ask. Ultimately, Rasyid refused the ability of non-Muslim academics to transcend their own religious identities, arguing instead that their "lenses" were always tainted by their Christian, Jewish, or secular presuppositions.

Building on Rasyid's argument that individual metaphysical beliefs molded research frameworks, *Media Dakwah* contributors rejected academic claims to neutrality and reconceptualized scholars instead as situated actors with institutional connections and political interests. Specifically, DDII writers usually identified Western academics according to their religious identities because they maintained that this information revealed important metaphysical biases. They stretched the same logic to scholars' national identities, seeking to equate ethnicity and citizenship with clear-cut political commitments. They assumed that all Jewish scholars threw their support behind the Israeli state and that all American scholars endorsed US foreign-policy aims, especially the goal of secularization. Clearly, these assumptions were essentialist, simplistic, and frequently anti-Semitic in nature. However, they underscore the extent to which *Media Dakwah* writers denied the possibility of scholarly agency in favor of highlighting the material realities and personal identities underpinning the production of academic knowledge.

Media Dakwah writers not only assumed that academics represented Western governmental interests but also worked to expose what they saw as politically motivated analyses of their magazine. In the August 1993 issue, Lukman Hakiem questioned the political undertones of Liddle's essay in particular. Why, he asked, did Western scholars such as Liddle so often study points of contestation within the Muslim community? Why didn't they examine cooperation and agreement instead? Hakiem suggested that Western academics prioritize studying discord because they seek to sow divisions and incite conflicts among Indonesian Muslims. Such allegations appear at first glance to be little more than anti-Western paranoia, but Hakiem was able to muster some concrete evidence. He pointed to Liddle's insinuation that despite public announcements to the contrary, *Media Dakwah* did not support the New Order's Pancasila-based state.⁹⁵ Hakiem vigorously denied the accusation and then moved to flip the tables on Liddle, reading between the lines of the political scientist's essay. He speculated that Liddle spread these malicious rumors because he disapproved of Suharto's recent rapprochement with DDII and hoped that labeling its major magazine as anti-Pancasila would spur the state to reverse course and resume suppression of Islamists. Hakiem concluded, "Inciting like this is indeed a unique approach of Western scholars who do not like to see the materialization of a harmonious relationship between the Muslim community and the state."⁹⁶ While he lacked evidence about Liddle's motives, Hakiem did have reason to fear the potential consequences of Liddle's words. Suharto had mandated that all organizations declare Pancasila as their "sole foundation" in the 1980s. As a result, accusing DDII of only feigning its support for Pancasila could lead to popular protests or even legal action against the organization. Moreover, Hakiem was right that many Western scholars of Indonesia expressed concern about Suharto's purported "conservative turn" in the 1990s. He sought to warn his readers about these political agendas so that they would fight the corrosive power of academic outsiders to influence Indonesian Islam.

Media Dakwah also blamed Western-educated Muslim intellectuals for acting as conduits, whether consciously or unconsciously, for American soft power. DDII writers believed that Muslims who studied Islam in the West disseminated academic frameworks such as secularization and contextual hermeneutics and hence furthered American political interests in Indonesia. In the 1990s, Nurcholish Madjid was a lightning rod for such criticisms. Several *Media Dakwah* contributors argued that Madjid's experiences at the University of Chicago deepened his secularist commitments. Hakiem even accused Leonard Binder of coaxing Madjid and other Indonesian scholars into writing dissertations that refuted the link between Islam and politics.⁹⁷ Despite being a student of Binder and a Chicago alumnus himself, Amien Rais waded into this conversation about the intersection of Western academia and American foreign policy. In one interview, Rais explained that the Fulbright program was part of a "mission on behalf of American governmental interests" to build a network of Indonesian intellectuals sympathetic to the United States.⁹⁸ *Media Dakwah* expanded this critique to include Rockefeller and Ford scholarships as well.⁹⁹ They wanted to expose these programs as pillars of American soft power. Rais certainly agreed that US political interests drove these fellowship programs, but his writings and career also signal that he remained hopeful that Indonesian Muslims could navigate the treacherous waters. DDII writers disagreed. They did not believe that Western-educated Muslim intellectuals could or should navigate the dangerous political currents below the surface of these exchange programs, so they advised Muslim students to steer clear of them altogether.

Feeling targeted by this form of soft power, *Media Dakwah* responded with the non-military means at its disposal: harsh, exclusionary language and conspiratorial narratives. Magazine contributors refused to see Orientalism and studying Islam in the West as merely interesting points for intellectual debate. Rather, they viewed Western academics as threats because they supposedly helped Western governments and development organizations to mold Indonesian Islam from within. DDII thus fought a war of words to expel Western influence from the country's Islamic sphere. They derided Western-educated intellectuals such as Madjid and worked to persuade Indonesian Muslims to disengage from Western academic networks. When Munawir Sjadzali retired from the Ministry of Religious Affairs in 1993, Daud Rasyid and his DDII allies launched a public campaign to dismantle Sjadzali's extensive exchange programs with Western universities.[100] They urged aspiring scholars to avoid Western academia and instead study Islam in Indonesia or the Middle East, where they would learn the true tenets of their religion from fellow Muslims. While fusionist epistemologies and networks continued to thrive in the 1990s, *Media Dakwah* was clear that they saw Western academics as unwelcome intruders in the Indonesian Islamic sphere and Western-educated Muslims as collaborators with American soft power.

By dedicating their August 1993 issue to "answering Liddle," the *Media Dakwah* staff clearly sought to talk back to Western academic scholars of Islam. In the process, they created a dilemma: should Western academics listen to these forceful criticisms? On the one hand, *Media Dakwah* provided several compelling reasons to exclude DDII writers from any meaningful conversations about the Western academic study of Islam. The magazine's writers articulated their responses to Liddle in highly discriminatory language, and they tended to eschew nuanced, evidence-based analysis in favor of one-dimensional, conspiratorial musings. In many ways, *Media Dakwah* articles functioned like a pre-internet version of trolling. Instead of taking them seriously, perhaps scholars should simply recognize them as one of the hazards of the academic profession. On the other hand, refusing to listen to the *Media Dakwah* response seems to perpetuate the very power imbalance against which DDII members were railing. After all, their "answers to Liddle" revolved around the central questions of who should have the right to speak and be heard in certain discursive spaces. DDII supporters were frustrated that Western academics such as Liddle had a voice in even an avowedly Islamic magazine such as *Ulumul Qur'an* and therefore fought to curtail this Western academic presence. Whereas they contested the existence of academic voices in their discursive sphere, *Media Dakwah* writers had very little voice at all in Western academic spaces in the 1990s. They certainly could not publish their criticisms of Western scholarship on Islam in an academic journal. Nor did the August 1993 issue elicit any direct responses from academics to their complaints. The relationship was clearly unequal. *Media Dakwah* contributors felt compelled to write in order to demand their intellectual autonomy vis-à-vis Western academia; Western academics, in turn, already enjoyed such autonomy and thus could choose whether or not to engage with Islamist critiques about academic imperialism.

After spending over thirty years at the helm of Indonesian politics, Suharto and his New Order government faced cascading crises at the close of the twentieth century. In August 1997, the Asian financial contagion spread south from Thailand in the form of a severe attack on the Indonesian rupiah. The value of the currency plummeted, leading to extreme inflation and a nationwide economic collapse. Three of out four Indonesian businesses fell into financial distress, and the GDP retracted by a devastating ten to fifteen percentage points.[101] The economic crisis soon boiled over into the political sphere. Hundreds of thousands of angry Indonesians took to the streets to protest Suharto's corrupt and authoritarian state. The mass protests shut down university campuses and urban thoroughfares alike. There were also sporadic outbreaks of violence against protestors, Chinese minorities, and other politically vulnerable groups. Observers began to worry about the prospect of civil war.

During these critical months, the Chicago alumni were front and center, but they were no longer on Suharto's side. Amien Rais emerged as one of the most visible opposition leaders. Since his forced resignation from ICMI in March 1997, Rais had taken increasingly bold steps against Suharto. In late September 1997, he declared his intention to run for president in the Surabaya-based newspaper *Jawa Pos*. The announcement rallied more university students to his cause.¹⁰² By May 1998, Rais was in the streets, leading million-person marches to demand Suharto's resignation. Whereas Rais helped mobilize the popular resistance to Suharto's New Order, Nurcholish Madjid preferred to exercise his influence as a leading Muslim intellectual in subtler ways. He reportedly met with high-ranking military leaders, including future president Susilo Bambang Yudhoyono (b. 1949), in March 1998 to discuss how to ensure a nonviolent transfer of power.¹⁰³ Madjid also issued public statements in support of a quick but peaceful transition. Then, as the protests reached a fever pitch, he was summoned to Suharto's private chambers on May 18 to counsel the embattled president on his options. Madjid told Suharto that he had run out of time to institute reforms and needed to resign. The next day, Madjid was once again invited to Suharto's residence, along with eight other Muslim leaders, to discuss the country's uncertain future. They refused to accept any of the president's desperate compromise proposals.¹⁰⁴ Two days later, Suharto resigned, handing the reins of the government to Vice President B. J. Habibie.

The three Chicago alumni entered the post-Suharto era in positions of substantial religious and political authority. Thanks to his prominent role in the anti-Suharto protests, Rais secured the most powerful legislative position in the country, the chair of the People's Consultative Assembly, in 1999. He earned a reputation as "king maker" for catapulting NU leader Abdurrahman Wahid to the presidency. Because Rais's national political ambitions made him an awkward fit for leading the avowedly nonpolitical Muhammadiyah, he agreed to step down as the chairman in 1998. This decision propelled a second Chicago alumnus into the national spotlight when Ahmad Syafii Maarif succeeded him as chairman of the mass modernist organization. In 1999, Madjid received Indonesia's highest civilian honor, Bintang Mahaputra Utama, for his role in mediating the transition. The third Chicago alumnus briefly threw his hat in the ring for the 2004 presidential election before falling ill with liver disease. When Madjid passed away in 2005, a host of Indonesian dignitaries lined up outside the Paramadina offices to pay their respects before his state burial.¹⁰⁵ Madjid was gone, but the Mazhab Ciputat continued to represent his legacy in the highest echelons of Indonesian religious and political leadership. In the end, the post-Suharto era brought political uncertainty and substantial new challenges to Indonesia in the shape of Reformasi and the onset of the global war on terror. However, as the careers of the Chicago alumni and other Western-educated Muslim intellectuals demonstrate, these developments did not dismantle the new model of Islamic religious authority that the past several decades had produced. On the contrary, fusionist thinking and the transnational networks that fostered it continued to thrive—albeit with new sources of opposition and controversy—well into the twenty-first century.[106]

CONCLUSION

The Future of Islamic Studies

THE SECOND HALF of the twentieth century saw Western academics become increasingly intertwined with modern Islamic thought in Indonesia and Indonesian Muslims, in turn, become regular participants in the academic study of Islam. The border between the two intellectual traditions, which had long been taken for granted, was nearing collapse. This trend raises a series of pressing questions about the very purpose of Islamic studies as a field: What type of relationships do Western academics seek to build with our "objects" of study? What place does and should supporting Islamic reformist projects have in the field? How can Western academic scholars of Islam navigate our current geopolitical landscape in an ethical and transparent manner?[1] This conclusion draws on both religious studies and postcolonial scholarship, first to formulate three distinct options for the future of Islamic studies and then to evaluate the relative strengths and weaknesses of each proposal in the hope that, taken together, they might help us envision a more viable path forward.

OPTION 1: DISCURSIVE BOUNDARY MAINTENANCE

The first scholarly camp diagnoses academic entanglement with Islamic thought as a sign of disciplinary distress and therefore campaigns to restore the perceived border between the two discursive traditions. Aaron W. Hughes has been the most vocal and persistent proponent of this position. Building on the work of Jonathan Z. Smith, Bruce Lincoln, and Russell T. McCutcheon, Hughes argues that Islamic studies has become far too permissive of normative, insider perspectives at the expense of more critical, historical scholarship. He offers this damning assessment of the field:

> The academic study of Islam as carried out in departments of religious studies has become so apologetic that it has largely ceased to function as an academic discipline, preferring instead to propagate a theological and apologetic representation of the religion. This discourse, which I call "Islamic Religious Studies," is largely theological in orientation, manipulative in its use of sources, and distortive in its conclusions.[2]

Hughes is not one to mince words. While he acknowledges the political and pedagogical challenges facing Islamic studies in the post-9/11 era, he criticizes Muslim and non-Muslim scholars alike for retreating into essentialism when they depict Islam as an innately peaceful, liberal, and gender-egalitarian religion. He takes particular aim at Tariq Ramadan, Omid Safi, and Carl Ernst for "writing hagiographies" rather than "academic books" about Muhammad.[3] He also charges John Esposito with producing "apologetical treatises" about Muslim women.[4] Because these scholars seek to define what Islam *really* is, Hughes argues that their work is deeply theological in nature. He insists that proper academic scholarship, in contrast, should avoid such essentialist claims and focus instead on how various Islams have been imagined, constructed, and propagated over the past fourteen hundred years. He writes, "Islams and the Muslim sources that produce them are our data, not our faith commitments" and thereby urges his fellow academics to "identify all those approaches that masquerade as critical scholarship for what they are."[5] By taking these steps, Hughes hopes to repair the collapsing boundary between Western academia and modern Islamic thought.

Hughes makes two important points in his many books. First, he highlights how Western academia has become more hospitable to what I call fusionism and what he calls "liberal Muslim theologizing."[6] As we have seen, fusionist thinkers at the McGill Institute faced substantial resistance from established Orientalists such as Joseph Schact in the 1950s and 1960s, but less than two decades later, Fazlur Rahman and Leonard Binder earned various professional accolades for their equally fusionist "Islam and Social Change" project. This shift is significant, but Hughes focuses so much energy on criticizing "Islamic religious studies" as a peculiarly problematic field that he misses the normative underpinnings of other academic disciplines, including history and the social sciences. These disciplines have been and remain thoroughly entangled with Islamic reformist projects; their practitioners simply articulate those aims through a more secularist language.[7] Second, Hughes proposes critical historical analysis as a corrective to essentialist scholarship. In one book he trades the search for the "real Muhammad" for studying how various Muslims (and non-Muslims) have used prophetic biographies to construct new group identities.[8] Hughes demonstrates how this mode of historical research foregrounds the diversity, dynamism, and agency possible within the Islamic discursive tradition. These are undoubtedly important scholarly aims, but, as we have seen Mohamad Rasjidi argue, they exhibit a certain secularizing ethos that carries its own normative baggage.

While he endorses an antiessentialist historical approach to Islam, Hughes oddly overlooks the diversity, dynamism, and agency possible within Western academia itself. After all, his two key terms, "academic" and "critical," also have contested histories and competing, situated definitions. For example, mid-twentieth-century Orientalists used essentialist constructs such as "the Arab mind" and "the Muslim personality" to frame their studies of Islam. While we now see these attempts at cultural psychoanalysis as deeply flawed and highly ethnocentric, H. A. R. Gibb and other prominent Orientalists argued that this form of analysis was, unlike its missionary predecessors, objective and hence properly academic. Modernization theory was likewise touted as objective, methodologically rigorous, and cutting-edge academic knowledge. Hughes himself points out the personal and political contexts driving Edward Said's critique of Orientalism.[9] Proponents of all three approaches claimed to be "academic" and "critical." Unless Hughes presumes that he possesses an objective, value-free yardstick to evaluate scholarship that previous generations lacked, then he should acknowledge that there is no one definition of these terms because what counts as "academic" and "critical" is decidedly fluid across time and space. After all, his own theses on method implore: "We should situate these data within their historical social, ideological, and material contexts even though the sources themselves tend to represent themselves as timeless and as ahistorical."[10] We must therefore ask: How have colonial and postcolonial politics shaped what it means to be "academic" and "critical" over the past several decades? Who has constructed the prevailing definitions of these terms; who has opposed those definitions; and why? Instead of asking these questions, Hughes aims to fix definitions for "academic" and "critical" as though these particular terms should—unlike "Islamic" or "Muslim"—have innate and stable meanings.

These oversights hint at a more fundamental problem with Hughes's work: he does not interrogate the history and politics of his own boundary-making project. It is a surprising slip coming from a scholar who cites Talal Asad as an ally. Asad has exposed "religion" as a historically constructed and peculiarly European category. Hughes even uses this Asadian insight to support his argument against a sui generis approach to Islam, but he then neglects Asad's extensive work on secular ontologies.[11] In *Formations of the Secular* (2003), Asad explains that "in my view, the secular is neither singular in origin nor stable in its historical identity, although it works through a series of particular oppositions" such as belief versus knowledge and fiction versus history.[12] In other words, Asad seeks to interrogate the very historical processes through which religious and secular boundaries have been drawn and redrawn, thereby exposing those boundaries as contingent and profoundly Eurocentric in nature.[13] Hughes, ironically, contributes to this history of boundary-making. As George Archer notes, Hughes "seems unaware" that "to identify the edges of theology is itself a theological argument. To argue against a canon is to establish another canon."[14] Hughes looks at Islam through his critical-historical lenses but then removes the glasses when advancing his own disciplinary ethics.

Whereas Hughes does not situate his boundary-making project, his colleague Russell T. McCutcheon tackles this issue head-on. In an insightful article, McCutcheon concedes that postmodernism and postcolonial theory have crippled objectivist arguments for distinguishing academic religious studies from theology. He even acknowledges that "today, the challenge is for those who maintain that there is a utility in demarcating the academic study of religion from religious practices and institutions."[15] McCutcheon accepts this challenge and works to articulate an alternative defense for what he calls "discursive boundary maintenance."[16] He writes:

> Discourses can be distinguished by their differing rules of formation, as well as their varying institutional settings. Although I agree that discursive relativism entails the loss of normative status for any one discourse— . . . all positions are implicated in "paradigmatic commitments to certain values, concepts, and methods"—this hardly does away with the ability to distinguish between discourses. Simply put, although we may all have prior commitments, not all our commitments are necessarily the same. [17]

To elaborate, McCutcheon draws an analogy to the idea that different sports have different sets of rules. No single sport can be deemed superior to another, but this does not mean that "anything goes" in any given game. A tennis match requires that all players agree to the established rules of tennis. The match will simply not take place if one person insists on playing basketball. By emphasizing that rules have their institutional settings, McCutcheon makes a persuasive point. The division of the Western academic and Islamic discursive traditions into different spheres does not *need* to imply that one is superior to the other; it may simply acknowledge their different histories, canons, and rules for discursive engagement. They can be separate but equal.

McCutcheon's analogy works in theory, but it breaks down in practice, as do most "separate but equal" arguments. To pursue the athletic analogy for a moment, sports and their various players do not all have the same resources at their disposal.[18] If the tennis team at Analogy Academy has new courts, a jumbotron, pristine locker rooms, and ten athletic scholarships at its disposal, it will likely recruit more players than a basketball team with one netless hoop and a participation fee will. And what if the tennis team has some expansionist aspirations? Fearing that basketball may eventually rise in popularity at Analogy Academy, the tennis coach may first petition the athletic director to drain any remaining resources from the basketball team and then, when the impoverished basketball coach invariably resigns, persuade the director to appoint his tennis partner as the new coach of the basketball team. Given these odd occurrences, two outcomes are likely. First, many basketball players will choose to take up tennis in light of the clear benefits of playing that game, but they will bring some of their basketball-related skills, such as jumping really high and playing full-contact defense, into tennis to the chagrin of the experienced tennis players. Second, the remaining members of the basketball team—now coached by a tennis player—will begin to adopt some aspects of tennis. They might begin to play on one of those new courts, thereby incorporating tennis-court boundaries into basketball. Ultimately, as the basketball players adjust to the unequal power dynamics between the two sports, they destabilize the established rules of both tennis and basketball. Hughes and McCutcheon would presumably respond by blaming the basketball players for violating the rules of tennis and then calling for "discursive boundary maintenance" to ensure the integrity of future tennis matches.

While most tennis coaches do not become so intertwined with basketball teams, we cannot say the same for Western academia and modern Islamic thought over the past two centuries. In no way have these two discursive traditions been either separate or equal. Proponents of "discursive boundary maintenance" must therefore account for the grossly unequal distribution of resources and political power in the postcolonial period if they are to make their proposal historically and ethically relevant for the field of Islamic studies. They must also explain why the altered forms of tennis and basketball (a.k.a. fusionist thinking) do not constitute valid and even beneficial modifications to the sports. Otherwise, this first option has too much in common with previous iterations of intellectual dualism, including the colonial bifurcation of educational systems and Schacht's exclusionary, identitarian response to Rahman.

OPTION 2: SELF-CRITICAL, CROSS-DISCURSIVE DIALOGUE

Whereas Hughes and McCutcheon see "discursive boundary maintenance" as crucial for preserving the "academic" integrity of Islamic studies, a second scholarly camp embraces the interconnections between Western academia and modern Islamic thought as an opportunity to forge a more intellectually diverse and cosmopolitan field. These scholars take postcolonial critiques of the academy as their point of departure. They accept that Islamic studies has long been complicit in colonial and postcolonial knowledge regimes and strive to redress these wrongs first by recognizing their own situatedness as Western scholars and second by inviting Muslim intellectuals to the table for open conversation. Accordingly, this second camp wants to reimagine Islamic studies as a field devoted to self-critical, cross-discursive dialogue.

Leonard Binder was one of the earliest advocates of this dialogic model. As we saw in chapter 4, Binder spent the early decades of his career as a modernization theorist but began, in the 1970s and 1980s, to cultivate a deep interest in postmodernism and postcolonial theory. He eventually eschewed social-scientific claims to objectivity in favor of theoretical criticism and personal self-reflection. Specifically, *Islamic Liberalism* endorsed Said's blistering critique of the field, but Binder also expressed a fundamental disagreement with Said over what academics must do next. He worried that, after so vigorously rejecting essentialist Orientalist representations of Islam, Said failed to say anything at all about the religion, thereby rendering Islam as little more than an empty signifier. Binder tried to give Said the benefit of the doubt on this glaring omission. He speculated that perhaps Said chose to say nothing about Islam in order to avoid producing his own reductive representation. After all, Said's analysis seemed to suggest that writing about the Other always constitutes an act of discursive aggression and even violence. Binder thus wondered aloud, "Is not silence preferable to the violence of academic discourse?"[19] But he answered his own question with a resounding "no." Even if all attempts to understand Islam produce dominating forms of knowledge, Binder pled that silence was worse. He borrowed from Jacques Derrida to suggest that the limited violence of discourse is "the only way to repress the worst violence, the violence of primitive and prelogical silence, of an unimaginable night which would not even be the opposite of nonviolence."[20] Said might have chosen that unimaginable night, but Binder refused to be lulled into such a dangerous and hopeless slumber.

To combat the violence of silence, Binder wrote *Islamic Liberalism* as a self-critical meditation on Middle Eastern politics. Its very first page reads:

> It is tempting to try to begin thus from the very beginning, urging the reader to forget everything he or she believes, and pretending that I have suppressed all that I believe. It is, however, difficult in practice, and probably impossible in theory, to build up the entire world out of nothing. It is easier, and possibly more candid, to start with what one thinks one believes, and then to proceed to engage with the reader in dialogue.[21]

With these words, Binder abandoned any pretense to neutrality. He declared his personal commitment to political liberalism and invited Muslim intellectuals to likewise bring their religious commitments to the table for an open conversation. It was through such dialogue that Binder hoped Western academics and Muslim intellectuals could strengthen liberalism in the Middle East together.[22] While optimistic about the potential of cross-discursive conversation, Binder also recognized that "dialogue can be coercive," especially when one side possesses greater material wealth and political power.[23] He attempted to mitigate this power differential by subjecting Western academic development theory to extensive "self-criticism" and engaging closely and deeply with Islamic thinkers.[24] Binder's dialogic model was thus equal parts postcolonial critique and cross-cultural optimism.

Richard C. Martin has also carried the proverbial torch for cross-discursive dialogue. Like Binder before him, Martin takes postcolonial criticism of Islamic studies to heart, acknowledging the field's tendency "to exert epistemological control over the self-understanding of colonized societies."[25] He aims to ameliorate this dismal colonial record by extending greater "sensitivity to the Muslim *subject* in Islamic studies, of being the *object* of study for the past century."[26] For Martin, this sensibility requires that scholars reimagine

Islamic studies as a Habermasian "global cosmopolitan arena" where Western academics engage with Muslim intellectuals as subjects—rather than only as objects—of knowledge production.[27] He explains: "Our urgent task is to learn how to make productive arguments on the cosmopolitan academic stage where our conversation partners are invested in increasingly diverse ideological and religious worldviews."[28] Martin foregrounds the pedagogical function of these encounters because he wants Western academics to loosen our collective grip on the roles of expert and teacher and to assume, at times, the roles of participant and student instead. By extension, the academy should not, according to Martin, belong only to those who can claim the title of "academic" but should rather function as a meeting ground for various intellectual traditions so that their adherents can practice cross-discursive collaboration.

Cross-discursive dialogue stands as a simultaneously pragmatic and optimistic model for Islamic studies. It is pragmatic because neither Binder nor Martin aspire to lofty standards of objectivity or critical distance. Rather, they embrace their situatedness as Western academics and acknowledge the colonial dynamics undergirding the field. They also retain their political and personal commitments. Binder certainly did not renounce political liberalism, and Martin never suggests that "critical scholarship" or even revisionist research into the Qur'an and the Prophet's life should be out of bounds for Western academics. It is also optimistic because Binder and Martin frame cross-discursive work as an intellectually exciting and politically inclusive future for the field. Unlike Hughes and McCutcheon, who seek a degree of discursive homogeneity within the academic study of religion, Binder and Martin welcome discursive plurality.

Despite its many strengths, the cross-discursive dialogue model runs into some complications regarding guest lists. Specifically, if the academy functions as a "global cosmopolitan arena," then who is invited to participate and on whose terms? More importantly, who exactly gets to send out the invitations? The *Media Dakwah* case, which we explored in chapter 5, exemplifies the conflicts that can arise over guest lists. Indonesian Muslims had serious disagreements over whether Ohio State political scientist William Liddle should have been invited to the discussion about Indonesian Islamic politics. Fusionist thinkers at *Ulumul Qur'an* happily published his essay, but *Media Dakwah* writers saw Liddle as an uninvited outsider who trespassed into Islamic discursive territory. Similar issues emerged on the academic side of the controversy. When *Media Dakwah* writers decided to "answer Liddle" in their August 1993 issue, they sought to continue the conversation by talking back, albeit in hostile language, to Western academics. Liddle and other Western academics did not respond. They chose instead either to ignore *Media Dakwah* altogether or to turn the magazine into an object of analysis.[29] This case demonstrates that the cross-discursive dialogue model only works when all parties agree on who should participate in the conversation. We live in a world where some people can presume the right to speak and be heard and others cannot, so advocates of this second approach must work toward devising fair and transparent ways to extend invitations for any future conversations.

OPTION 3: RADICAL INTROSPECTION

Wael Hallaq represents a third scholarly camp that views the collapsing border between Western academia and modern Islamic thought as a major manifestation of epistemological imperialism.[30] This radical critique begins with the argument that modern knowledge is not merely representational in nature; it is also performative. Indeed, Hallaq pushes back against the prevailing Saidian assessment that the primary problem with Islamic studies was/is that Western scholars misrepresent Islam as a backward, misogynistic, violent, and yet exotic monolith. Said exposed how these essentialist representations fostered a European culture of racial superiority and Islamophobia that were, first and foremost, about Europe. While he, too, criticizes such essentialist representations, Hallaq is far more concerned with the performative power of modern knowledge, or its ability to "construct action" and "create a reality."[31] He traces how Orientalists deployed their knowledge to "remold, refashion, and, in short, re-create" Muslim subjectivities over the past two centuries.[32] For example, he enumerates how European Orientalists and officials destroyed the *waqf* (religious endowment)-based Islamic economic system and codified shariʿa into a state-based, rigid legal system, thereby fundamentally altering the socio-moral structures of Muslim communities.[33] Hallaq therefore describes "colonialism as a modern project of total transformation, one that perpetually aims at reengineering the subject," and he denounces these forced transformations as nothing short of structural genocides.[34]

Instead of targeting Orientalism for special criticism as Said had done, Hallaq casts blame for epistemological imperialism on Western academia as a whole. He condemns business schools, economics departments, the natural and social sciences, philosophy, and history for all possessing "an underlying structure of thought that is inherently colonialist."[35] He also characterizes academia as "a state entity" that produces only docile, capitalist, nationalist citizens.[36] While painting this bleak picture of modern knowledge, Hallaq insists that intellectual resistance is still possible and points hopefully to the figure of the "subversive author." According to Hallaq, subversive authors "must consciously stand outside the paradigmatic structures" and "interrogate the foundational assumptions and epistemological mainstays of the discursive formations as well as the larger system of power that sustains them."[37] They must, in other words, work to expose and attack the very roots of the modern, imperialist academy.

Hallaq proposes that subversive authors practice "introspective orientalism" as a form of radical resistance.[38] "Introspective orientalism" requires scholars first to repudiate existing disciplinary norms. Focusing on history in particular, Hallaq argues:

> If it is true that human beings are predisposed to history, then history must be written for one's own society and must remain within that society. It must not be allowed to transcend to the Other. To write history in order to judge the Other, or worse, to instruct or dominate the Other, is to consciously engage in a thought-structure that raises fundamental ethical objections.[39]

Put another way, subversive authors must refuse to deploy their authority as Western academics to evaluate and hence reshape the Muslims whom they study. These are "extroverted" moves that direct knowledge outward for the sake of domination, violence, and structural genocide.[40] Hallaq's second step entails redirecting Orientalist knowledge inward. Specifically, he suggests that scholars study the premodern Islamic (or another religious) tradition in order to practice a "heuristic retrieval" of alternative ways of knowing and living in the world.[41] Scholars can then use their knowledge of this alternative tradition to critique our modern society and to refashion modern individuals into more ethical subjects. Hallaq admits that "introspective orientalism" is an "ethically self-centered process," but it is grounded in a humble rather than a narcissistic ethos.[42] Hallaq explains, "If we write history and write it for ourselves, a perfectly valid and ethical engagement, then it is to learn something from it."[43] Ultimately, Hallaq seeks to turn the power of Orientalist knowledge to "remold, refashion, and re-create" inward.

Hallaq models radical introspection in *The Impossible State: Islam, Politics, and Modernity's Moral Predicament* (2013). The book draws on his decades of research into the history of Islamic law but refuses to use this knowledge to criticize shariʿa for its purported incompatibility with modernity, as many previous scholars have done. Instead, Hallaq reverses the critical gaze and presents shariʿa as an alternative social model so that his Western readers can better understand the limitations of our own, state-based social order. He argues that morality was central in shariʿa-based societies because Muslims saw their greatest responsibility as serving God through ethical behavior. All other concerns, including loyalty to one's ruler and economic gain, took a backseat to fulfilling one's responsibilities to God. Hallaq juxtaposes this shariʿa-based society with the modern state-based society. Because the modern state serves no higher metaphysical ideal than that of its own survival, it cultivates amoral citizens who maintain "my country, right or wrong."[44] Hallaq uses shariʿa heuristically to expose the modern state's failings and demonstrate that more viable "forms of ethically sustainable living" are possible.[45]

Interestingly, Hallaq insists that radical introspection is the *only* "ethically justifiable reason" for studying the Other.[46] It is this categorical statement that many scholars, including those who fall into the first two camps, would characterize as a threat to academic freedom because it clearly restricts what and how academics research. To underscore the differences among these three camps, let us consider revisionist histories of the Qurʾan and Muhammad's life for a moment. Hughes praises revisionist historiography for applying historical criticism to the Qurʾan and Muhammad instead of treating these source texts with a theological-style reverence.[47] Martin suggests that while Western academics should cultivate "sensitivity to the Muslim subject," they certainly retain the right to conduct critical research on Islamic source texts and other religiously sensitive subjects.[48] Academics must simply be more prepared to discuss and defend their methods in a cross-discursive dialogue.[49] Despite their profound differences on other matters, Hughes and Martin agree that academic freedom should be protected in any future Islamic studies. Hallaq resolutely disagrees. Not only would he condemn revisionist historians for producing unabashedly "extroverted" knowledge, but he would also trouble the very notion of academic freedom. Indeed, Hallaq argues that intellectual freedom merely "translates into precisely the kind of questions whose answers yield the destructive effects of oppression, colonialism, and genocide."[50] In this manner, Hallaq ties "freedom" to academic imperialism and implores scholars to trade both postures for a more ethical form of knowledge production.

This move to prioritize academic ethics over freedom enables Hallaq to resolve the guest-list dilemma that Binder and Martin's cross-discursive dialogue model left unanswered. Returning to the *Media Dakwah* case, Hallaq would surely suggest that Liddle violated the cardinal ethical rule when he used his Western academic authority to evaluate the Islamist magazine's content and therefore "to judge the Other." Liddle did not seek to "learn something from" the *Media Dakwah* staff, as Hallaq advises, but instead wielded his discursive power vis-à-vis the magazine's writers. While *Media Dakwah* responded with hostile and prejudicial language, they did not initiate the confrontation. Liddle was the aggressor. Hallaq would stress that Western academics have no innate rights to be on the guest lists for conversations in other cultural or discursive spaces. If we violate our ethical limits, then we should be prepared to face hostile resistance for trespassing.

Hallaq's radical introspection offers a way to reduce epistemological imperialism, but his proposal raises questions about how (much) to subvert modern knowledge systems. On the one hand, he articulates and models a clear vision for subversion at the level of scholarly ideas. Academic research should be aimed at cross-discursive learning rather than teaching. Scholars should focus on exposing the intellectual and moral weaknesses of their own societies and learning from the ethical practices that underpin other societies. *The Impossible State* stands as an example of such work. On the other hand, Hallaq offers little advice on how to navigate the material structures that enable academic imperialism. For example, should exchange programs with Indonesian Muslims be shut down to prevent opportunities for further academic domination? Should academic essays and books not be translated into non-European languages? To answer either of these questions in the affirmative seems extreme. After all, the decision to end exchange programs and discourage translation would rob Indonesian Muslim intellectuals of the opportunity to make their own decisions about where to study and what to read for the sake of some paternalistic version of postcolonialism. Nevertheless, Hallaq's dire diagnosis of academic knowledge seems to suggest that ideas alone, without some kind of accompanying structural action, are insufficient to meet the challenge.

In the end, the increasing interconnections between Western academia and modern Islamic thought pose a set of dilemmas for academic scholars of Islam that lack easy answers. None of the three options outlined above is perfect or straightforward to implement. They all require academics to reevaluate our priorities, to weigh competing concerns about academic freedom, critical methods, religious diversity, and academic imperialism against one another, and to forge a new balance for the future of the field. Still, it is more important now than ever to confront these dilemmas. The 9/11 attacks, the subsequent war on terror, and the rise of Islamophobia in the West have thrown academic scholars of Islam into a political maelstrom, and the waves do not seem to be dying down anytime soon. The tumultuous political climate requires that we ask difficult questions about the purpose and the ethics of Islamic studies and that we seek answers to them together.

NOTES

INTRODUCTION

1. For one example, see Mujiburrahman, *Humor, Perempuan, dan Sufi*, 181.
2. Jabali and Jamhari, *Modernization of Islam*, 20–21.
3. Jabali and Jamhari, *Modernization of Islam*, 36.
4. For several prominent examples, see Mottahedeh, *Mantle of the Prophet*; Zaman, *Modern Islamic Thought*; and Moosa, *What Is a Madrasa?*
5. For notable scholarship on colonial-era Islamic education, see Metcalf, *Islamic Revival*; Mitchell, *Colonizing Egypt*, 63–94; Messick, *Calligraphic State*; and Zaman, *Ulama in Contemporary Islam*, 60–86.
6. For research on the postcolonial politics of Islamic education, see Starrett, *Putting Islam to Work*; Zeghal, "Religion and Politics," 371–99; Hefner and Zaman, *Schooling Islam*; Ahmad, *Islamism and Democracy*, 83–136; and Hefner, *Making Modern Muslims*.
7. Some other scholars have also noticed this collapse. For example, Michael Feener observes that "for well over a century now, the blending of emic and etic discourses on Islam has been a complex and creative dynamic in Muslim thought"; see "Cross-Cultural Contexts," 273. And Carool Kersten refers to Western-educated Muslim intellectuals as "working in the interstices between and betwixt cultures and academic traditions"; see *Cosmopolitans and Heretics*, 1.
8. For previous uses of the term *dualism* in this context, see Rahman, *Islam and Modernity*, 58, 62, 96; Hashim, *Educational Dualism in Malaysia*; and Azyumardi Azra, Dina Afrianty, and Robert W. Hefner, "Pesantren and Madrasa: Muslim Schools and National Ideals in Indonesia," in Hefner and Zaman, *Schooling Islam*, 182–91.
9. Talal Asad and Shahab Ahmed have both conceptualized Islam, despite its undeniably diverse and contested existence, as a coherent tradition. I follow their lead. Asad, *Idea of an Anthropology of Islam*; Ahmed, *What Is Islam?*, 270–97.
10. MacIntyre, *Whose Justice?*, 8.
11. MacIntyre, 12.
12. Admittedly, MacIntyre argues that academic philosophy alone houses multiple and competing traditions of inquiry. He would therefore presumably challenge my designation of Western academia as an overarching intellectual tradition. While acknowledging the existence of profound intellectual differences, I argue that

academics do share some core principles—among them, a respect for reason-based inquiry, scholarly agency, and individual creativity—*and* work within the common institutional space of the modern university. This latter fact shapes the material realities of academic life in myriad ways, from access to funding to the tenure and promotion process. These are the tangible markers of academic community, and they largely transcend intellectual and disciplinary commitments. MacIntyre, *Three Rival Versions*.

13. Jung, *Orientalists*; Laffan, *Makings of Indonesian Islam*; Purohit, *Aga Khan Case*; Datla, *Language of Secular Islam*, 20–55; Aydin, *Muslim World*.

14. Jung, *Orientalists*, 7.

15. Aydin, *Muslim World*, 69.

16. Aydin, 69.

17. MacIntyre, *Whose Justice?*, 167.

18. MacIntyre, 164.

19. Ibrahim, *Improvisational Islam*, 8, 11.

20. Gyan Prakash makes a similar argument about Indian elites and their ability to translate between British scientific epistemologies and indigenous Indian forms of knowledge. Prakash, *Another Reason*.

21. For recent discussions of Islamic authenticity, see Lee, *Overcoming Tradition*; and Lukens-Bull, *Islamic Higher Education*, 71–3.

22. Abbas, "Western Academia and Pakistan," 736–68; Zaman, *Islam in Pakistan*, 66–74.

23. Hirschkind, "Heresy or Hermeneutics," 35–50; Najjar, "Islamic Fundamentalism," 177–200.

24. Roberts and Turner, *Sacred and the Secular*, 11.

25. Roberts and Turner, 43–106; Marsden, *Soul of the American University*.

26. For an introduction to the insider-outsider problem, see McCutcheon, *Insider/Outsider Problem*.

27. Other notable advocates of this position include Jonathan Z. Smith and Donald Wiebe.

28. McCutcheon, "Study of Religion," 14.

29. Lincoln, *Gods and Demons*, 1.

30. McCutcheon, *Critics Not Caretakers*.

31. Orsi, *Between Heaven and Earth*, 7.

32. For other comments on the relative isolation of Islamic studies from wider trends in religious studies, see Adams, "History of Religions," 177–93; and Richard C. Martin, "Islam and Religious Studies: An Introductory Essay," in *Approaches to Islam*, 1–18.

33. The insider-outsider problem has also impacted the study of Hinduism, Sikhism, and Native American religions in distinctly postcolonial ways. Patton, *Who Owns Religion?*

34. Said, *Orientalism*. The late 1970s also saw Patricia Crone and Michael Cook's publication of *Hagarism*, a revisionist history of Islam's origins that brazenly

declared itself "a book written by infidels for infidels." The book—and that quote in particular—produced its own heated discussion about insider-outsider politics in the field. Crone and Cook, *Hagarism*, vii-viii.

35. Said, *Orientalism*, 322.
36. Lewis, "Question of Orientalism," 49–56.
37. Martin, "Islam and Religious Studies," 9.
38. Hughes, *Situating Islam*; Hughes, "Study of Islam," 314–36; Hughes, *Theorizing Islam*; Hughes, *Islam*.
39. Hughes, *Theorizing Islam*, 5.
40. *Method and Theory in the Study of Religion* devoted an entire 2012 issue (vol. 24) to Hughes's provocation and several scholarly responses. Internet-based discussions include Safi, "Reflections," and a series of 2014 posts in *The Bulletin for the Study of Religion* blog at http://bulletin.equinoxpub.com.
41. Hallaq, *Restating Orientalism*, 101. For more discussion of Hallaq, see this book's conclusion.
42. Hallaq, *Impossible State*; Hallaq, *Restating Orientalism*; Mahmood, "Secularism, Hermeneutics, Empire," 323–47; Mahmood, *Religious Difference*.
43. Ahmad, *Islamism and Democracy*; Rudnyckyj, *Spiritual Economies*; Ibrahim, *Improvisational Islam*.
44. Recent books on twenty-first-century intersections between religion and development include Fountain, Bush, and Feener, *Religion*; Clarke and Halafoff, *Religion*; and Scheer, Fountain, and Feener, *Mission of Development*.
45. For detailed studies of Cold War–era foundations, see Berman, *Influence*; and Parmar, *Foundations*.
46. Mahmood Mamdani offers some trenchant analysis of how the U.S. government distinguished between "good" and "bad" Muslims during the Cold War and its immediate aftermath. Mamdani, *Good Muslim, Bad Muslim*.
47. Mahmood, "Secularism, Hermeneutics, Empire," 329.

CHAPTER 1

1. The literal translation of Sekolah Tinggi Islam is "Islamic High School." However, the level of instruction and entry requirements made it more akin to a college.
2. Hatta, "Sifat Sekolah Tinggi Islam," in Supardi, *Setengah Abad UII*, 33.
3. Hatta, 34.
4. Hatta, 36.
5. Noer, *Mohammad Hatta*, 13–28.
6. Ahmad, *Islamic Modernism*, 31–56; Troll, *Sayyid Ahmad Khan*; Lelyveld, "Disenchantment at Aligarh," 85–102.
7. Hourani, *Arabic Thought*, 161–92; Sedgwick, *Muhammad Abduh*.
8. Zaman, *Modern Islamic Thought*, 174.
9. Noer, *Modernist Muslim Movement*, 25; Ricklefs, *Polarizing Javanese Society*, 58–60.
10. Laffan, *Islamic Nationhood*.

11. Noer, *Modernist Muslim Movement*, 31–33; Laffan, *Islamic Nationhood*, 106–13.
12. Sedgwick, *Muhammad Abduh*, 95–102.
13. Noer, *Modernist Muslim Movement*, 73–83; Idris, "Kiyai Haji Ahmad Dahlan," 23–25.
14. Noer, *Modernist Muslim Movement*, 37–38; Abdullah, *Schools and Politics*, 21–23.
15. Abdullah, *Schools and Politics*, 44–45, 72.
16. Idris, "Kiyai Haji Ahmad Dahlan," 172–78.
17. Idris, 173–74.
18. Abdullah, *Schools and Politics*, 145–50.
19. Roff, "Indonesian and Malay Students," 73–74.
20. Laffan, *Islamic Nationhood*, 215–7.
21. Kinsey, "Efforts for Educational Synthesis," 175–76.
22. As quoted in Abdullah, *Schools and Politics*, 172.
23. For more on Yunus's early life, see Abdullah, *Schools and Politics*, 160–73; Srimulyani, *Mahmud Yunus' Islamic Educational Thought*, 21–5; Rochwulaningsih, "Mahmud Yunus," 168–75.
24. Abdullah, *Schools and Politics*, 242–45; Natsir, *Capita Selecta*, 66–79.
25. Van Niel, *Emergence*, 31–32.
26. Van Niel, *Emergence*, 54–5.
27. Ricklefs, *Polarizing Javanese Society*, 215.
28. Shiraishi, *Age in Motion*, 64–68, 168.
29. Shiraishi, 106–7; Ricklefs, *Polarizing Javanese Society*, 228.
30. Van Niel, *Emergence*, 56.
31. Ali, *Islam and Colonialism*, 258.
32. Laffan, *Makings of Indonesian Islam*, 123–74.
33. Laffan, *Islamic Nationhood*, 181–89; Kahfi, *Islam and Nationalism*, 20–27.
34. Kahfi, *Islam and Nationalism*, 121.
35. Kahfi, 127.
36. Kahin, *Islam, Nationalism, and Democracy*, 1–13.
37. Natsir, *Capita Selecta*, 60.
38. Kahin, *Islam, Nationalism, and Democracy*, 28–30.
39. For a detailed exploration of pesantren culture, see Dhofier, *Pesantren Tradition*, 1–40.
40. Ali, *Islam and Colonialism*, 55.
41. Dhofier, *Pesantren Tradition*, 80–83.
42. Dhofier, 83–84; Zaini, "Kyai Haji Abdul Wahid Hasyim," 11–29, 54–67.
43. Benda, *Crescent and the Rising Sun*.
44. Latif, *Indonesian Muslim Intelligentsia*, 167–68, 232.
45. Supardi, *Setengah Abad UII*, 25–29, 54–55; Jamhari, "IAIN Jakarta," in Yatim and Nasuhi, *Membangun Pusat Keunggulan*, 20–21.
46. Hatta, "Sifat Sekolah Tinggi Islam," 36.

47. "Pidato Menteri Agama K. H. Wahid Hasyim," in *Perguruan Tinggi Agama Islam Negeri*, 21–22.

48. "Pidato Menteri Agama Hasyim," 22.

49. Menteri Agama Republik Indonesia, "Surat Putusan tentang Panitya Perguruan Tinggi Islam," dated July 7, 1950, folder 64, Sekretariat Negara RI Yogyakarta Collection, ANRI; "Penjelasan atas Peraturn Presiden No. 11/1960 tentang Pembentukan Institut Agama Islam Negeri," in *Himpunan Perundang-undangan Direktorat Jenderal Bimbingan Maysarakat Islam*, folder 39, Departemen Agama II, ANRI.

50. Yunus, *Pokok-Pokok Pendidikan*, 9–10.

51. Yunus, 9.

52. Yunus, 9.

53. Yunus, 5–8.

54. Yunus, 8.

55. Yunus, *Sejarah Pendidikan Islam*, xv.

56. Srimulyani, *Yunus*, 64–73.

57. Armai Arief, "Prof. Dr. H. Mahmud Yunus," in Yatim and Nasuhi, *Membangun Pusat Keunggulan*, 60–64.

58. Yunus, *Sejarah Pendidikan*, 447–53; Arief, "Prof. Dr. H. Mahmud Yunus," 63.

59. Yunus, *Sejarah Pendidikan*, 31–39.

60. Yunus, *Metodik Chusus*; Srimulyani, *Yunus*, 46–9.

61. Yunus, *Metodik Chusus*, 3; Yunus, *Pokok-Pokok Pendidikan*, 89–113.

62. Many Muslim contemporaries, most notably Pakistani Islamist Abul A'la Mawdudi(1903–78), made similar assumptions about the "value neutral" status of science. Nasr, *Mawdudi*, 52–53.

63. Kahin, *Islam, Nationalism, and Democracy*, 24.

64. Jung, *Orientalists*; Aydin, *Idea of the Muslim World*.

65. Jung, *Orientalists*, 7.

66. Natsir, *Capita Selecta*, 4.

67. Natsir, 12.

68. Natsir, *Islam Sebagai Ideologie*, 7.

69. Natsir, 7–22.

70. Natsir, *Capita Selecta*, 3.

71. Natsir, *Islam Sebagai Ideologie*, 7.

72. Natsir, *Capita Selecta*, 13–15.

73. Feener, *Muslim Legal Thought*, 86. For additional discussion of Natsir's reliance on Western Orientalists, see Feener, "Constructions of Religious Authority," 139–51; and Feener, "Cross-cultural Contexts," 272–75.

74. It was published in Istanbul as *Orta Asyada Arap fütuhatı*.

75. Qutb, *Social Justice in Islam*, 266–67; Jung, *Orientalists*, 215–16.

76. For discussion of several more examples, see Feener, *Muslim Legal Thought*, 86n22–3.

77. Laffan, "Straight from Mecca," 265–83.

78. Natsir, *Capita Selecta*, 3.

79. In contrast, Sayyid Qutb did not characterize Gibb as an objective scholar. Instead, he wrote, "Such men [Orientalists like Gibb] are unable fully to comprehend the Islamic spirit, but confine themselves rather to a review of its practical benefits." Qutb, *Social Justice*, 268.

80. Natsir, *Capita Selecta*, 37–40.

81. Natsir, 37.

82. Madinier, *Islam and Politics*, 29.

83. "Penjelasan atas Peraturn Presiden No. 11/1960," dated May 9, 1960, *Himpunan Perundang-undangan*, ANRI.

84. "Amanat P.J.M. Presiden Republik Indonesia dalam Upatjara Dies Natalis Ke II Institut Agama Islam Negeri pada Tanggal 4 Agustus 1962 di Jakarta," *Al-Djamiah* 2, no. 1 (January–February 1963): 3–4.

85. *Sewindu Institut Agama Islam Negeri*, 55.

86. Fealy, "Ulama and Politics," 85.

87. Fealy, 83–110; Bush, *Nahdlatul Ulama*, 24–64; Kahin, *Islam, Nationalism, and Democracy*, 93–96; Madinier, *Islam and Politics*, 135–46, 375–80.

88. Kahin, *Islam, Nationalism, and Democracy*, 99.

89. Kahin, 114–153; Madinier, *Islam and Politics*, 248–80.

90. Fealy, "Ulama and Politics," 184–225.

91. Muhaimin Abdul Ghofur, "KH Saifuddin Zuhri: Eksistensi Agama dalam Nation Building," in Azra and Umam, *Menteri-Menteri Agama RI*, 203–241.

92. Zuhri, *Berangkat*, 505.

93. Zuhri, 505–6.

94. *Sewindu Institut Agama Islam Negeri*, 25–39.

95. Machasin, "Prof. Mr. R. H. A. Soenarjo," in Damami, *Lima Tokoh Pengembangan*, 53–78.

96. Dewan Mahasiswa IAIN Jogjakarta, "Buku Putih," dated August 17, 1963, file 1086, Abdul Gani Personal Collection, ANRI; Dewan Mahasiswa IAIN Jakarta, "Buku Putih," dated October 5, 1963, file 1086, Abdul Gani Personal Collection, ANRI.

97. Dewan Mahasiswa IAIN Jakarta, "Buku Putih," ANRI.

98. For more detailed analysis of the October 10 incident, see Abbas, "Battling over the Bureaucracy," 207–25.

99. Saridjo, *Jabatan untuk Umat*, 9–21.

100. Saridjo, 22–24.

101. *Sewindu Institut Agama Islam Negeri*, 491–96.

102. For example, see Zaim Uchrowi and Ahmadie Thaha, "Riwayat Hidup Prof. Dr. Harun Nasution," in *Refleksi Pembaharuan Pemikiran Islam*, 39.

103. Yunus, *Sejarah Pendidikan*, 454–61.

104. *Sewindu Institut Agama Islam Negeri*, 25–28.

105. Abdul Basit Adnan and Abdulhayi Adnan, "K. H. R. Mohammad Adnan," in Damami, *Lima Tokoh Pengembangan*, 39–40.

106. For sample course syllabi, see *Sewindu Institut Agama Islam Negeri*, 159–300.

CHAPTER 2

1. F. Cyril James, "Impressions of Java and Bali, August 1957," file 6866, box 229, records group (RG) 2, McGill University Archives.
2. James, "Impressions."
3. Wilfred Cantwell Smith letter to Cyril James, dated April 17, 1956, folder 6251, box 180, RG 2, McGill University Archives; "Interviews: CG, Professor WC Smith, September 30, 1957, Telephone," folder 100, box 11, series 427.R, RG 1.2, Rockefeller Foundation Archives, RAC.
4. Jabali and Jamhari, *Modernization of Islam*, 20–1.
5. "History of the McGill-IAIN Relationship."
6. Novick, *That Noble Dream*, 1–20.
7. Lockman, *Contending Visions*, 100–103; Lockman, *Fieldnotes*, 1–19.
8. Lockman, *Fieldnotes*, 20–71.
9. *Program for Near Eastern Studies*, 8.
10. *Program for Near Eastern Studies*, 17.
11. Johnson and Tucker, "Middle East Studies Network," 8.
12. Webster, *Fire and the Full Moon*, 92–93.
13. Webster, *Fire and the Full Moon*, 100. For the role of Sufism at the Institute, see Hick, "Comparative Religion," 141–69.
14. Gibb, *Mohammedanism: A Historical Survey*, v–vii.
15. Cragg, *Call of the Minaret*, viii.
16. Waardenburg, "Louis Massignon," 325–29.
17. Gibb, *Modern Trends in Islam*, ix.
18. Gibb, *Mohammedanism*, vi.
19. Von Grunebaum, *Modern Islam*, 46, 147.
20. Schacht, *Origins*, 149.
21. Schacht, 140–41.
22. Schacht, 152–55.
23. Guillaume, "Review of *Muhammad at Mecca*," 609–10; Von Grunebaum, "Review of *Muhammad at Mecca*," 223–24; Schacht, "Review of *Muhammad at Mecca*," 231–33.
24. Gibb, *Modern Trends*, 6–7.
25. Gibb, *Mohammedanism*, 145–46.
26. Gibb, *Modern Trends*, 109–29.
27. Von Grunebaum, *Modern Islam*, 129–257.
28. "Interviews: JM with Philip Hitti Princeton, November 1, 1951," folder 3520, box 408, series 200R, RG 1.2, Rockefeller Foundation Archives, RAC.
29. Cuyler Young letter to J. A. Williams, dated January 18, 1962, folder Jan. 1962, box 3, archive collection 164, series Oriental Studies, Princeton University Archives. For similar comments about Iranian participation in a Ford-sponsored conference in the country, see Lockman, *Fieldnotes*, 151–52.
30. Majid Khadduri, Muhsin Mahdi, and Albert and George Hourani all had academic appointments during this era.

31. "Excerpt from Trustee's Confidential Report: The Institute of Islamic Studies," April 1, 1954, folder 93, box 10, series 427, Record Group (RG) 1.2, Rockefeller Foundation Archives, RAC.

32. Smith, *Faith of Other Men*, 9–23; Sheila McDonough, "Wilfred Cantwell Smith in Lahore, 1940–1951," in Aitken and Sharma, *Legacy*, 147–61.

33. Smith, *Modern Islam*, viii.

34. Wilfred Cantwell Smith letter to John Marshall, dated May 29, 1951, folder 93, box 10, series 427, RG 1.2, Rockefeller Foundation Archives, RAC.

35. Smith, *Modern Islam in India*, 75.

36. Smith, 211.

37. McDonough, "Smith in Lahore," 161–68.

38. Smith, *Pakistan*, 33.

39. Wilfred Cantwell Smith letter to Cyril James, dated October 12, 1948, folder 5586, box 208, RG 2, McGill University Archives.

40. Smith letter to James, dated October 12, 1948.

41. Wilfred Cantwell Smith letter to Cyril James, dated June 6, 1951, folder 5586, box 208, RG 2, McGill University Archives.

42. Wilfred Cantwell Smith, "Comparative Religion," 31–50.

43. Smith letter to James, dated June 6, 1951.

44. Wilfred Cantwell Smith letter to Cyril James, dated May 7, 1951, folder 5586, box 208, RG 2, McGill University Archives.

45. Smith letter to James, dated May 7, 1951.

46. Wilfred Cantwell Smith letter to Cyril James, dated May 25, 1951, folder 93, box 10, series 427.R, RG 1.2, Rockefeller Foundation Archives, RAC.

47. Howard Federspiel, personal interview, March 17, 2012.

48. "The Institute of Islamic Studies Report," August 16, 1955, folder 99, box 11, series 427.R, RG 1.2, Rockefeller Foundation Archives, RAC.

49. Italics added by author. Rahbar, *Memories and Meanings*, 269.

50. Smith, *Islam in Modern History*, 93.

51. Smith, *Islam in Modern History*, 122.

52. Wilfred Cantwell Smith memo to Cleon Swayzee, "Interim Note on Scope and Objective," dated December 7, 1954, folder 5869, box 169, RG 2, McGill University Archives.

53. Smith, "Review of *Islam and the West*," 438.

54. Smith, "Review of *Islam—The Straight Path*," 311.

55. Smith, 310.

56. Federspiel, personal interview.

57. Federspiel, "Collected Papers," 6.

58. Smith letter to James, dated June 6, 1951.

59. "Interview: RHN, Visit to Institute of Islamic Studies, McGill University," dated October 8, 1958, folder 100, box 11, series 427R, RG 1.2, Rockefeller Foundation Archives, RAC.

60. Federspiel, personal interview.

61. "Interview: RHN, Visit to Institute of Islamic Studies," dated October 8, 1958.

62. Federspiel, personal interview.

63. Smith continued this habit during his years at Harvard's Center for the Study of World Religions. Aitken and Sharma, *Legacy*, 107–8, 210–11.

64. John Marshall letter to Wilfred Cantwell Smith, dated November 20, 1956, folder 1772, box 7, RG 36, McGill University Archives.

65. Inter-Office Correspondence from JM, dated September 14, 1955, folder 99, box 11, series 427.R, RG 1.2, Rockefeller Foundation Archives, RAC.

66. Inter-Office Correspondence, dated September 14, 1955; Wilfred Cantwell Smith letter to Chadbourne Gilpatric, dated September 25, 1954, folder 97, box 10, series 427.R, RG 1.2, Rockefeller Foundation Archives, RAC.

67. Wilfred Cantwell Smith letter to John Marshall, dated December 1, 1956, folder 1772, box 7, RG 36, McGill University Archives.

68. "Excerpt from JM Diary, McGill University, Institute of Islamic Studies," dated September 20, 1954, folder 97, box 10, series 427.R, RG 1.2, Rockefeller Foundation Archives, RAC.

69. Wilfred Cantwell Smith, "The Institute of Islamic Studies" dated August 16, 1955, folder 99, box 11, series 427.R, RG 1.2, Rockefeller Foundation Archives, RAC.

70. H. Soebagijo I.N., "Dari Saridi ke Rasjidi," in Ananda, *70 Tahun Prof. Dr. H.M. Rasjidi*, 3–35.

71. "Grant in Aid, Account RF 54153-H," dated August 5, 1955, folder 69, box 6, series 652.R, RG 1.2, Rockefeller Foundation Archives, RAC.

72. "Excerpt from CBF diary, Place: Jakarta, Indonesia," dated May 4, 1955, folder 69, box 6, series 652, RG 1.2, Rockefeller Foundation Archives, RAC; "A Call from M. Rasjidi, Paris," dated February 4, 1956, folder 69, box 6, series 652, RG 1.2, Rockefeller Foundation Archives, RAC; Syamsuddin, *Professor Dr. HM Rasjidi*, 44.

73. "Memorandum Submitted to the Asia Foundation by WC Smith," June 16, 1956, folder: Asia Foundation, 1956, box 61, RG 84, McGill University Archives.

74. Kenneth W. Morgan, "Prof. Rasjidi Has Served His Country and the International Islamic Community with Distinction," in Ananda, *70 Tahun Prof. Dr. H.M. Rasjidi*, 173–74.

75. Rasjidi, *Falsafat Agama*, 92–125.

76. "Interview: RHN, Visit to Institute of Islamic Studies," dated October 8, 1958, Rockefeller Foundation Archives, RAC.

77. Federspiel, personal interview.

78. "Interviews: BRC with Wilfred C. Smith, McGill University," dated November 7, 1960, folder 101, box 11, series 427.R, RG 1.2, Rockefeller Foundation Archives, RAC.

79. Rasjidi, "Islam," 105–38.

80. Azyumardi Azra, "H.M. Rasjidi, BA; Pembentukan Kementerian Agama dalam Revolusi," in Azra and Umam, *Menteri-Menteri Agama RI*, 20.

81. Howard Federspiel confirmed Rasjidi's account of cancelled classes and an institute-wide discussion.

82. Rasjidi, *Koreksi terhadap Drs. Nurcholish Madjid*, 59- 61.

83. For a biography of Faruqi, see Shafiq, *Growth of Islamic Thought*. The other founder of the Islamization of Knowledge movement, Naquib al-Attas, also studied at McGill briefly.

84. Wilfred Cantwell Smith letter to RHN, dated March 9, 1959, folder 92, box 10, series 427R, RG 1.2, Rockefeller Foundation Archives, RAC.

85. Faruqi, *On Arabism: Urubah and Religion*; Faruqi, *Christian Ethics*.

86. Federspiel, personal interview.

87. "Interviews: RHN; Paul Romeril, Institute of Islamic Studies McGill University," dated April 7, 1959, folder 92, box 10, series 427R, RG 1.2, Rockefeller Foundation Archives, RAC; Federspiel, personal interview.

88. "Excerpt from P.E.A. Romeril's Final Report on Near East re: Isma'il Faruqi," dated May 20, 1959, folder 92, box 10, series 427R, RG 1.2, Rockefeller Foundation Archives, RAC.

89. Smith letter to RHN, dated March 9, 1959, RAC.

90. Federspiel, personal interview.

91. Faruqi, "*Structure of the Ethical Terms*," 154.

92. "Interview: JM; Fazlur el Rahman, June 7, 1954," folder 96, box 10, series 427.R, RG 1.2, Rockefeller Foundation Archives, RAC.

93. Schacht, *Origins*, 2.

94. Schacht, *Origins*, 138.

95. Rahman, *Islam*, 47–48.

96. Rahman, *Islamic Methodology*, 85–147.

97. Rahman, 5–6.

98. Rahman, *Islam*, 52.

99. He also tied *ijma* (consensus) to these terms, making it an organic triad. Rahman, *Islamic Methodology*, 22–24.

100. Rahman, vi.

101. Rahman, 141.

102. Rahman, 87.

103. Rahman, vi.

104. For other analyses of Mukti Ali's intellectual career, see Steenbrink, "Study of Comparative Religion," 153–61; Munhanif, "Islam," 84–126; Pohl, "On the Role of Interreligious Dialogue," 59–66.

105. M. Damami et al., "H.A. Mukti Ali: Ketaatan, Kesalehan, dan Kecendekiawan," in Abdurrahman and Djam'annuri, *Agama dan Masyarakat*, 21.

106. Damami, *Agama dan Masyarakat*, 21–24.

107. Damami, 25–6.

108. Damami, 29.

109. Damami, 27.

110. Ali Munhanif, "Prof. Dr. A. Mukti Ali: Modernisasi Politik-Keagamaan Orde Baru," in Azra and Umam, *Menteri-Menteri Agama RI*, 283.

111. Ali, *Ilmu Perbandingan Agama*, 32.

112. Wilfred Cantwell Smith letter to Mrs. Pollard, dated February 23, 1957, folder: Asia Foundation 1957, box 61, RG 84, McGill University Archives.

113. Ali, *Ilmu Perbandingan Agama*, 38.

114. Ali, 6–7.

115. Ali, 8–11, 19–32.

116. Ali, 7.

117. Ali, 14.

118. Ali, 19.

119. Ali, 14–5.

120. Ali, 7–8.

121. Ali, 39–40.

122. Ali, 38–41.

123. Zaim Uchrowi and Ahmadi Thaha, "Menyeru Pemikiran Rasional Muʿtazilah," in *Refleksi Pembaharuan Pemikiran Islam*, 33. For other discussions of Nasution's education and his efforts to resurrect Muʿtazilism, see Muzani, "Muʿtazilite Theology," 91–131; Martin, Woodward, and Atmaja, *Defenders of Reason*, 139–96; Saleh, *Modern Trends*, 196–218.

124. Uchrowi and Thaha, "Menyeru Pemikiran Rasional Muʿtazilah," 5–12.

125. Uchrowi and Thaha, 15.

126. Uchrowi and Thaha, 15–26.

127. Uchrowi and Thaha, 27–30.

128. Uchrowi and Thaha, 34.

129. Nasution, "Islamic State in Indonesia."

130. Uchrowi and Thaha, "Menyeru Pemikiran Rasional Muʿtazilah," 34.

131. Nasution, "Place of Reason," 267.

132. Nasution, "Place of Reason," 13.

133. Nasution, *Falsafat Islam*; Nasution, *Teologi Islam*.

134. Uchrowi and Thaha, "Menyeru Pemikiran Rasional Muʿtazilah," 38.

135. In contrast, Aaron Hughes argues that Smith and Rahman were successful in reorienting Islamic studies as a discipline away from the academic ideal of objectivity and toward more overtly theological commitments. However, he overlooks the extensive criticism that they, and especially Rahman, received from prominent scholars. Hughes, *Situating Islam*, 58–71.

136. Rahman, *Islam*, xiii.

137. Serjeant, "Review of *Islam*," 76; Schimmel, "Review of *Islamic Studies*," 266.

138. Schacht, "Review of *Islamic Methodology*," 394–95.

139. Burton, "Review of *Islam*," 392–95.

140. Hourani, "Review of *Islam in Modern History*," 633–35.

141. Ricketts, "Review of *Faith of Other Men*," 744–45.

142. Wilfred Cantwell Smith letter to Rocke Robertson, dated March 18, 1963, folder 11235, box 304, RG 2, McGill University Archives.

143. Wiebe, "Role of 'Belief,'" 247–48.

144. Wilfred Cantwell Smith to Chadbourne Gilpatric, dated February 19, 1955, folder 98, box 10, series 427.R, RG 1.2, Rockefeller Foundation Archives, RAC.

145. David R. Smock, "Evaluation of Grants to McGill University's Institute of Islamic Studies," dated December 30, 1975, Grant 6200227, reel 2478, Ford Foundation Archives, RAC.

146. Francis X. Sutton note, dated March 2, 1975, Grant 6200227, reel 2478, Ford Foundation Archives, RAC.

CHAPTER 3

1. These are Ridwan's recollections. Abdul Hadi and Mudjimanto, "Biografi H. Kafrawi Ridwan: Berangkat dari Pesantren Kembali ke Pesantren," in Saridjo, *Jabatan untuk Umat*, 43.

2. Ricklefs, *Islamisation*, 116–18, 150–9.

3. Hassan, *Muslim Intellectual Responses*; Hefner, *Civil Islam*; Porter, *Managing Politics*, 24–129; Ricklefs, *Islamisation*, 116–203.

4. For an authoritative history of the 1965–66 anti-Communist massacres, see Robinson, *Killing Season*.

5. For examples of anti-Sukarno discourse, see Murtopo, *Dasar-Dasar Pemikiran*, 37–42, 74; Prawiro, *Indonesia's Struggle*, 21–24.

6. MacDougall, "Technocratic Model of Modernization," 1166–83; Simpson, *Economists with Guns*.

7. Prawiro, *Indonesia's Struggle*, 87–8.

8. Nitisastro, *Indonesian Development Experience*, 3–17, 104–14.

9. Nitisastro, 25–97.

10. Prawiro, *Indonesia's Struggle*, 21–54.

11. Simpson, "Indonesia's 'Accelerated Modernization,'" 475–78.

12. Murtopo, *Dasar-Dasar Pemikiran*, 92–7.

13. Murtopo, *Dasar-Dasar Pemikiran*, 95–7. M. C. Ricklefs notes that the "floating mass" concept was actually first proposed by Nurcholish Madjid. Ricklefs, *Islamisation*, 163.

14. The New Order did not banish all ideologies from the Indonesian political landscape. Drawing a distinction between damaging partisan ideologies and a unifying national ideology, Murtopo reaffirmed Pancasila and the 1945 Constitution as the official ideology of the Indonesian nation-state. Murtopo, *Dasar-Dasar Pemikiran*, 11–25.

15. This new brand of modernism has attracted a fair share of scholarly attention and, with it, some competing names. Several Indonesianists refer to this loose school of thought as "neo-modernism" to emphasize its relationship with and yet distinction from modernism. Other scholars of Islam prefer to use the term "liberal Muslim" to denote its intersections with Western-style liberalism. While these two terms have their merits, they remain too nebulous for the purpose of this book. For use of the "neo-modernist" label, see Ali and Effendy, *Merambah Jalan Baru Islam*, 175–95; Barton, "Emergence of Neo-Modernism"; Saleh, *Modern Trends*, 196–294. For use of

the term "liberal Muslim," see Kurzman, *Liberal Islam*; Ibrahim, *Improvisational Islam*, 69–70.

16. Porter, *Managing Politics and Islam*, 38–75; Ricklefs, *Islamisation*, 150–62.
17. Hassan, *Muslim Intellectual Responses*, 78–116; Hefner, *Civil Islam*, 113–19.
18. There are some notable exceptions to the rule, including Muzani, "Muʿtazilite Theology," 123–31; and Feener, *Shariʿa and Social Engineering*, 263–67.
19. Gaus, *Sang Pelintas Batas*, 76–77.
20. Wahib, *Pergolakan*, 146–50. See also Barton, "Neo-Modernism," 11–12, 27–28; Kersten, *Cosmopolitans and Heretics*, 64–65.
21. Wahib, *Pergolakan*, 164–65; Barton, "Neo-Modernism," 27–28.
22. Hadi and Mudjimanto, "Biografi Kafrawi Ridwan," 41.
23. Zain Uchrowi and Ahmadi Thaha, "Menyeru Pemikiran Rasional Muʿtazilah" in *Refleksi Pembaharuan Pemikiran Islam*, 39.
24. Kull, *Piety and Politics*, 37–53.
25. Madjid, "Keharusan Pembaharuan," 5.
26. Madjid, 6.
27. Madjid, 6.
28. Madjid, 5–6. For more analysis of Madjid's argument about secularization and the resulting controversy, see Barton, "Neo-Modernism," 17–21; Hefner, *Civil Islam*, 116–19; Kull, *Piety and Politics*, 58–62; Feener, *Muslim Legal Thought*, 133–37; and Kersten, *Cosmopolitans*, 52–67.
29. Nurcholish Madjid, "Sekali Lagi tentang Sekularisasi," in Rasjidi, *Koreksi terhadap Drs. Nurcholish Madjid*, 36–8; Barton, "Neo-Modernism," 21–24.
30. Wahib, *Pergolakan*, 23; Barton, "Neo-Modernism," 34–37.
31. Wahib, *Pergolakan*, 162.
32. Muljanto Sumardi, "Pak Wi, Ada Saja Gagasannya," in Saridjo, *Jabatan untuk Umat*, 106–7; Munhanif, "Islam and the Struggle," 101–3. Interestingly, Munhanif gives Sumardi a larger role in the negotiations with Murtopo than did Sumardi, who emphasized Ridwan's leadership.
33. Munhanif, "Islam and the Struggle," 103–9; Ricklefs, *Islamisation*, 132–38. Ali also endured a major controversy over Indonesia's marriage law; see Azra, "Indonesian Marriage Law," 76–95.
34. Ali, *Agama dan Pembangunan di Indonesia*, 1:15.
35. Ali, 1:1–20.
36. Ali, 4:137–44; Ali, 5:64–67.
37. Achmad Syahid and Abas Al-Jauhari, "Pengantar Editor," in Syahid and Al-Jauhari, *Bahasa, Pendidikan, dan Agama*, ix–xxiv.
38. Ali uses the English "creative minority" in an otherwise Indonesian text. Italics and quotation marks are original. Ali, *Agama dan Pembangunan di Indonesia*, 1:59.
39. Ali, 4:19–25.
40. Ali, 2:15–24.
41. Ali, 2:25–27.

42. For other discussions of IAIN reform under Mukti Ali, see Saeed, "Towards Religious Tolerance," 183–86; Azyumardi Azra, Dina Afrianty, and Robert Hefner, "Pesantren and Madrasa: Muslim Schools and National Ideals in Indonesia," in Hefner and Zaman, *Schooling Islam*, 185–91; Kersten, *Cosmopolitans*, 64–65; and Lukens-Bull, *Islamic Higher Education*, 46–7.

43. *Sewindu Institut Agama Islam Negeri*, 25–39.

44. Husni Rahim, "Penerobos Kejenuhan IAIN," in Syahid and Al-Jauhari *Bahasa, Pendidikan, dan Agama*, 3.

45. Rahim, "Penerobos Kejenuhan IAIN," 3–4.

46. "Laporan Singkat Pelaksanaan Tugas Departemen Agama RI," October 1973, folder 645, series 40.a, ANRI.

47. "Laporan Singkat Pelaksanaan Tugas Departemen Agama RI," August 1974, folder 645, series 40.a, ANRI. IAIN Sunan Gunung Jati in Bandung did not manage to eliminate two of its branch campuses, specifically the Shari'a Faculty in Serang and the Education Faculty in Cirebon. Rahim, "Penerobos Kejenuhan IAIN," 4.

48. Internal Report on Ministry of Religion Grant for $16,700, undated, grant number 07450678, reel 3087, Ford Foundation Archives, RAC.

49. Wilfred Cantwell Smith, "Recommendation to Canadian International Development Agency," grant number 07450678, reel 3087, Ford Foundation Archives, RAC.

50. Smith, "Recommendation." CIDA did not fund the project because, in Smith's assessment, it did not see religion as an integral aspect of economic development. Smith letter to Rosser, dated Oct. 26, 1973, grant number 07450678, reel 3087, Ford Foundation Archives, RAC.

51. These nine scholar-bureaucrats were A. Hafidz Dasuki (1974), Zaini Muchtarom (1975), Murni Djamal (1975), Muhammad Idris (1975), Nourouzzaman Shiddiqi (1975), Bisri Affandi (1976), Saifuddin Anshari (1976), A. Farichin Chumaidy (1976), and Muhammad Asyari (1976). Jabali and Jamhari, *Modernization of Islam*, 21.

52. "IAIN Di Antara Ulama dan Sarjana," *Panji Masyarakat* 217 (February 15, 1977): 19.

53. Ali, *Agama dan Pembangunan di Indonesia*, 9:142–43; *Almanak Sewindu Litbang Agama*, 117–20.

54. Penelitian Agama Pamphlet, grant number 07450678, reel 3380, Ford Foundation Archives, RAC.

55. Badan Penelitian dan Pengembangan Agama, *Laporan Seminar Pengembangan Penelitian Agama*, 1–2.

56. Sumardi also supported scholarly conversations about the nature of religious research with publications such as Sumardi, *Penelitian Agama*.

57. Muljanto Sumardi, "Documentation Center on Islamic Education in Indonesia: An Abstract of a Project Proposal," grant number 07450678, reel 5080, Ford Foundation Archives, RAC.

58. Sumardi, "Documentation Center."

59. Sumardi, *Sedjarah Singkat Pendidikan Islam di Indonesia*, 99–111.

60. In August 1973 alone, the Ministry reported that thirty-five Indonesian students had departed for religious study in Egypt, Saudi Arabia, and Syria. "Laporan Singkat Pelaksanaan Tugas Departemen Agama RI," August 1973, folder 645, series 40.a, ANRI.

61. Muhbib Abdul Wahab, "Prof. Dr. Bustami A. Gani," and Yusuf Rahman, "Prof. H.M. Toha Yahya Omar, MA," in Yatim and Nasuhi, *Membangun Pusat Keunggulan*, 115–59.

62. Nasution served as Omar's assistant rector and helped to run the IAIN campus when Omar fell ill. Rahman, "Prof. H.M. Toha Yahya Omar," 148–49.

63. Nasution, *Akal dan Wahyu dalam Islam*; Nasution, *Islam Rasional*.

64. Nasution, *Islam Rasional*, 393.

65. Uchrowi and Thaha, *Refleksi Pembaharuan*, 43.

66. Nasution, *Islam Rasional*, 146.

67. Uchrowi and Thaha, *Refleksi Pembaharuan*, 45–49; Muzani, "Mu'tazilite Theology," 120–23; Porter, *Managing Politics*, 57–58.

68. Uchrowi and Thaha, *Refleksi Pembaharuan*, 48–49.

69. For other analyses of Nasution's reforms, see Muzani, "Mu'tazilite Theology," 101–6; Lukens-Bull, *Islamic Higher Education*, 47–49.

70. The meeting lasted for a week in late August 1973, and in addition to curricular matters, the rectors also discussed the ongoing rationalization plan. "Laporan Singkat Pelaksanaan Tugas Departemen Agama RI," August 1973, folder 645, series 40.a, ANRI; "Dr. Harun Nasution tentang: Pelaksanaan Rasionalisasi di IAIN Jakarta," *Panji Masyarakat* 146 (March 1, 1974): 27.

71. Uchrowi and Thaha, *Refleksi Pembaharuan*, 41; Porter, *Managing Politics*, 56.

72. Nasution, *Islam Ditinjau*, 1:4–5.

73. The second chapter of the book is titled "Islam Dalam Pengertian yang Sebenarnya," which translates into English as "Islam in Its Genuine Understanding." Nasution, *Islam Ditinjau*, 1:24.

74. Nasution, 2:38–42.

75. Nasution, 2:43.

76. Nasution, 2:43.

77. Nasution, 1:92–96.

78. Nasution, 1:96–105.

79. Nasution, 1:101.

80. Nasution, 1:97.

81. Nasution, 2:44–45.

82. Sumardi, "Documentation Center;" Peter D. Weldon Memo to Reuben Frodin, "Islamic Research," dated January 7, 1974, grant number 07450678, reel 5080, Ford Foundation Archives, RAC.

83. Weldon Memo to Frodin, dated January 7, 1974.

84. "IAIN Di Antara Ulama dan Sarjana," *Panji Masyarakat* 217 (February 15, 1977): 19.

85. Komaruddin Hidayat, "Sebagai Guru Sekaligus Orang Tua," in *Refleksi Pembaharuan Pemikiran Islam*, 291–98.
86. Hidayat, 292–93.
87. Hidayat, 292–93.
88. Hefner, *Civil Islam*, 107.
89. Feener, *Muslim Legal Thought*, 111–14.
90. Hasan, *Laskar Jihad*, 39.
91. Rasjidi, *Islam Menetang Komunisme*; Rasjidi, *Islam dan Socialisme*; Rasjidi, *Mengapa Aku Tetap Memeluk Agama Islam*; Rasjidi, *Empat Kuliah Agama Islam Pada Perguruan Tinggi*.
92. Rasjidi, *Koreksi Terhadap Drs. Nurcholish Madjid*, 14–18.
93. Rasjidi, 12–27.
94. Rasjidi, 58–59.
95. Rasjidi, *Koreksi Terhadap Dr. Harun Nasution*, 13–4. For other discussions of Rasjidi's criticisms of Nasution, see Muzani, "Muʿtazilite Theology," 106–15; Saleh, *Modern Trends*, 201–3; and Kersten, *Cosmopolitans*, 67.
96. Rasjidi, *Koreksi Terhadap Dr. Harun Nasution*, 32–35.
97. Rasjidi, 44–50.
98. Rasjidi, 15.
99. Rasjidi, 16.
100. Rasjidi, 53.
101. Rasjidi, 104–12.
102. Rasjidi, 108.
103. Rasjidi, 56–57.
104. Rasjidi, 61–71.
105. Rasjidi, 61.
106. Rasjidi, 150.
107. Rasjidi, 25–26.
108. Rasjidi, 12.
109. Rasjidi, "Antara Saya dan Harun Nasution," in *Refleksi Pembaharuan Pemikiran Islam*, 269.
110. Rasjidi, 269.
111. Sidney Jones, "Memo: Meeting with Minister Alamsyah of Department Agama, dated March 1, 1979, Grant 770–0499, reel 5004, Ford Foundation Archives, RAC.

CHAPTER 4

1. Leonard Binder and Fazlur Rahman, "Report on Feasibility Investigation with regard to the University of Chicago Grant Proposal on Islam and Social Change," dated February 6, 1973, grant number 07400141, reel 3087, Ford Foundation Archives, RAC.
2. Sidney Jones, "Evaluation of Grant #740–0141 to the University of Chicago for Project on Islam and Social Change," dated April 12, 1983, grant number 07400141, reel 3087, Ford Foundation Archives, RAC.

3. Leonard Binder Letter to Reuben Frodin, dated July 3, 1974, grant number 07400141, reel 3087, Ford Foundation Archives, RAC.
4. Lockman, *Contending Visions*, 121–47; Lockman, *Fieldnotes*, 72–159.
5. Lockman, *Contending Visions*, 134.
6. Lockman, 134.
7. As quoted in Gilman, *Mandarins*, 8.
8. Gilman, 56–62.
9. Gilman, 77–79.
10. Gilman, 59.
11. Geertz, *Peddlers and Princes*.
12. In addition to Lockman and Gilman, see Gendzier, *Managing Political Change*; Eckbladh, *Great American Mission*; and Latham, *Right Kind of Revolution*.
13. Rostow, *Stages of Economic Growth*.
14. Simpson, *Economists with Guns*.
15. As quoted in Gilman, *Mandarins*, 2.
16. Gilman, 61.
17. Lerner, *Passing of Traditional Society*, 45–47.
18. Lerner, 43–75.
19. Lerner, 349, 405–10.
20. Lerner, 43.
21. Halpern, *Politics of Social Change*, 35.
22. Lerner, *Passing*, 43–5; Halpern, *Politics of Social Change*, 30–5; Safran, *Egypt*, 245–54.
23. Lerner, *Passing*, 407.
24. Geertz, *Islam Observed*, 69.
25. Geertz, 74.
26. Mitchell, "Middle East," 88–89.
27. Binder, *Religion and Politics in Pakistan*.
28. Binder, "Islamic Tradition and Politics," 256.
29. Almond diagnosed traditional societies as suffering from "mixed political cultures, in which a 'Western system' with its various imported structural elements coexisted uneasily with the 'pre-Western' or 'traditional' elements." He contended that this collision of political cultures shattered the stability of tradition and instead produced new anxieties and feelings of rootlessness. Almond, "Comparative Political Systems," 391–409.
30. Binder, *Iran*, 60–89.
31. Binder, 346–50.
32. Binder, *Ideological Revolution*.
33. For more on Rahman's experiences in Pakistan, see Abbas, "Between Western Academia and Pakistan," 748–59; Zaman, *Islam in Pakistan*, 66–74.
34. Leonard Binder, personal interview, August 28, 2012.
35. Rahman, "Islamic Modernism," 327–32.
36. Leonard Binder and Fazlur Rahman, "Islam and Social Change: A Research Proposal," undated, grant number 07400141, reel 3087, Ford Foundation Archives, RAC.

37. Binder and Rahman, "Research Proposal."
38. Binder and Rahman, "Research Proposal."
39. Italics added by author. Binder and Rahman, "Research Proposal."
40. Binder and Rahman, "Research Proposal."
41. Narrative Report for Project Year 1974, undated, grant number 07400141, reel 3087, Ford Foundation Archives, RAC.
42. Courtney Nelson memo to Wayne Fredericks, dated February 16, 1973, grant number 07400141, reel 3087, Ford Foundation Archives, RAC.
43. Robert Edwards memo to David Smock, dated March 5, 1974, grant number 07400141, reel 3087, Ford Foundation Archives, RAC.
44. Frank Miller letter to John Bresnan, dated August 9, 1974, grant number 07400141, reel 3087, Ford Foundation Archives, RAC.
45. Peter Weldon letter to Leonard Binder, dated April 15, 1975, grant number 07400141, reel 3087, Ford Foundation Archives, RAC.
46. Leonard Binder and Fazlur Rahman, "Islam and Social Change Project: An Interim Report," dated September 6, 1977, grant number 07400141, reel 3087, Ford Foundation Archives, RAC.
47. Binder and Rahman, "Interim Report" (1977).
48. In addition to the project codirectors, team members and associates included Mumtaz Ahmad, Shahrough Akhavi, Bahattin Aksit, Asim al-Dassoqui, Huseyin Atay, Robert Bianchi, Donna Lee Bowen, Edward Danforth, Evelyn Early, Chris Eccel, Michael Fischer, Jerrold Green, Marcia Hermanson, Stephen Humphreys, Nasim Ahmad Jawed, Dwight King, Henry Munson, Jr, and, of course, the two Indonesians: Nurcholish Madjid and M. Amien Rais. For details, see Leonard Binder and Fazlur Rahman, "Islam and Social Change: Final Report," dated January 7, 1980, grant number 07400141, reel 3087, Ford Foundation Archives, RAC.
49. Leonard Binder and Fazlur Rahman, "Islam and Social Change: Interim Report," dated June 1976, grant number 07400141, reel 3087, Ford Foundation Archives, RAC.
50. Binder and Rahman, "Final Report."
51. Binder and Rahman, "Final Report."
52. Binder and Rahman, "Final Report."
53. Binder and Rahman, "Final Report."
54. Rahman, *Islam and Modernity*, 89.
55. Rahman, 110–18.
56. Rahman, 5.
57. Rahman, 6.
58. Rahman, 7.
59. Rahman, 141.
60. Rahman, 4, 151.
61. Binder, *Islamic Liberalism*, 5.
62. Binder, 19.
63. Binder, 2.

64. Binder, 170–205.
65. Binder, 205.
66. Binder, 294.
67. Binder, 20.
68. Binder, 9.
69. Denny, "Review of *Major Themes of the Qur'an*," 62–63; Gaffney, "Review of *Major Themes of the Qur'an*," 88–90; Graham, "Review of *Major Themes of the Qur'an*," 445–47; Lewis, "Revolt of Islam," 35–38. Many of these reviewers were Wilfred Cantwell Smith's or even Rahman's own students.
70. Bulliet, *Under Siege*; Esposito and Voll, *Islam and Democracy*.
71. Eickelman, "Inside the Islamic Reformation," 80–89; Wright, "Iranian Luther."
72. Rahman, *Islam and Modernity*, 124.
73. Daud, *Rihlah Ilmiah*, 70, 86.
74. Daud, *Rihlah Ilmiah*, 76.
75. At the time, the population of Muslim university students was growing not only at Chicago but across the United States. By 1965 the number of foreign students studying at American universities from Muslim-majority countries had reached thirteen thousand, a fivefold increase over the number two decades before. Some of these Muslim students were politically active. For example, Muslim student-activists at the University of Illinois, Urbana-Champaign founded the first chapter of the Muslim Student Association (MSA) in 1963. Kambiz GhaneaBassiri, *History of Islam in America*, 264–65.
76. Greg Barton is certainly correct to note that Rahman was "not the originator" of Madjid's modernism; see Greg Barton, "International Context," 81.
77. Gaus, *Api Islam Nurcholish Madjid*, 142–47.
78. Kersten, *Cosmopolitans*, 69–84, 95–100.
79. Madjid, "Issue of Modernization," 383. Barton persuasively suggests that Madjid wrote the paper after reading Muhammad Kamal Hassan's critical account of the Indonesian renewalist movement. Barton, "Neo-Modernism," 10–11, 66.
80. Madjid and Roem, *Tidak Ada Negara Islam*, 54.
81. Madjid, "Fazlur Rahman," x.
82. Madjid, "Ibn Taymiyya," 218–26.
83. Madjid, 226–9.
84. Kersten, *Cosmopolitans*, 76.
85. Madjid, "Ibn Taymiyya," 232–33.
86. Madjid, 233.
87. Madjid, *Khazanah Intelektual Islam*, 3–70; Kull, *Piety and Politics*, 113–4.
88. Madjid, *Khazanah*, 4.
89. Madjid, 34.
90. Madjid, 67.
91. Rahman "Social Change and Early Sunnah," 205–26; Rahman, *Islam and Modernity*, 23–25.
92. Rais, *Inilah Jalan Hidup Saya*, v–vii.

93. Rais, 26–27.
94. Rais, 30.
95. Assyaukanie, *Islam and the Secular State*, 113. Nurcholish Madjid also emphasized Rais's early support for an Islamic State in his letters to Mohammad Roem from 1983. Madjid and Roem, *Tidak Ada Negara Islam*, 17–18.
96. Rais, *Inilah Jalan Hidup Saya*, 38–42.
97. Binder and Rahman, "Interim Report" (1977).
98. Leonard Binder, personal interview, August 28, 2012.
99. M. Amien Rais, "Runtuhnya Sendi-Sendi Orientalisme," in *Cakrawala Islam*, 234. Rais's views on Orientalism and postcolonial theory are discussed in detail in chapter 5.
100. Daud, *Rihlah Ilmiah*, 86–88.
101. Italics in the original. Rais, *Inilah Jalan Hidup Saya*, 48–49.
102. Rais, 45–49.
103. Rais, "Muslim Brotherhood in Egypt," 1–8.
104. Rais, 17.
105. Rais, 27.
106. Rais, 143–44.
107. Rais, 144.
108. Rais, 147.
109. Rais, 145.
110. Rais, 148.
111. Ismail, "Islam, Politics, and Ideology"; Ramage, *Politics in Indonesia*, 35–39; Ricklefs, *Islamisation*, 221–25.
112. Amien Rais, "Tidak Ada Negara Islam," *Panji Masyarakat* 376 (November 1, 1982): 17–18. Rais expanded on his views on the Islamic state in other contemporaneous writings. Amien Rais, "Indonesia dan Demokrasi," in Carvallo and Dasrizal, *Aspirasi Umat Islam Indonesia*, 65–78; Rais, *Cakrawala Islam*, 36–49.
113. Assyaukanie, *Islam and the Secular State*, 112–13.
114. Agus Fadjar, "Amien Rais dan Negara Islam," *Panji Masyarakat* 379 (December 1, 1982): 5.
115. Mohamad Roem, "Tidak ada Negara Islam," *Panji Masyarakat* 386 (February 11, 1983): 30.
116. Roem, "Tidak ada Negara Islam," 30–32.
117. Ismail, "Islam, Politics, and Ideology," 259.
118. Madjid and Roem, *Tidak Ada Negara Islam*, 12–43.
119. Maarif, *Otobiografi Ahmad Syafii Maarif*, 88–89.
120. Maarif, 103–89.
121. Maarif, 192.
122. Maarif, 196–203.
123. Maarif, 209.
124. Maarif, 210–15.

125. Maarif, 139.

126. For more analysis of Maarif's "conversion" at Chicago, see Burhani, "Transmission of Islamic Reform," 29–47.

127. Maarif, *Otobiografi Ahmad Syafii Maarif*, 224.

128. Maarif, 227–8.

129. Rahman, *Islam and Modernity*, 141. See also Fazlur Rahman, "Approaches to Islam in Religious Studies: Review Essay," in *Approaches to Islam in Religious Studies*, ed. Richard C. Martin (Oxford: Oneworld Publications, 1985), 195–97.

130. Maarif, "Islam as the Basis of State," 116.

131. Maarif, 132.

132. Maarif, 26–27.

133. Maarif, 307.

134. Maarif, 310.

135. Maarif, 12.

136. Ahmad Syafii Maarif, "Islam, Politik, dan Demokrasi di Indonesia," in Carvallo and Dasrizal, *Aspirasi Umat Islam Indonesia*, 37–64; Maarif, *Al-Qur'an, Realitas Sosial, dan Limbo Sejarah: Sebuah Refleksi* (Bandung: Pustaka, 1985).

137. Maarif, *Islam dan Masalah Kenegaraan*.

138. Bahtiar Effendy, Hendro Prasetyo, and Arief Subhan, "Munawir Sjadzali, MA: Pencairan Ketegangan Ideologis," in Azra and Umam, *Menteri-Menteri Agama RI*, 367–412; Feener, *Muslim Legal Thought*, 137–46.

139. Sjadzali, *Pendidikan Agama*, 17–25.

140. Sjadzali, 64.

141. Fazlur Rahman letter to Mochtar Bukhari, dated June 15, 1985, grant 855-0866A, reel 4344, Ford Foundation Archives, RAC.

142. Fazlur Rahman, "Recommendations for the Improvement of IAIN Curriculum and Method of Instruction," dated August 23, 1985, grant 855-0866A, reel 4344, Ford Foundation Archives, RAC.

143. Rahman, "Recommendations"; Feener, *Muslim Legal Thought*, 138–9.

144. Rahman, "Recommendations."

145. Rahman, "Recommendations."

146. Mudzhar, *Belajar Islam di Amerika*, 8.

147. *Across the Archipelago*, 44.

148. Kartanegara, *Seni Mengukir Kata*, 241.

149. Syamsuddin, "Religion and Politics in Islam," v.

150. "Seminar Pikiran-Pikiran Fazlur Rahman" (unpublished conference papers, Jakarta, 1988).

151. Kersten, "Bourgeois Islam and Muslims," 168–80.

152. The creation of INIS formalized a series of exchanges that had occurred between 1969 and 1984. During those fifteen years, three separate groups of IAIN lecturers had received short-term scholarships for language training and research at Leiden University. "History of the Cooperation between Indonesia and the Netherlands," 5–9.

153. Donald Little, Margaret Gillet, and Rebecca Aiken, "IAIN Institutional Development Project Feasibility/Design Mission Report," dated February 1988, folder 2659, box 159, records group 84, McGill University Archives.

154. Munawir Sjadzali letter to Vice President Sudharmono, "Laporan Program Tugas Belajar ke Luar Negeri," dated August 23, 1989, folder 20, series Departemen Agama II, ANRI.

155. "IAIN Institutional Development Project Feasibility/Design Mission Report," folder 2659, box 159, records group 84, McGill University Archives.

156. *Research on the Role of the McGill University Islamic Studies Alumni*, 3.

157. A. Uner Turgay, Institute of Islamic Studies Annual Report 1992–93, dated June 30, 1993, folder 15318, box 912, records group 3, McGill University Archives.

158. Maarif, Otobiografi, 266–68.

CHAPTER 5

1. Rais, *Cakrawala Islam*, 234.
2. Rais, 239.
3. Rais, 240–42.
4. Said, *Orientalism*, 323–24.
5. Ricklefs, *Islamisation*, 208.
6. Hefner, "Islam, State, and Civil Society," 1–35; Ricklefs, *Islamisation*, 206–21; Latif, *Indonesian Muslim Intelligentsia*, 419–25.
7. Ricklefs, *Islamisation*, 206–11.
8. Latif, *Indonesian Muslim Intelligentsia*, 421–22.
9. Rais, *Cakrawala Islam*, 175–233.
10. M. Amien Rais, "Muhammadiyah dan Pembaharuan," in *Pendidikan Muhammadiyah*, 68.
11. Rais, *Inilah Jalan Hidup Saya*, 100.
12. Rais, 105–6.
13. "Muhammadiyah Politik Berpayung Amal Saleh," *Jurnal Ulumul Qur'an* 6, no. 2 (1995): 36–37.
14. "Muhammadiyah Politik Berpayung," 36–83.
15. M. Amien Rais, "Kata Pengantar," viii-x.
16. Burhani, "Transmission of Islamic Reform," 29–47.
17. Jurdi, *Satu Abad Muhammadiyah: Gagasan Pembaruan Sosial Keagamaan*, 290.
18. "Muhammadiyah Politik Berpayung," 37.
19. Ricklefs, *Islamisation*, 361–68; Kersten, *Islam in Indonesia*, 71–72.
20. Gaus, *Api Islam Nurcholish Madjid*, 149–50.
21. Madjid, *Islam, Kemodernan, dan Keindonesiaan*; Kersten, *Cosmopolitans*, 78–84.
22. Gaus, *Api Islam Nurcholish Madjid*, 157–58.
23. Sjadzali, "Reaktualisasi Ajaran Islam," 1–11; Feener, *Muslim Legal Thought*, 137–46.

24. Gaus, *Api Islam Madjid*, 181–82.
25. Kull, *Piety and Politics*, 210–12; Kersten, *Islam in Indonesia*, 52–57.
26. Dwifatma, *Cerita Azra*, 8–67.
27. Latif, *Indonesian Muslim Intelligentsia*, 432.
28. Latif, 433–44.
29. Ramage, *Politics in Indonesia*, 75.
30. Hefner, "Islam, State, and Civil Society," 1–35; Liddle, "Islamic Turn in Indonesia," 613–34; Ramage, *Politics in Indonesia*, 75–121; Porter, *Managing Politics*, 87–129; Latif, *Indonesian Muslim Intelligentsia*, 416–65.
31. Porter, *Managing Politics*, 91–92.
32. Latif, *Indonesian Muslim Intelligentsia*, 438–40.
33. Mudzhar, *Belajar Islam di Amerika*; Asmin, *Pengalaman Belajar Islam di Kanada*.
34. Faisal Ismail, "Studi Islam di Barat: Fenomena Menarik," in Asmin, *Pengalaman Belajar Islam di Kanada*, 40–42.
35. Azra, "Studi Islam di Timur," 8–9.
36. Fuad Jabali, "Mengapa ke Barat?," in Asmin, *Pengalaman Belajar Islam di Kanada*, 25.
37. Rais, *Cakrawala Islam*, 69–70.
38. Ali and Effendy, *Merambah Jalan Baru Islam*, 258–62.
39. Rais, *Cakrawala Islam*, 36.
40. Rais, 37.
41. Rais, 75.
42. Rais, 77–78.
43. Rais, 86.
44. Rais seems to have borrowed from Ali Shariati's writings on tawhid to develop his conception of "social monotheism."
45. Saleh, *Modern Trends*, 177.
46. Rais, *Cakrawala Islam*, 45–49.
47. Rais, "Kata Pengantar," ix.
48. In one of his few explicit nods to Rahman, Rais praised the elder scholar's position on zakat. Rais, "Muslim Brotherhood in Egypt," 146–48.
49. Rais, *Tauhid Sosial*, 126–36.
50. Barton, "International Context," 77–79; Kull, *Piety and Politics*, 135, 162; Saleh, *Modern Trends*, 256–57; Van Bruinessen, "Liberal and Progressive Voices," 192–5.
51. Kersten, *Cosmopolitans*, 72–84.
52. Nurcholish Madjid, "Beberapa Renungan Kehidupan Keagamaan untuk Generasi Mendatang," in Effendy, *Dekonstruksi Islam: Mazhab Ciputat*, 18–27.
53. For his engagement with Bellah's work, see Madjid, *Islam*, xl, lxxiv; Madjid, *Islam, Kemodernan, dan Keindonesiaan*, 62–74. For Bellah's essay and note about his brief foray into Islamic studies, see Bellah, *Beyond Belief*, 146–67.
54. Nurcholish Madjid, "Ibn Taymiyya," 58.
55. Madjid, *Pintu-Pintu*, 46–7.

56. Madjid, *Pintu-Pintu*, 8.
57. Kull, *Piety and Politics*, 48.
58. Madjid, "Islamic Roots," 70.
59. Madjid, *Islam*, 468–91.
60. Smith, *Meaning and End*, 80–118.
61. Madjid, *Islam*, 436.
62. Madjid, 428.
63. Madjid, "Beberapa Renungan," 34.
64. Madjid, 34.
65. Madjid, 40–44.
66. This phrase is a reference to the title of Madjid's 1994 edited collection, *Pintu-Pintu Menuju Tuhan*.
67. For one example, see Madjid, "Islamic Roots," 67–8.
68. Kull, *Piety and Politics*, 227–40.
69. *Jurnal Ulumul Qur'an* 5, no. 1 (1994).
70. Feener, *Muslim Legal Thought*, xvii.
71. There is very little scholarship on Abdullah's career. One notable exception is Carool Kersten, who has analyzed Abdullah's more recent (i.e., post-1998) writings and institutional leadership at IAIN Yogyakarta. Kersten, *Islam in Indonesia*, 264–75.
72. Abdullah, *Studi Agama*, 202–5.
73. Abdullah, 206–8.
74. Abdullah, *Falsafah Kalam*, 79–80.
75. Abdullah, 82.
76. Abdullah, 84–88; Abdullah, *Studi Agama*, 101–4, 121–37.
77. On this point, Abdullah reconfirmed the eternal and universal nature of the Qur'an but insisted that Islamic theology and other interpretative disciplines were decidedly human activities. Abdullah, *Studi Agama*, 124–25.
78. Abdullah, 124–28.
79. Abdullah, 131–32.
80. Abdullah, 108–17.
81. Abdullah, *Falsafah Kalam*, 106–9.
82. Abdullah, 109–13.
83. Azyumardi Azra, "Pasca-Modernisme, Islam, dan Politik: Kecenderungan dan Relevansi," *Jurnal Ulumul Qur'an* 5, no. 1 (1994): 6–7.
84. Liddle, "*Media Dakwah* Scripturalism," 324.
85. Liddle, 329–32.
86. Liddle, 329.
87. Liddle, 332.
88. Bernhard Platzdasche convincingly argues that "liberal bias" against Islamists is endemic in scholarship on Indonesian Islam. Platzdasche, *Islamism in Indonesia*, 2–6.
89. "R. William Liddle Profile."

90. Lukman Hakiem, "William Liddle Mau Mengulang Sejarah Lama Memecah Belah Umat," *Media Dakwah* (August 1993): 41. Walking back the statement, Rais later claimed that he had been misquoted and that he had actually called Liddle a "rotten American." Barton, "Islam and Politics," 37–38.

91. Burhanuddin, "Conspiracy of Jews," 53–76; Reid, "Entrepreneurial Minorities," 63–4; Siegel, *Objects and Objections*, 42–75.

92. Brown, *Regulating Aversion*, 187–88.

93. Rasyid, *"Pembaruan" Islam*, 14.

94. Rasyid, 109–10.

95. Liddle suggested that *Media Dakwah* retained ambitions to establish an Islamic state in Indonesia but worked to disguise those sentiments with subtle language and comparisons to other countries, such as Malaysia. Liddle, "*Media Dakwah* Scripturalism," 332–35.

96. Lukman Hakiem, "William Liddle Menghasut!," *Media Dakwah* (August 1993): 46.

97. Lukman Hakiem, "Nabi Gagal Menjalankan Missinya?," *Media Dakwah* (December 1992): 41.

98. Noni Halimi, "Menolak Studi Amerika Menengok ke Timur dan Islam," *Media Dakwah* (October 1992): 12.

99. Halimi, "Menolak Studi Amerika," 12.

100. Rasyid, *"Pembaruan" Islam*, 99–106.

101. Stiglitz, *Globalization and Its Discontents*, 112.

102. Hefner, *Civil Islam*, 199.

103. Kull, *Piety and Politics*, 82–83.

104. Hefner, *Civil Islam*, 207–8; Latif, *Indonesian Muslim Intelligentsia*, 449–50.

105. Kull, *Piety and Politics*, 87–8.

106. For major developments in Indonesian Islamic thought, especially in IAIN circles, after the fall of Suharto, see Lukens-Bull, *Islamic Higher Education*; Kersten, *Islam in Indonesia*; and Van Bruinessen, *Contemporary Developments*.

CONCLUSION

1. These questions overlap with those posed by Laurie Patton, and yet, as Patton herself suggests, I have also modified them to fit the particular contexts of twentieth- and twenty-first-century Islamic studies. Patton, *Who Owns Religion?*, 250–63.

2. Hughes, *Theorizing Islam*, 3.

3. Hughes, 10–31.

4. Hughes, 78.

5. Hughes, 128.

6. Hughes, 5.

7. Hughes does discuss the influx of social scientists into Middle Eastern Area Studies in the wake of World War II. However, he focuses his critique on how Orientalists doubled down on religious essentialism to defend their territory as experts on Islam rather than examining the reformist ambitions and therefore "liberal

theologizing" of modernization theorists and other social scientists. Hughes, *Situating Islam*, 33–48.

8. Hughes, *Theorizing Islam*, 32–59.
9. Hughes, *Situating Islam*, 11, 28–29.
10. Hughes, *Theorizing Islam*, 129.
11. Hughes, *Islam*, 51–53.
12. Asad, *Formations of the Secular*, 25.
13. Hughes even cites Asad on the history of boundary-making between the religious and the secular to argue against religious essentialism but does not acknowledge how these theoretical insights—and the quoted Asad line that "it is this assumption that allows us to think of religion as 'infecting' the secular domain"—apply to his own work. Hughes, *Islam*, 51–52.
14. George Archer, "Review of *Islam and the Tyranny of Authenticity*."
15. McCutcheon, *Critics Not Caretakers*, 104.
16. McCutcheon, 104.
17. McCutcheon, 107.
18. For a similar point, see Arnal, "What If I Don't Want to Play Tennis?," 61–66.
19. Binder, *Islamic Liberalism*, 122.
20. Binder, 127.
21. Binder, 1.
22. Binder, 2.
23. Binder, 7.
24. Binder, 8–9.
25. Martin, "Uses and Abuses," 375.
26. Martin, 375.
27. Martin, 380.
28. Martin, 382.
29. Mark Woodward, "Introduction," 12–3.
30. Talal Asad, Saba Mahmood, and many of their postsecularist interlocutors follow the same general "radical introspective" principles as Hallaq does.
31. Hallaq, *Restating Orientalism*, 61.
32. Hallaq, 101.
33. Hallaq, 112–37.
34. Hallaq, 215.
35. Hallaq, 24.
36. Hallaq, 102–4.
37. Hallaq, 164, 174.
38. Hallaq, 246.
39. Italics removed from original for the sake of clarity. Hallaq, "On Orientalism," 439.
40. Hallaq, *Restating Orientalism*, 246.
41. Hallaq, 244.
42. Hallaq, 257.

43. Hallaq, "On Orientalism," 439.
44. Hallaq, *Impossible State*.
45. Hallaq, "On Orientalism," 439.
46. Hallaq, 439. See also Hallaq, *Restating Orientalism*, 257.
47. Hughes, *Situating Islam*, 1–32.
48. Martin, "Uses and Abuses," 373–77. Binder seems to diverge, at least partially, from Martin on this point because he eviscerates Crone and Cook's *Hagarism* (1977). Binder, *Islamic Liberalism*, 103–7.
49. Patton arrives at a similar stance as Martin's regarding the value of academic freedom and the need for scholars to prepare for resistance from the objects of their research. Patton, *Who Owns Religion?*, 250–63.
50. Hallaq, *Restating Orientalism*, 265. I suspect that Hallaq would reverse McCutcheon's and Hughes's distinction between critics and caretakers by arguing that so-called critical historians merely serve as caretakers of secular empire.

BIBLIOGRAPHY

ARCHIVES

Indonesian National Archives (Arsip Nasional Republik Indonesia [ANRI]), Jakarta, Indonesia
    Abdul Gani Personal Collection
    Departemen Agama I and II Collections
    Sekretariat Negara RI Yogyakarta Collection
McGill University Archives, McLennan Library, Montreal, Canada
    Faculty of Graduate Studies and Research
    Institute of Islamic Studies
    Office of the Principal and Vice-Chancellor Records
Princeton University Archives, Seeley G. Mudd Library, Princeton, New Jersey
    Department of Oriental Studies Records
Rockefeller Archive Center, Sleepy Hollow, New York
    Ford Foundation Collection
    Rockefeller Foundation Collection

INTERVIEWS AND CORRESPONDENCE

Leonard Binder, personal interview at UCLA, August 28, 2012.
Phillip Buckley, personal interview at McGill University, March 19, 2012.
Bahtiar Effendy, personal interview at IAIN Jakarta, June 26, 2013.
Howard Federspiel, personal interview at AAS Conference in Toronto, March 17, 2012.
Stephen Humphreys, personal interview at UC Santa Barbara, August 30, 2012.
Fuad Jabali, personal interview at IAIN Jakarta, June 25, 2013.
Paul Walker, personal interview at the University of Chicago, November 15, 2012.
John A. Williams, personal correspondence via email, June 22, 2012.
John Woods, personal interview at the University of Chicago, November 16, 2012.

PERIODICALS

Al-Djamiah
Gema Islam
Media Dakwah
Panji Masyarakat
Jurnal Ulumul Qur'an

PUBLISHED SOURCES

Abbas, Megan Brankley. "Battling over the Bureaucracy: The 10 October Incident and Intra-Muslim Conflict under Sukarno's Guided Democracy." *Indonesia and the Malay World* 43, no. 126 (2015): 207–25.

———. "Between Western Academia and Pakistan: Fazlur Rahman and the Fight for Fusionism." *Modern Asian Studies* 51, no. 3 (May 2017): 736–68.

Abdullah, Amin. *Falsafah Kalam di Era Post-Modernisme*. Yogyakarta: Pustaka Pelajar, 1995.

———. *Studi Agama Normativitas atau Historistas?* Yogyakarta: Pustaka Pelajar, 1996.

Abdullah, Taufik. *Schools and Politics: The Kaum Muda Movement in West Sumatra, 1927–1933*. Classic Edition. Jakarta: Equinox, 2009.

Abdurrahman, Burhanuddin Daya, and Djam'annuri, eds. *Agama dan Masyarakat: 70 Tahun H.A. Mukti Ali*. Yogyakarta: IAIN Sunan Kalijaga Press, 1993.

Across the Archipelago, from Sea to Shining Sea: Commemorating the 60/20 Anniversary of Fulbright Indonesia and Aminef. Jakarta: American-Indonesian Exchange, 2012.

Adams, Charles J. "The History of Religions and the Study of Islam." In *The History of Religions: Essays on the Problem of Understanding*, edited by Joseph M. Kitagawa, 177–94. Chicago: University of Chicago Press, 1967.

Ahmad, Aziz. *Islamic Modernism in India and Pakistan, 1857–1964*. London: Oxford University Press, 1967.

Ahmad, Irfan. *Islamism and Democracy in India: The Transformation of Jamaat-e-Islami*. Princeton, NJ: Princeton University Press, 2009.

Ahmed, Shahab. *What Is Islam?: The Importance of Being Islamic*. Princeton, NJ: Princeton University Press, 2015.

Aitken, Ellen Bradshaw, and Arvind Sharma, eds. *The Legacy of Wilfred Cantwell Smith*. Albany: State University of New York Press, 2017.

Ali, Fachry, and Bahtiar Effendy. *Merambah Jalan Baru Islam: Rekonstruksi Pemikiran Islam Indonesia Masa Orde Baru*. Bandung: Mizan, 1986.

Ali, Muhamad. *Islam and Colonialism: Becoming Modern in Indonesia and Malaya*. Edinburgh: Edinburgh University Press, 2015.

Ali, A. Mukti. *Agama dan Pembangunan di Indonesia*. 9 vols. Jakarta: Departemen Agama Republik Indonesia, 1972–83.

———. *Ilmu Perbandingan Agama: Sebuah Pembahasaan tentang Methodos dan Sistima*. Yogyakarta: P. T. al-Falah, 1965.

Almanak Sewindu Litbang Agama. Jakarta: Departemen Agama, 1983.

Almond, Gabriel. "Comparative Political Systems." *The Journal of Politics* 18, no. 3 (August 1956): 391–409.

Ananda, Endang Basri, ed. *70 Tahun Prof. Dr. H. M. Rasjidi*. Jakarta: Harian Umum Pelita, 1985.

Archer, George. "Review of *Islam and the Tyranny of Authenticity* by Aaron W.

Hughes." *Reading Religion*, August 8, 2016. http://readingreligion.org/books/islam-and-tyranny-authenticity.

Arnal, William E. "What If I Don't Want to Play Tennis?: A Rejoinder to Russell McCutcheon on Postmodernism and Theory of Religion." *Studies in Religion* 27, no. 1 (1998): 61–66.

Asad, Talal. *The Idea of an Anthropology of Islam*. Washington, DC: Center for Contemporary Arab Studies Georgetown University, 1986.

Asmin, Yudian, ed. *Pengalaman Belajar Islam di Kanada*. Yogyakarta: Titian Ilahi Press, 1997.

Assyaukanie, Lufti. *Islam and the Secular State in Indonesia*. Singapore: ISEAS, 2009.

Aydin, Cemil. *The Idea of the Muslim World: A Global Intellectual History*. Cambridge, MA: Harvard University Press, 2017.

Azra, Azyumardi. "The Indonesian Marriage Law of 1974: An Institutionalization of the Shariʿa for Social Changes." In *Shariʿa and Politics in Modern Indonesia*, edited by Azyumardi Azra and Arskal Salim, 76–95. Singapore: ISEAS, 2003.

———. "Studi Islam di Timur dan Barat: Pengalaman Selintas." *Jurnal Ulumul Qur'an* 5, no. 3 (1994): 4-11.

Azra, Azyumardi, and Saiful Umam, eds. *Menteri-Menteri Agama RI: Biografi Sosial-Politik*. Jakarta: Pusat Pengajian Islam dan Masyarakat PPIM, 1998.

Badan Penelitian dan Pengembangan Agama. *Laporan Seminar Pengembangan Penelitian Agama*. Jakarta: Departemen Agama RI, 1978.

Barton, Greg. "The International Context for the Emergence of Islamic Neo Modernism in Indonesia." In *Islam in the Indonesian Social Context*, edited by M. C. Ricklefs, 69–82. Clayton VIC, Australia: Centre for Southeast Asian Studies at Monash University, 1991.

———. "Islam and Politics in the New Indonesia." In *Islam in Asia: Changing Political Realities*, edited by Jason F. Isaacson and Colin Rubenstein, 1–90. New York: Routledge, 2002.

———. "Neo-Modernism: A Vital Synthesis of Traditionalist and Modernist Islamic Thought in Indonesia." *Studia Islamika* 2, no. 3 (1995): 1–76.

Bellah, Robert N. *Beyond Belief: Essays on Religion in a Post-traditionalist World*. Berkeley: University of California Press, 1970.

Benda, Harry J. *The Crescent and the Rising Sun: Indonesian Islam under the Japanese Occupation 1942-1945*. The Hague: W. van Hoeve, 1958.

Berman, Edward H. *The Influence of the Carnegie, Ford, and Rockefeller Foundations on American Foreign Policy: The Ideology of Philanthropy*. Albany: State University of New York Press, 1983.

Binder, Leonard. *The Ideological Revolution in the Middle East*. New York: John Wiley & Sons, 1964.

———. *Iran: Political Development in a Changing Society*. Berkeley: University of California Press, 1962.

———. *Islamic Liberalism: A Critique of Development Ideologies*. Chicago: The University of Chicago Press, 1988.

———. "Islamic Tradition and Politics: The Kijaji and the Alim." *Comparative Studies in Society and History* 2, no. 2 (January 1960): 250–56.

———. *Religion and Politics in Pakistan*. Berkeley: University of California Press, 1961.

Brown, Wendy. *Regulating Aversion: Tolerance in the Age of Identity and Empire*. Princeton, NJ: Princeton University Press, 2006.

Bulliet, Richard W., ed. *Under Siege: Islam and Democracy*. New York: Columbia University Press, 1993.

Burhani, Ahmad Najib. "Transmission of Islamic Reform from the United States to Indonesia." *Indonesia and the Malay World* 41, no. 119 (2013): 29–47.

Burhanuddin. "The Conspiracy of Jews: The Quest for Anti-Semitism in Media Dakwah." *Graduate Journal of Asia-Pacific Studies* 5, no. 2 (2007): 53–76.

Burton, John. "Review of *Islam* by Fazlur Rahman." *Bulletin of the School of Oriental and African Studies, University of London* 31, no. 2 (1968): 392–95.

Bush, Robin. *Nahdlatul Ulama and the Struggle for Power within Islam and Politics in Indonesia*. Singapore: ISEAS, 2009.

Carvallo, Bosco, and Dasrizal, eds. *Aspirasi Umat Islam Indonesia*. Jakarta: Lembaga Penunjang Pembangunan Nasional, 1983.

Clarke, Matthew, and Anna Halafoff. *Religion and Development in the Asia-Pacific: Sacred Places as Development Spaces*. New York: Routledge, 2017.

Cragg, Kenneth. *The Call of the Minaret*. Oxford: Oxford University Press, 1959.

Crone, Patricia, and Michael Cook. *Hagarism: The Making of the Islamic World*. Cambridge: Cambridge University Press, 1977.

Damami, Mohammad, ed. *Lima Tokoh Pengembangan IAIN Sunan Kalijaga Yogyakarta*. Yogyakarta: Pusat Penelitian IAIN Sunan Kalijaga, 1998.

Datla, Kavita. *The Language of Secular Islam: Urdu Nationalism and Colonial India*. Honolulu: University of Hawai'i Press, 2013.

Daud, Wan Mohd Nor Wan. *Rihlah Ilmiah Wan Mohd Nor Wan Daud: Dari Neo-Modernisme ke Islamisasi Ilmu*. Jakarta: CASIS and INSISTS, 2012.

Denny, Frederick. "Review of *Major Themes of the Qur'an* by Fazlur Rahman." *Middle Eastern Studies Association Bulletin* 15, no. 1 (July 1981): 62–63.

Dhofier, Zamakhsyari. *The Pesantren Tradition: The Role of the Kyai in the Maintenance of Traditional Islam in Java*. Tempe: Arizona State University Press, 1999.

Dwifatma, Andina. *Cerita Azra: Biografi Cendekiawan Muslim Azyumardi Azra*. Jakarta: Penerbit Erlangga, 2011.

Eckbladh, David. *The Great American Mission: Modernization and the Construction of an American World Order*. Princeton, NJ: Princeton University Press, 2011.

Effendy, Edy A., ed. *Dekonstruksi Islam: Mazhab Ciputat*. Bandung: Zaman Wacana Mulia, 1999.

Eickelman, Dale. "Inside the Islamic Reformation." *Wilson Quarterly* 22, no. 1 (Winter 1998): 80–89.

Esposito, John L., and John Voll. *Islam and Democracy*. Oxford: Oxford University Press, 1996.

Faruqi, Isma'il R. al-. *Christian Ethics: A Historical and Systematic Analysis of Its Dominant Ideals*. Montreal: McGill-Queens University Press, 1967.
———. *On Arabism: Urubah and Religion*. Amsterdam: Djambatan, 1962.
———. "The Structure of the Ethical Terms in the Koran by Toshihiko Izutsu." *Islamic Studies* 1, no. 2 (June 1962): 148–54.
Feener, R. Michael. "Constructions of Religious Authority in Indonesian Islamism: 'The Way and the Community' Re-imagined." In *Islamic Legitimacy in a Plural Asia*, edited by Anthony Reid and Michael Gilsenan, 139–53. New York: Routledge, 2007.
———. "Cross-cultural Contexts of Modern Muslim Intellectualism," *Die Welt des Islams* 47, no. 3 (2007): 264–82.
———. *Muslim Legal Thought in Modern Indonesia*. Cambridge: Cambridge University Press, 2007.
———. *Shariʿa and Social Engineering: The Implementation of Islamic Law in Contemporary Aceh, Indonesia*. Oxford: Oxford University Press, 2013.
Fountain, Philip, Robin Bush, and R. Michael Feener, eds. *Religion and the Politics of Development*. New York: Springer, 2015.
Gaffney, Patrick. "Review of *Major Themes of the Qur'an* by Fazlur Rahman and *Les Grandes Themes du Coran* by Jacques Jonnier." *The Journal of Religion* 62, no. 1 (January 1982): 88–90.
Gaus, Ahmad. *Api Islam Nurcholish Madjid: Jalan Hidup Seorang Visioner*. Jakarta: Buku Kompas, 2010.
———. *Sang Pelintas Batas: Biografi Djohan Effendi*. Jakarta: Indonesia Conference on Religion and Peace, 2009.
Geertz, Clifford. *Islam Observed: Religious Development in Morocco and Indonesia*. Chicago: University of Chicago Press, 1971.
———. *Peddlers and Princes: Social Change and Economic Modernization in Two Indonesian Towns*. Chicago: University of Chicago Press, 1963.
Gendzier, Irene L. *Managing Political Change: Social Scientists and the Third World*. Boulder: Westview Press, 1985.
GhaneaBassiri, Kambiz. *A History of Islam in America*. Cambridge: Cambridge University Press, 2010.
Gibb, H. A. R. *Modern Trends in Islam*. Chicago: University of Chicago Press, 1947.
———. *Mohammedanism: A Historical Survey*. New York: Galaxy Books, 1966.
Gilman, Nils. *Mandarins of the Future: Modernization Theory in Cold War America*. Baltimore, MD: John Hopkins University Press, 2003.
Graham, William A. "Review of *Major Themes of the Qur'an* by Fazlur Rahman." *Journal of the American Oriental Society* 103, no. 2 (April–June 1983): 445–47.
Guillaume, Alfred. "Review of *Muhammad at Mecca* by W. Montgomery Watt." *Bulletin of the School of Oriental and African Studies* 16, no. 3 (1954): 609–10.
Hallaq, Wael B. *The Impossible State: Islam, Politics, and Modernity's Moral Predicament*. New York: Columbia University Press, 2013.
———. "On Orientalism, Self-consciousness, and History." *Islamic Law and Society* 18, no. 3–4 (2011): 387–439.

———. *Restating Orientalism: A Critique of Modern Knowledge.* New York: Columbia University Press, 2018.
Halpern, Manfred. *The Politics of Social Change in the Middle East and North Africa.* Princeton, NJ: Princeton University Press, 1963.
Hasan, Noorhaidi. *Laskar Jihad: Islam, Militancy, and the Quest for Identity in Post–New Order Indonesia.* Ithaca, NY: Cornell University Press, 2006.
Hashim, Rosnani. *Educational Dualism in Malaysia: Implications for Theory and Practice.* Oxford: Oxford University Press, 1996.
Hassan, Muhammad Kamal. *Muslim Intellectual Responses to "New Order" Modernization in Indonesia.* Kuala Lumpur: Dewan Bahasa dan Pustaka, 1980.
Hefner, Robert W. *Civil Islam: Muslims and Democratization in Indonesia.* Princeton, NJ: Princeton University Press, 2000.
———. "Islam, State, and Civil Society: ICMI and the Struggle for the Indonesian Middle Class." *Indonesia* 56 (October 1993): 1–35.
Hefner, Robert W., ed. *Making Modern Muslims: The Politics of Islamic Education in Southeast Asia.* Honolulu: University of Hawai'i Press, 2009.
Hefner, Robert W., and Muhammad Qasim Zaman, eds. *Schooling Islam: The Culture and Politics of Modern Muslim Education.* Princeton, NJ: Princeton University Press, 2007.
Hick, Rosemary Hick. "Comparative Religion and the Cold War Transformation of Indo-Persian 'Mysticism' into Liberal Islamic Modernity." In *Secularism and Religion-Making*, edited by Markus Dressler and Arvind-Pal S. Mandair, 141–69. Oxford: Oxford University Press, 2011.
Hirschkind, Charles. "Heresy or Hermeneutics: The Case of Nasr Hamid Abu Zayd." *Stanford Humanities Review* 5, no. 1 (1996): 35–50.
"History of the Cooperation between Indonesia and the Netherlands in the Field of Islamic Studies." *INIS Newsletter* 1 (1989): 5–9.
"History of the McGill-IAIN Relationship," McGill University, accessed June 10, 2018. www.mcgill.ca/indonesia-project/about/history.
Hourani, Albert. *Arabic Thought in the Liberal Age, 1798–1939.* Cambridge: Cambridge University Press, 1983.
———. "Review of *Islam in Modern History* by Wilfred Cantwell Smith." *Bulletin of the School of Oriental and African Studies* 21, no. 1 (1958): 633–35.
Hughes, Aaron W. *Islam and the Tyranny of Authenticity: An Inquiry into Disciplinary Apologetics and Self-Deception.* Sheffield, UK: Equinox, 2015.
———. *Situating Islam: The Past and Future of an Academic Discipline.* London: Equinox, 2007.
———. "The Study of Islam before and after 9/11: A Provocation." *Method and Theory in the Study of Religion* 24 (2012): 314–36.
———. *Theorizing Islam: Disciplinary Deconstruction and Reconstruction.* New York: Routledge, 2012.
Ibrahim, Nur Amali. *Improvisational Islam: Indonesian Youth in a Time of Possibility.* Ithaca, NY: Cornell University Press, 2018.

Jabali, Fu'ad, and Jamhari. *The Modernization of Islam in Indonesia: An Impact Study of the Cooperation between the IAIN and McGill University*. Montreal: Indonesia-Canada Islamic Higher Education Project, 2003.

Johnson, Peter, and Judith Tucker. "Middle East Studies Network in the United States." *MERIP Reports*, no. 38 (June 1975): 3–20, 26.

Jung, Dietrich. *Orientalists, Islamists, and the Global Public Sphere*. Sheffield, UK: Equinox, 2011.

Jurdi, Syarifuddin, ed. *Satu Abad Muhammadiyah: Gagasan Pembaruan Sosial Keagamaan*. Jakarta: Buku Kompas, 2010.

Kahfi, Erni Haryanti. *Islam and Nationalism: Agus Salim and Nationalist Movement in Indonesia during the Early Twentieth Century*. Jakarta: Logos Wacana Ilmu, 2001.

Kahin, Audrey R. *Islam, Nationalism, and Democracy: A Political Biography of Mohammad Natsir*. Singapore: National University of Singapore Press, 2012.

Kartanegara, R. Mulyadhi. *Seni Mengukir Kata: Kiat-kiat Menulis Efektif-Kreatif*. Bandung: Mizan Learning Center, 2006.

Kersten, Carool. "Bourgeois Islam and Muslims without Mosques: Muslim Liberalism and Its Discontents in Indonesia." In *Islam after Liberalism*, edited by Faisal Devji and Zaheer Kazmi, 168–80. Oxford: Oxford University Press, 2017.

———. *Cosmopolitans and Heretics: New Muslim Intellectuals and the Study of Islam*. New York: Columbia University Press, 2011.

———. *Islam in Indonesia: The Contest for Society, Ideas, and Values*. London: Hurst and Company, 2015.

Kinsey, David C. "Efforts for Educational Synthesis under Colonial Rule: Egypt and Tunisia." *Comparative Education Review* 15, no. 2 (June 1971): 172–87.

Kull, Ann. *Piety and Politics: Nurcholish Madjid and His Interpretation of Islam in Modern Indonesia*. Lund, Sweden: Lund University, 2005.

Kurzman, Charles, ed. *Liberal Islam: A Sourcebook*. New York: Oxford University Press, 1998.

Laffan, Michael F. *Islamic Nationhood and Colonial Indonesia: The Umma below the Winds*. New York: Routledge, 2003.

———. *The Makings of Indonesian Islam: Orientalism and the Narration of a Sufi Past*. Princeton, NJ: Princeton University Press, 2011.

———. "Straight from Mecca: Medan, Hamka, and the Coming of Islam to Indonesia." In *The Post-colonial Moment in South and Southeast Asia*, edited by Gyan Prakash, Michael Laffan, and Nikhil Menon, 265–83. London: Bloomsbury Academic, 2018.

Latham, Michael. *The Right Kind of Revolution: Modernization, Development, and U.S. Foreign Policy from the Cold War to the Present*. Ithaca, NY: Cornell University Press, 2011.

Latif, Yudi. *Indonesian Muslim Intelligentsia and Power*. Singapore: ISEAS, 2008.

Lee, Robert D. *Overcoming Tradition and Modernity: The Search for Islamic Authenticity*. New York: Westview Press, 1997.

Lelyveld, David. "Disenchantment at Aligarh: Islam and the Realm of the Secular in Late Nineteenth-Century India." *Die Welts des Islam* 22 (1982): 85–102.

Lerner, Daniel. *The Passing of Traditional Society: Modernizing the Middle East.* Glencoe, IL: Free Press, 1958.

Lewis, Bernard. "The Question of Orientalism." *New York Review of Books*, June 24, 1982, 49–56.

———. "The Revolt of Islam." *New York Review of Books*, June 30, 1983, 35–38.

Liddle, R. William. "The Islamic Turn in Indonesia: A Political Explanation." *The Journal of Asian Studies* 55, no. 3 (August 1996): 613–34.

———. "*Media Dakwah* Scripturalism: One Form of Islamic Political Thought and Action in New Order Indonesia." In *Toward a New Paradigm: Recent Developments in Indonesian Islamic Thought*, edited by Mark R. Woodward, 323–56. Tempe: Arizona State University, 1996.

Lincoln, Bruce. *Gods and Demons, Priests and Scholars: Critical Explorations in the History of Religions.* Chicago: University of Chicago Press, 2012.

Lockman, Zackary. *Contending Visions of the Middle East: The History and Politics of Orientalism.* New York: Cambridge University Press, 2004.

———. *Fieldnotes: The Making of Middle East Studies in the United States.* Stanford, CA: Stanford University Press, 2016.

Lukens-Bull, Ronald. *Islamic Higher Education in Indonesia: Continuity and Conflict.* New York: Palgrave MacMillan, 2013.

Maarif, Ahmad Syafii. *Islam dan Masalah Kenegaraan: Studi tentang Percaturan dalam Konstituante.* Jakarta: LP3ES, 1985.

———. *Otobiografi Ahmad Syafii Maarif: Titik-Titik Risau di Perjalananku.* Yogyakarta: Ombak, 2006.

———. *Al-Qur'an, Realitas Sosial, dan Limbo Sejarah: Sebuah Refleksi.* Bandung: Pustaka, 1985.

MacDougall, John James. "The Technocratic Model of Modernization: The Case of Indonesia's New Order." *Asian Survey* 16, no. 12 (December 1976): 1166–83.

MacIntyre, Alasdair. *Three Rival Versions of Moral Enquiry: Encyclopaedia, Geneology, and Tradition.* Notre Dame, IN: University of Notre Dame Press, 1990.

———. *Whose Justice? Which Rationality?* Notre Dame, IN: University of Notre Dame Press, 1988.

Madinier, Remy. *Islam and Politics in Indonesia: The Masyumi Party between Democracy and Integralism*, translated by Jeremy Desmond. Singapore: National University of Singapore Press, 2015.

Madjid, Nurcholish. "Fazlur Rahman dan Rekonstruksi Etika al-Qur'an." In *Kontroversi Pemikiran Fazlur Rahman*, edited by H. Muhaimin, vii-xx. Cirebon, Indonesia: Pustaka Dinamika, 1999.

———. *Islam: Doktrin dan Peradaban.* Jakarta: Yayasan Wakaf Paramadina, 1992.

———. *Islam, Kemodernan, dan Keindonesiaan.* Bandung: Mizan, 1987.

———. "Islamic Roots of Modern Pluralism: Indonesian Experiences." *Studia Islamika* 1, no. 1 (April–June 1994): 55–78.

———. "The Issue of Modernization among Muslims in Indonesia: A Participant's Point of View." In *Readings on Islam in Southeast Asia*, edited by Ahmad Ibrahim, 379–87. Singapore: ISEAS, 1985.

———. *Khazanah Intelektual Islam*. Malaysia edition. Kuala Lumpur: Ikraq, 1983.

———. "Keharusan Pembaharuan Pemikiran Islam dan Masalah Integrasi Ummat," *Panji Masyarakat* 51 (February 1970): 5.

———. *Pintu-Pintu Menuju Tuhan*. Jakarta: Paramadina, 1994.

Madjid, Nurcholish, and Mohamad Roem. *Tidak Ada Negara Islam: Surat-Surat Politik Nurcholish Madjid-Mohamad Roem*, 2nd ed., edited by Laksmi Pamuntjak. Jakarta: Djambatan, 2000.

Mahmood, Saba. *Religious Difference in a Secular Age: A Minority Report*. Princeton, NJ: Princeton University Press, 2016.

———. "Secularism, Hermeneutics, Empire: The Politics of Islamic Reformation." *Public Culture* 18, no. 2 (2006): 323–47.

Mamdani, Mahmood. *Good Muslim, Bad Muslim: America, the Cold War, and the Roots of Terror*. New York: Three Leaves Press, 2005.

Marsden, George M. *The Soul of the American University*. New York: Oxford University Press, 1994.

Martin, Richard C., ed. *Approaches to Islam in Religious Studies*. Oxford: Oneworld, 1985.

———. "The Uses and Abuses of Criticism in the Study of Islam: A Response to Aaron Hughes." *Method and Theory in the Study of Religion* 24 (2012): 371–88.

Martin, Richard C., Mark R. Woodward, and Dwi S. Atmaja. *Defenders of Reason in Islam: Muʿtazilism from Medieval School to Modern Symbol*. Oxford: Oneworld, 1997.

McCutcheon, Russell T. *Critics Not Caretakers: Redescribing the Public Study of Religion*. Albany: State University of New York Press, 2001.

McCutcheon, Russell T., ed. *The Insider/Outsider Problem in the Study of Religion: A Reader*. New York: Continuum, 1999.

———. "The Study of Religion as an Anthropology of Credibility." In *Religious Studies, Theology, and the University: Conflicting Maps, Changing Terrain*, edited by Linell E. Cady and Delwin Brown. Albany: State University of New York Press, 2002.

Messick, Brinkley. *The Calligraphic State: Textual Domination and History in a Muslim Society*. Berkeley: University of California Press, 1993.

Metcalf, Barbara Daly. *Islamic Revival in British India: Deoband, 1860–1900*. Princeton, NJ: Princeton University Press, 1982.

Mitchell, Timothy. *Colonizing Egypt*. Berkeley: University of California Press, 1988.

———. "The Middle East in the Past and the Future of Social Science." In *The Politics of Knowledge: Area Studies and the Disciplines*, edited by David L. Szanton, 74–118. Berkeley: University of California Press, 2004.

Moosa, Ebrahim. *What Is a Madrasa?* Chapel Hill: University of North Carolina Press, 2015.

Mottahedeh, Roy. *The Mantle of the Prophet: Religion and Politics in Iran*. Rev. ed. London: Oneworld, 2000.

Mudzhar, M. Atho. *Belajar Islam di Amerika*. Jakarta: Pustaka Panjimas, 1991.

Mujiburrahman. *Humor, Perempuan, dan Sufi*. Jakarta: PT Elex Media Komputindo, 2017.

Munhanif, Ali. "Islam and the Struggle for Religious Pluralism in Indonesia: A Political Reading of the Religious Thought of Mukti Ali." *Studia Islamika* 3, no. 1 (1996): 84–126.

Murtopo, Ali. *Dasar-Dasar Pemikiran tentang Akslerasi Modernisasi Pembangunan 25 Tahun*. 2nd ed. Jakarta: Center for Strategic and International Studies, 1973.

Muzani, Saiful. "Muʿtazilite Theology and the Modernization of the Indonesian Muslim Community: Intellectual Portrait of Harun Nasution." *Studia Islamika* 1, no. 1 (April–June 1994): 91–131.

Najjar, Fauzi M. "Islamic Fundamentalism and the Intellectuals: The Case of Nasr Hamid Abu Zayd." *British Journal of Middle Eastern Studies* 27, no. 2 (2000): 177–200.

Nasr, Seyyed Vali Reza. *Mawdudi and the Making of Islamic Revivalism*. New York: Oxford University Press, 1996.

Nasution, Harun. *Akal dan Wahyu dalam Islam*. Jakarta: Penerbit Universitas Indonesia, 1982.

———. *Falsafat Islam: Kuliah-kuliah dan Ceramah yang Diberikan di IKIP Jakarta, IAIN, dan Universitas Nasional*. Jakarta: Kelompok Diskusi tentang Agama Islam, 1972.

———. *Islam Ditinjau dari Berbagai Aspeknya*, 2 vols. 2nd ed. Jakarta: Penerbit Universitas Indonesia, 1978.

———. *Islam Rasional: Gagasan dan Pemikiran*. Bandung: Mizan, 1995.

———. *Teologi Islam: Aliran-aliran Sejarah Analisa Perbandingan*. Jakarta: Penerbit Universitas Indonesia, 1972.

Natsir, Mohammad. *Capita Selecta Volume One*. Bandung: W. Van Hoeve, 1954.

———. *Islam Sebagai Ideologie*. 2nd ed. Jakarta: Pustaka Aida, 1950.

Nitisastro, Widjojo. *The Indonesian Development Experience: A Collection of Writings and Speeches of Widjojo Nitisastro*. Singapore: ISEAS, 2011.

Noer, Deliar. *The Modernist Muslim Movement in Indonesia, 1900–1942*. Singapore: Oxford University Press, 1973.

———. *Mohammad Hatta: Conscience of a Nation, 1902–1980*. Jakarta: Djambatan, 2002.

Novick, Peter. *That Noble Dream: The "Objectivity Question" and the American Historical Profession*. New York: Cambridge University Press, 1988.

Orsi, Robert A. *Between Heaven and Earth: The Religious Worlds People Make and the Scholars Who Study Them*. Princeton, NJ: Princeton University Press, 2005.

Parmar, Inderjeet. *Foundations of the American Century: The Ford, Carnegie, and Rockefeller Foundations in the Rise of American Power*. New York: Columbia University Press, 2012.

Patton, Laurie L. *Who Owns Religion?: Scholars and their Publics in the Late Twentieth Century*. Chicago: University of Chicago Press, 2019.
Perguruan Tinggi Agama Islam Negeri. Jakarta: Kementerian Agama, 1951.
Platzdasche, Bernhard. *Islamism in Indonesia: Politics in the Emerging Democracy*. Singapore: ISEAS, 2009.
Pohl, Florian. "On the Role of Interreligious Dialogue in the Religious Studies Programs at Indonesian State Islamic Universities." *Journal of Ecumenical Studies* 50, no. 1 (Winter 2015): 159–66.
Porter, Donald. *Managing Politics and Islam in Indonesia*. London: Routledge Curzon, 2002.
Prakash, Gyan. *Another Reason: Science and the Imagination of Modern India*. Princeton, NJ: Princeton University Press, 1999.
Prawiro, Radius. *Indonesia's Struggle for Economic Development: Pragmatism in Action*. Kuala Lumpur: Oxford University Press, 1998.
A Program for Near Eastern Studies in the United States: Report of the Committee on Near Eastern Studies. New York: American Council of Learned Societies, 1949.
Purohit, Teena. *The Aga Khan Case: Religion and Identity in Colonial India*. Cambridge, MA: Harvard University Press, 2012.
Qutb, Sayyid. *Social Justice in Islam*, translated by John B. Hardie. Oneonta, NY: Islamic Publications International, 2000.
Rahbar, Daud. *Memories and Meanings*. Boston: D. Rahbar, 1985.
Rahman, Fazlur. *Islam*. 3rd ed. Chicago: University of Chicago Press, 2002.
———. *Islam and Modernity: Transformation of an Intellectual Tradition*. Chicago: University of Chicago Press, 1982.
———. *Islamic Methodology in History*. Karachi: Central Institute of Islamic Research, 1965.
———. "Islamic Modernism: Its Scope, Method, and Alternatives." *International Journal of Middle East Studies* 1, no. 4 (October 1970): 317–33.
———. "Social Change and the Early Sunnah." *Islamic Studies* 2, no. 2 (June 1963): 205–26.
Rais, M. Amien. *Cakrawala Islam: Antara Cita dan Fakta*. Bandung: Mizan, 1987.
———. *Inilah Jalan Hidup Saya: Autobiografi*, edited by Bagus Mustakim and Nurhuda Kurniawan. Yogyakarta: Insan Madani, 2010.
———. "Kata Pengantar." In *Embrio Cendekiawan Muhammadiyah*, edited by Mukhaer Pakkanna, viii–x. Jakarta: Pers Suara Ikatan Mahasiswa Muhammadiyah, 1995.
Rais, M. Amien, ed. *Pendidikan Muhammadiyah dan Perubahan Sosial*. Yogyakarta: Pusat Latihan Penelitian dan Pengembangan Masyarakat, 1985.
———. *Tauhid Sosial: Formula Menggempur Kesenjangan*. Bandung: Mizan, 1998.
Ramage, Douglas. *Politics in Indonesia: Democracy, Islam, and the Ideology of Tolerance*. New York: Routledge, 1995.
Rasjidi, H. Mohamad. *Empat Kuliah Agama Islam Pada Perguruan Tinggi*. Jakarta: Bulan Bintang, 1974.

———. *Falsafat Agama*. 2nd ed. Jakarta: Bulan Bintang, 1970.
———. "Islam." In *The Meaning of Life in Five Great Religions*, edited by R. C. Chalmers and John A. Irving, 105–38. Philadelphia: Westminster Press, 1965.
———. *Islam dan Sosialisme*. Jakarta: Yayasan Islam Studi Club, 1966.
———. *Islam Menetang Komunisme*. Jakarta: Islam Studi Club Indonesia, 1966.
———. *Koreksi Terhadap Dr. Harun Nasution tentang Islam Ditinjau dari Berbagai Aspeknya*. Jakarta: Bulan Bintang, 1977.
———. *Koreksi Terhadap Drs. Nurcholish Madjid tentang Sekularisasi*. Jakarta: Bulan Bintang, 1972.
———. *Mengapa Aku Tetap Memeluk Agama Islam*. Jakarta: Hudaya, 1968.
Rasyid, Daud. *"Pembaruan" Islam dan Orientalisme dalam Sorotan*. Jakarta: Usamah Press, 1993.
Refleksi Pembaharuan Pemikiran Islam: 70 Tahun Harun Nasution. Jakarta: Lembaga Studi Agama dan Filsafat, 1989.
Reid, Anthony. "Entrepreneurial Minorities, Nationalism, and the State." In *Essential Outsiders: Chinese and Jews in the Modern Transformation of Southeast Asia and Central Europe*, edited by Daniel Chirot and Anthony Reid, 33–71. Seattle: University of Washington Press, 2011.
Research on the Role of the McGill University Islamic Studies Alumni in Academics, Bureaucracy, and Society. Jakarta: IAIN Jakarta, 1996.
Ricketts, Mac. "Review of *Faith of Other Men* and *The Meaning and End of Religion* by Wilfred Cantwell Smith." *Journal of Asian Studies* 25, no. 4 (August 1966): 744–45.
Ricklefs, M. C. *Islamisation and Its Opponents in Java: A Political, Social, Cultural, and Religious History, c. 1930 to the Present*. Singapore: National University of Singapore Press, 2012.
———. *Polarizing Javanese Society: Islamic and Other Visions*. Singapore: National University of Singapore Press, 2007.
Roberts, Jon H., and James Turner. *The Sacred and the Secular University*. Princeton, NJ: Princeton University Press, 2000.
Robinson, Geoffrey. *The Killing Season: A History of the Indonesian Massacres, 1965–66*. Princeton, NJ: Princeton University Press, 2018.
Rochwulaningsih, Yety. "Mahmud Yunus: Islamic Religious Instruction in the Public School." In *Reclaiming the Conversation: Islamic Intellectual Tradition in the Malay Archipelago*, edited by Rosnani Hashim, 167–86. Kuala Lumpur: Other Press, 2010.
Roff, William R. "Indonesian and Malay Students in Cairo in the 1920s." *Indonesia* 9 (April 1970): 73–88.
Rostow, W. W. *The Stages of Economic Growth: A Non-Communist Manifesto*. 3rd ed. Cambridge: Cambridge University Press, 1990.
Rudnyckyj, Daromir. *Spiritual Economies: Islam, Globalization, and the Afterlife of Development*. Ithaca, NY: Cornell University Press, 2011.
"R. William Liddle Profile," Department of Political Science, Ohio State University, accessed July 30, 2018. https://polisci.osu.edu/people/liddle.2.

Saeed, Abdullah. "Towards Religious Tolerance through Reform in Islamic Education: The Case of the State Institute of Islamic Studies in Indonesia." *Indonesia and the Malay World* 27, no. 79 (1999): 177–91.

Safi, Omid. "Reflections on the State of Islamic Studies." *Jadaliyya*, January 31, 2014. www.jadaliyya.com/Details/30175/Reflections-on-the-State-of-Islamic-Studies.

Safran, Nadav. *Egypt in Search of Political Community: An Analysis of the Intellectual and Political Evolution of Egypt, 1804–1952*. Cambridge, MA: Harvard University Press, 1961.

Said, Edward *Orientalism*. 25th anniversary edition. New York: Vintage, 1994.

Saleh, Fauzan. *Modern Trends in Islamic Theological Discourse in 20th Century Indonesia: A Critical Survey*. Leiden: Brill, 2001.

Saridjo, Marwan, ed. *Jabatan untuk Umat: 70 Tahun H. Kafrawi Ridwan*. Jakarta: Yayasan Pustaka Ummat, 2002.

Schacht, Joseph. *The Origins of Muhammadan Jurisprudence*. London: Oxford University Press, 1950.

———. "Review of *Islamic Methodology in History* by Fazlur Rahman." *Bulletin of the School of Oriental and African Studies, University of London* 29, no. 2 (1966): 394–95.

———. "Review of *Muhammad at Mecca* by W. Montgomery Watt." *Arabica* 2, no. 2 (May 1955): 231–33.

Scheer, Catherine, Philip Fountain, and R. Michael Feener, eds. *The Mission of Development: Religion and Technopolitics in Asia*. Leiden: Brill, 2018.

Schimmel, Annmarie. "Review of *Islamic Studies*, June 1962–November 1963." *Die Welts des Islams* 9 (1964): 265–70.

Sedgwick, Mark. *Muhammad Abduh*. Oxford: Oneworld, 2010.

Serjeant, R. B. "Review of *Islam* by Fazlur Rahman." *Journal of the Royal Asiatic Society of Great Britain and Ireland* 1–2 (April 1968): 76–77.

Sewindu Institut Agama Islam Negeri Sunan Kalidjaga Jogjakarta, 1960–1968. Yogyakarta: Institut Agama Islam Negeri, 1968.

Shafiq, Muhammad. *Growth of Islamic Thought in North America: Focus on Ismai'l Raji al Faruqi*. Brentwood, MD: Amana, 1994.

Shiraishi, Takashi. *An Age in Motion: Popular Radicalism in Java, 1912–1926*. Ithaca, NY: Cornell University Press, 1990.

Siegel, James T. *Objects and Objections of Ethnography*. New York: Fordham University Press, 2011.

Simpson, Bradley. *Economists with Guns: Authoritarian Development and US-Indonesia Relations, 1960–68*. Stanford, CA: Stanford University Press, 2008.

———. "Indonesia's 'Accelerated Modernization' and the Global Discourse of Development, 1960–1975." *Diplomatic History* 33, no. 3 (June 2009): 467–86.

Sjadzali, Munawir. *Pendidikan Agama dan Pengembangan Pemikiran Keagamaan*. Jakarta: Biro Hukum dan Humas, 1984.

———. "Reaktualisasi Ajaran Islam." In *Polemik Reaktualisasi Ajaran Islam*, edited by Iqbal Abdurrauf Saimima, 1–11. Jakarta: Pustaka Panjimas, 1988.

Smith, Wilfred Cantwell. "Comparative Religion: Whither and Why?" In *The History of Religions: Essays in Methodology*, edited Mircea Eliade and Joseph Kitagawa, 31–50. Chicago: University of Chicago Press, 1959.
———. *The Faith of Other Men*. New York: New American Library, 1963.
———. *Islam in Modern History*. Princeton, NJ: Princeton University Press, 1957.
———. *The Meaning and End of Religion*. Minneapolis: Fortress Press, 1991.
———. *Modern Islam in India: A Social Analysis*. 2nd rev. ed. New Delhi: Usha, 1946.
———. *Pakistan as an Islamic State*. Lahore: Ashraf Press, 1951.
———. "Review of *Islam and the West: Proceedings of the Harvard Summer Conference on the Middle East, July 25–27, 1955*, by Richard N. Frye." *Middle East Journal* 11, no. 4 (Autumn 1957): 437–38.
———. "Review of *Islam—The Straight Path: Islam Interpreted by Muslims*, by Kenneth W. Morgan." *Journal of the American Oriental Society* 78, no. 4 (1958): 309–11.
Srimulyani, Eka. *Mahmud Yunus' Islamic Educational Thought*. Banda Aceh, Indonesia: Ar-Raniry Press Darussalam, 2008.
Starrett, Gregory. *Putting Islam to Work: Education, Politics, and Religious Transformation in Egypt*. Berkeley: University of California Press, 1998.
Steenbrink, Karel A. "The Study of Comparative Religion by Indonesian Muslims: A Survey." *Numen* 37, no. 2 (December 1990): 153–61.
Stiglitz, Joseph E. *Globalization and Its Discontents*. New York: W.W. Norton, 2002.
Sumardi, Mulyanto, ed. *Penelitian Agama: Masalah dan Pemikiran*. Jakarta: Sinar Harapan, 1982.
———. *Sedjarah Singkat Pendidikan Islam di Indonesia*. Jakarta: Departemen Agama, 1977.
Supardi, ed. *Setengah Abad UII: Sejarah Perkembangan Universitas Islam Indonesia*. Yogyakarta: UII Press, 1994.
Syahid, Achmad, and Abas Al-Jauhari. *Bahasa, Pendidikan, dan Agama: 65 Tahun Prof. Dr. Muljanto Sumardi*. Jakarta: Logos, 2002.
Syamsuddin, Muhammad. *Professor Dr. HM Rasjidi: Perjuangan dan Pemikirannya*. Jakarta: Aziziah, 2004.
Troll, Christian W. *Sayyid Ahmad Khan: A Reinterpretation of Muslim Theology*. New Delhi: Vikas, 1978.
Van Bruinessen, Martin, ed. *Contemporary Developments in Indonesian Islam: Explaining the 'Conservative Turn.'* Singapore: ISEAS, 2013.
———. "Liberal and Progressive Voices in Indonesian Islam." In *Reformist Voices of Islam: Mediating Islam and Modernity*, edited by Shireen Hunter. Armonk, NY: M. E. Sharpe, 2009.
Van Niel, Robert. *The Emergence of the Modern Indonesian Elite*. The Hague: W. Van Hoeve, 1960.
Von Grunebaum, G. E. *Modern Islam: The Search for Cultural Identity*. New York: Vintage, 1964.
———. "Review of *Muhammad at Mecca* by W. Montgomery Watt." *The Journal of Religion* 34, no. 3 (July 1954): 223–24.

Waardenburg, Jacques. "Louis Massignon (1883–1962) as a Student of Islam." *Die Welt des Islams* 45, no. 3 (2005): 312–42.
Wahib, Ahmad. *Pergolakan Pemikiran Islam: Catatan Harian Ahmad Wahib*, edited by Djohan Effendi and Ismed Natsir. Jakarta: LP3ES, 1981.
Webster, David. *Fire and the Full Moon: Canada and Indonesia in a Decolonizing World*. Vancouver: University of British Columbia Press, 2009.
Wiebe, Donald. "The Role of 'Belief' in the Study of Religion: A Response to W. C. Smith." *Numen* 26, no. 2 (December 1979): 234–49.
Woodward, Mark. "Introduction: Talking across Paradigms—Indonesia, Islam, and Orientalism." In *Toward a New Paradigm: Recent Developments in Indonesian Islamic Thought*, edited by Mark Woodward, 1–45.Tempe: Arizona State University, 1996.
Wright, Robin. "An Iranian Luther Shakes the Foundations of Islam." *The Guardian*, February 1, 1995. www.drsoroush.com/English/News_Archive/E-NWS-19950201-1.html.
Yatim, Badri, and Hamid Nasuhi, eds. *Membangun Pusat Keunggulan Studi Islam: Sejarah dan Profil Pimpinan IAIN Syarif Hidayatullah, Jakarta, 1957–2002*. Jakarta: IAIN Jakarta Press, 2002.
Yunus, Mahmud. *Metodik Chusus Pendidikan Agama*. Jakarta: Al-Hidajah, 1965.
———. *Pokok-Pokok Pendidikan dan Pengadjaran: Hasil Kuliah Pada Fakultas Tarbijah Institut Agama Islam Negeri Jakarta*. Jakarta: Pustaka Mahmudiah, 1962.
———. *Sejarah Pendidikan Islam di Indonesia*, 3rd ed. Jakarta: Mahmud Yunus Wadzurriyyah, 2008.
Zaman, Muhammad Qasim. *Islam in Pakistan: A History*. Princeton, NJ: Princeton University Press, 2018.
———. *Modern Islamic Thought in a Radical Age: Religious Authority and Internal Criticism*. New York: Cambridge University Press, 2012.
———. *The Ulama in Contemporary Islam: Custodians of Change*. Princeton, NJ: Princeton University Press, 2002.
Zeghal, Malika. "Religion and Politics in Egypt: The Ulema of al-Azhar, Radical Islam, and the State." *International Journal of Middle Eastern Studies* 31, no. 3 (August 1999): 371–99.
Zuhri, K. H. Saifuddin. *Berangkat dari Pesantren*. Jakarta: Gunung Agung, 1987.

UNPUBLISHED THESES AND PAPERS

Barton, Greg. "The Emergence of Neo-Modernism: A Progressive, Liberal Movement of Islamic Thought in Indonesia." PhD diss., Monash University, 1995.
Fealy, Greg. "Ulama and Politics in Indonesia: A History of Nahdlatul Ulama, 1952–1967." PhD diss., Monash University, 1998.
Federspiel, Howard. "Collected Papers of Howard M. Federspiel, Set I: Graduate School Papers and Theses at McGill University." Self-compiled, 1994.
Idris, Muhammady. "Kiyai Haji Ahmad Dahlan: His Life and Thought." Master's thesis, McGill University, 1975.

Ismail, Faisal. "Islam, Politics, and Ideology in Indonesia: A Study of the Process of Muslim Acceptance of Pancasila." PhD diss., McGill University, 1995.

Maarif, Ahmad Syafii. "Islam as the Basis of State: A Study of the Islamic Political Ideas as Reflected in the Constituent Assembly Debates in Indonesia." PhD diss., University of Chicago, 1983.

Madjid, Nurcholish. "Ibn Taymiyya on Kalam and Falsafa: A Problem of Reason and Revelation in Islam." PhD diss., University of Chicago, 1984.

Nasution, Harun. "The Islamic State in Indonesia: The Rise of the Ideology, the Movement for Its Creation, and the Theory of the Masjumi." Master's thesis, McGill University, 1965.

———. "The Place of Reason in 'Abduh's Theology: Its Impact on His Theological System and Views." PhD diss., McGill University, 1968.

Rais, M. Amien. "The Muslim Brotherhood in Egypt: Its Rise, Demise, and Resurgence." PhD diss., University of Chicago, 1981.

"Seminar Pikiran-Pikiran Fazlur Rahman." Unpublished conference papers, Jakarta, 1988.

Syamsuddin, Muhammad. "Religion and Politics in Islam: The Case of Muhammadiyah in Indonesia's New Order." PhD diss., UCLA, 1991.

Zaini, Achmad. "Kyai Haji Abdul Wahid Hasyim: His Contribution to Muslim Educational Reform and to Indonesian Nationalism during the Twentieth Century." Master's thesis, McGill University, 1998.

INDEX

Abduh, Muhammad, 4, 23, 25–26, 29, 85–86, 100, 113, 175
Abdullah, Amin, 20, 157, 160–62, 165, 224n71, 224n77; academic imperialism, concern over, 174; on Islamic studies, 175; Islamic theological revolution, call for, 175–76; Muslim acculturation, defense of, 174; as postmodernist, 174, 176
Abdullah, Taufik, 105, 132
Abdulrahim, Muhammad Imaduddin, 162–63
Abu Zayd, Nasr Hamid: as apostate, 9–10; notoriety of, 9
Adams, Charles, 89, 153
Adnan, K. H. Mohammad, 35
Afghanistan, 158
Ahmad, Mumtaz, 138, 218n48
Ahmed, Shahab, 201n9
Akademi Dinas Ilmu Agama (ADIA), 38–39, 44, 81
al-Afghani, Jamal al-Din, 4
al-Ashʿari, Abu al-Hasan, 141
al-Attas, Syed Muhammad Naquib, 2, 210n83
al-Azhar, 23, 27, 44–45, 83, 159
Alfian, 105
al-Ghazali, Abu Hamid, 31, 141, 160, 175
Aligarh, 23, 44–45
Ali, Mukti, 1, 18–19, 53, 55, 90, 92–93, 98–99, 101–3, 105–6, 108–9, 114, 121, 123, 132, 149–50, 164, 168, 174, 213n33; and apologetics, 82; comparative religion, 81–83; as Father of Comparative Religion, 79; as fusionist, 74, 81, 94, 104, 122; McGill academic culture, difficult adjustment to, 80–81; objectivity, 81–82; Western academia encounter, as transformative, 81
Ali, Syed Ameer, 82
Al-Kulijat ul Islamiyah, 28
Almond, Gabriel, 125, 128, 166, 217n29
al-Shafiʿi, Imam, 31, 75–77
American Council of Learned Societies (ACLS), 55
Americanization, 127. *See also* modernization
American University of Cairo, 83
Amin, Uthman, 66
Amrullah, Abdul Malik Karim, 42
Amrullah, Shaikh H. A. Karim, *See* Hadji Rasul
anthropology: insider-outsider problem, 10
anti-Semitism, 178–79, 181
apologists, 12, 56–57, 65–66, 71–72, 82, 86
Arabism, 72
Archer, George, 190
Aristotle, 42
Arkoun, Mohammed, 2
Asad, Talal, 120, 190, 201n9, 226n30; boundary-making, 226n13
Ashʿari school, 111, 175
Ash-Shiddieqy, T. M. Hasbi, 35

Asia Foundation, 70, 80
Asmin, Yudian, 164
Asyʿari, Hasyim, 31–32
Auberdene, Patricia, 170
authenticity, 9–10, 13, 15, 58, 75, 130, 133, 135, 138–39, 141, 143, 149
Aydin, Cemil, 6, 40
Azizy, Qodri, 151
Azra, Azyumardi, 162, 164, 176

Bagley, William, 80
Banda Aceh, 46, 105
Barton, Greg, 219n76, 219n79
Basyir, Azhar, 159
Bellah, Robert, 169–70
Berkes, Niyazi, 64, 68, 71, 80
Binder, Leonard, 14, 19, 122–23, 128–29, 134, 137, 139, 142–43, 149–52, 154, 161, 166, 182, 188, 194, 227n48; bimodal approach of, 130–31, 133; cross-discursive dialogue model, 198; fieldwork, conducting of, 132; fusionist alliance between social sciences and Islamic thought, 124; interdisciplinary inquiry, encouraging of, 138; Islamic liberalism, 135; as modernization theorist, 192; political liberalism, commitment to, 136; researchers, recruiting of, 131–32; self-critical cross-discursive dialogue, 192–93
Bintang Mahaputra Utama, 185
Boland, B. J., 98
Bosnia, 154
Brawijaya University, 162
Brown, Wendy, 179
Burton, John, 88

Cairo (Egypt), 27, 35–36, 69, 84
Cairo University, 9
Cambridge University, 23
Campbell, Joseph, 170
Canadian International Development Agency (CIDA), 16, 105–6, 153, 214n50

Ceric, Mustafa, 138, 154
Chotib, Achmad, 48
Christianity, 41, 115, 176
Cold War, 14–16, 55–56, 95–96, 125–27, 203n46
colonialism, 6, 11–12, 14, 73, 82, 95, 166, 174, 195–97; language of, 5
Columbia University, 56, 90, 151
Committee for the Comparative Study of New Nations, 128
communism, 16, 41, 95, 115, 125
Council of Indonesian Muslim Associations. *See* Masyumi
Cox, Harvey, 100, 169
Cragg, Kenneth, 57

Dahlan, Ahmad, 25–26
Dahlan, Zaini, 48
Dalhousie University, 105–6
Dar al-Ulum, 27, 69
Daud, Wan Mohd Nor Wan, 138, 154
decolonialization, 11
democratization, 126
Deobandi revivalists, 4; ʿulama, 74
Derrida, Jacques, 193
development, 2, 9, 14–20, 60, 78, 104, 107, 118, 122, 183; criticism of, 102; as dangerous, 37; developmental psychology, 38, 44; as holistic process, 102; and Islam, 123–24, 129–30, 135, 138–39, 141, 149–51, 153, 193; modernization theory, 126, 143; New Order, 97, 157; as progress, 102–3; religious, 127–28, 131; as science, 96; Suharto, developmentalist vision of, 93, 95–96, 102, 109, 174
Djaelani, Anton Timur, 1, 53, 102–3, 106, 122
Djajadiningrat, Achmad, 29
Djajadiningrat, Hussein, 29
Djamal, Murni, 1, 150, 214n51
Durkheim, Emile, 81
Dutch East Indies, 24; Ethical Policy, 28.
Dutch Native School, 28, 30

Easton, David, 125
Edward W. Hazen Foundation, 70
Effendi, Djohan, 98–99, 101, 103–4, 161–62
Effendy, Bahtiar, 162, 178
Egypt, 44–45, 56, 59–60, 69, 108, 130–32, 135, 142–43, 215n60; dualism, struggle against, 23
Eickelman, Dale, 137
Einstein, Albert, 175
Ernst, Carl, 188
Esposito, John, 188
essentialism, 60–61, 68, 188–89, 225–26n7, 226n13

Fadjar, Agus, 145
falsafa, 140
Faruqi, Ismail al-, 2, 74, 180; as anti-Western, accusations of, 73; and Arabism, 72
fascism, 41
Federspiel, Howard, 67, 72–73, 209n81
Feener, Michael, 42, 115, 174, 201n7
fiqh, 2, 27, 51, 99–100
First New Nation, The (Lipset), 126–27
Five-Year Development Plans, 96
Ford Foundation, 9, 16, 19, 56, 63, 89–90, 96, 105, 107, 113, 121, 123, 129, 131–33, 138, 150, 182
Forman Christian College, 60
Foucault, Michel, 120, 156, 174, 176
Freud, Sigmund, 40–41, 70
Fromm, Erich, 170
Frost, Stanley Brice, 72
fusionism, 10, 11–12, 18–20, 77, 79, 81, 84–85, 103–4, 107, 110, 122, 129, 146, 150, 152, 154, 160, 163, 171, 192, 194; Cold War development politics, intertwined with, 15; colonial and postcolonial geopolitics, intersecting with, 14; commensurability, striving for, 7, 13, 53, 75, 90; and conflict, 54–55; and creativity, 54–55; critiques of, 90; dualism, combatting of, 53–54; first generation of, 15–16; Islamic modernism, connection to, 7–8; knowledge, approach to, 53, 55, 116, 168; knowledge, cross-discursive forms, 9, 14; knowledge, forms of, 55; at McGill University, 18, 74, 86–87, 90, 188; opposition to, 94, 180; postcolonial theory, 156–57, 164, 173, 177, 198; reason and revelation, relationship between, 8; setbacks to, 89; social and political influence of, 8; social sciences and Islamic thought, alliance between, 124; soft power, 17; spread of, 136; as term, 53; thriving of, 186; at University of Chicago, 123–24, 137–38, 141, 149; Western academia, 188
Fyzee, Asaf Ali Asghar, 73

Gani, Bustami A., 108
Geertz, Clifford, 125, 127–28
Gellner, Ernest, 141
genocide, 197; structural, 195–96
Georgetown University, 151
George Washington University, 165
Ghurbal, Shafiq, 66
Gibb, H. A. R., 14, 41–44, 56, 57–58, 65, 82, 90, 155, 189, 206n79
Goldziher, Ignaz, 75
Golkar, 97, 102, 158
Government Religious Academy. *See* Akademi Dinas Ilmu Agama (ADIA)
Gramsci, Antonio, 174
Guillaume, Alfred, 42, 58, 75
Guizot, François, 23

Habibie, B. J., 163, 185
hadith, 34–36, 58, 87–88, 169; historical authenticity, debates over, 75–78, 140–41
Hadji Rasul, 26–27
Hagarism (Crone and Cook), 202–3n34, 227n48

hajj, 24–25
Hakiem, Lukman, 181–82
Hallaq, Wael, 13, 195–96, 226n30, 227n50; Other, studying of, 197; as subversive author, 198
Halpern, Manfred, 127, 129–30
Hamim, Toha, 152
Hanafi, Hassan, 2
Hartford Theological Seminary, 55
Harvard University, 56–57, 90; Center for the Study of World Religions, 89
Hassan, Ahmad, 30
Hasyim, Wahid, 32–33, 35, 45, 47
Hatta, Mohammad, 21–22, 33–35, 40
Hefner, Robert, 115
Hidayat, Komaruddin, 114
Hijaz, 24
Hinduism, 115, 202n33
Hitti, Phillip, 59
Hodgson, Marshall, 141, 169
Hourani, Albert, 88
Hughes, Aaron W., 12–13, 189, 194, 203n40, 211n135, 225–26n7, 226n13, 227n50; boundary making, 190; discursive boundary maintenance, 191–92; on Islamic studies, 187–88, 197
Hurgronje, Snouck, 29

IAIN. *See* State Islamic Institute system
IAIN Jakarta, 18–19, 48, 53, 81, 98–100, 107–9, 114, 150, 161–62, 174; Functional Group, 102. *See also* State Islamic Institute system (IAIN)
IAIN North Sumatra, 180. *See also* State Islamic Institute system (IAIN)
IAIN Yogyakarta, 47–49, 79, 98, 105, 142, 149, 224n71. *See also* State Islamic Institute system (IAIN)
Ibn Miskawayh, 40–41
Ibn Rushd, 141
Ibn Sina, 42, 75
Ibn Taymiyya, 139–41, 145, 149, 170
Ibrahim, Nur Amali, 7

ijtihad, 8, 25, 77, 98, 140–41, 150, 161–62, 169
imperialism: academic, 20, 133, 166, 174, 177, 184, 197–99; British, 60; epistemological, 20, 164, 174, 195, 198; political, 74; Western, 40, 156, 164
India, 6, 44–45; partition of, 60–61
Indonesian Association, 22
Indonesian Association of Muslim Intellectuals (ICMI), 162–63, 168, 184
Indonesian Communist Party (PKI), 84, 95
Indonesian Dawah Council (DDII), 93, 114–15, 177–79, 181–84
Indonesian-Netherlands Islamic Studies (INIS), 152–53, 221n152
Indonesian Revolution, 17, 33, 40, 79
industrialization, 125–26
intellectual dualism, 4–5, 17, 22, 39–40, 44, 89, 192; campaign against, 23–24, 27; combatting of, 53–54; as dangerous, 26; debates over, 24; Islam-West binary, 6–7; struggle against, 27–28, 35, 50–51
Investigatory Committee to Prepare for Independence, 33
Iqbal, Muhammad, 60, 147, 175
Iran, 11, 63, 130, 132; hostage crisis, 16; political cultures in, 128–29
Iranian Revolution, 16, 136–37
Islam (Rahman), 75, 87–88
Islam: Doctrine and Civilization (Madjid), 154
Islamic College, 17, 21–24, 40, 79. *See also* State Islamic Institute (IAIN)
Islamic law, 196–97; inheritance law, 161–62
Islamic liberalism, 135–36
Islamic Liberalism: A Critique of Development Ideologies (Binder), 134–37, 149, 152, 192–93
Islamic Methodology in History (Rahman), 78, 87

Islamic Normal School, 28, 39
Islamic reform, 2, 7, 9, 13–14, 16–17, 28, 75, 94, 124, 129, 149–50, 153, 169, 187–89; "Muslim Luthers," 137; Reformation, as model, 127–28
Islamic Research Institute, 9, 16, 129, 132
Islamic Reformation, 63
Islamic renewal, 97, 99
Islamic schools, 37–38; recitation and memorization, focus on, 21; reform, call for, 26
Islamic State, 84, 145, 22n95
Islamic Union (PERSIS), 30–31, 39–40
Islamic University of Indonesia (UII), 34
"Islam as an Ideology" (Natsir), 99
Islamism, 145; liberal bias against, 224n88; Western fears about, 16
Islam in Modern History (Smith), 65, 88
Islam and Modernity: Transformation of an Intellectual Tradition (Rahman), 133, 136–37, 147, 149, 151
Islamophobia, 199
"Islam and Social Change" (project), 19, 122–24, 129, 134, 136, 138, 142, 188, 218n48
Islam as Viewed from Its Various Aspects (Nasution), 110, 114, 121
Ismail, Faisal, 164
Israel Defense Forces, 128
Israeli-Palestinian War, 128
Izutsu, Toshihiko, 68, 90; critique of, 73–74; focus-words, 85; linguistic methods of, 73, 85

Jabali, Fuad, 162, 164–65
Jakarta, 30, 86, 92, 99, 102–3, 122, 152; McGill mafia in, 1
James, Cyril, 52–53, 61, 63
Japan, 33, 83
jilbab, 157
Johns Hopkins University, 56
Johnson, Lyndon B., 126

Jordan, 128
Jung, Dietrich, 40

Kafrawi, K. H. Fathurahman, 35
Kahfi, Erni Haryanti, 29–30
Kahin, Audrey, 40
kalam, 140, 174–75
Kant, Immanuel, 36–37, 160
Karachi (Pakistan), 79
Kartanegara, R. Mulyadhi, 151–52
Kaum Muda movement, 26–27, 98
Kennedy, John F., 126
Kersten, Carool, 138–39, 169, 201n7, 224n71
Khan, Ayub, 9, 129
Khan, Sayyid Ahmad, 4, 23
Khan, Zafarullah, 66
Kharijites, 110–12
Khatib al-Minankabawi, Ahmad, 25–26, 29
Kuhn, Thomas, 175–77

Lahore (Pakistan), 60
Laroui, Abdallah, 135
Latif, Yudi, 158, 162–63
Latin America, 125
Leiden University, 106–8, 152–53, 221n152
Lerner, David, 127
Lewis, Bernard, 12
liberalism: Islamic, 135–37; political, 135–36, 193–94; Western, 14, 143, 212–13n15
Liddle, William, 177–79, 181–84, 194–95, 198, 225n90, 225n95
Limited Group, 98–99, 101, 103–4, 152, 161
Lincoln, Bruce, 11–13, 187
Lipset, Martin, 126–27
Litbang Agama, 106–7. *See also* Office of Religious Research and Development
Little, Donald, 153
Lockman, Zachary, 124
Lufti, Muchtar, 28
Luther, Martin, 127

Maarif, Ahmad Syafii, 1, 19–20, 123–24, 149, 153–54, 157, 160–61, 165, 185; as fusionist, 138; Islamic state, 146, 148; religio-political conversion of, 147
MacIntyre, Alasdair, 5, 7, 201–2n12
Madinier, Remy, 43
Madjid, Nurcholish, 2, 19–20, 100–101, 116, 120, 123–24, 132, 139–41, 145, 149, 153–57, 161, 163, 165, 176–78, 182–83, 218n48, 219n76, 219n79, 220n95; death of, 185; faith v. reason, 171; as fusionist, 138, 146, 171; inclusive spirituality, embrace of, 172–73; Islamic reform, vision of, 169; Islamic universalism, 171; knowledge v. faith, 171; methodology, disinterest in, 169–70; radical Islamic universalism, conception of, 169, 172–73; religious fundamentalism, as dangerous social addiction, 172; social sciences, fallibility of, 170–71; truth, as shared possession, 172
madrasas schools, 2–4, 6, 26
Mahmood, Saba, 17, 226n30
Mahmud, Zaki Naguib, 135
Majelis Tarjih, 160
Malaysia, 95, 152, 154, 160, 225n95
Mardin, Serif, 150–51
Margoliouth, D. S., 75, 87
Marshall, John, 68
Martin, Richard C., 12, 193–94, 197–98, 227n48, 227n49
Marxism, 60, 70, 143
Massignon, Louis, 57, 69
Masuzawa, Tomoko, 120
Masyumi, 33, 40–41, 43–46, 94, 97–98, 100, 114, 147; downfall of, 70; Islamic State, conception of, 84; Sukarno, toxic relationship with, 93
Maturidi school, 175
Mawdudi, Abul A'la, 146–47, 205n62
Mazhab Ciputat, 162, 174, 178, 185
McCutcheon, Russell T., 11–13, 187, 194, 227n50; discursive boundary maintenance, 190–92

McGill Institute of Islamic Studies, 1, 53–54, 70, 72–73, 75, 79–81, 84, 89, 105, 113, 123, 129, 149, 160, 164–65; academic culture, as alienating, 90; as creative space, 86; critical historical analysis, 90; cross-discursive encounters, 74; dialogue across cultural and religious lines, fostering of, 67–68; founding of, 56, 62; fusionist thinking at, 18, 74, 86–87, 90, 188; historical analysis, emphasis on, 66; IAIN exchange program, 153; Indonesian Islamic thought, as site for, 154; intellectual encounter and exchange at, 67; as intellectual space, 91; inter-religious community of, 66–67; legacy of, 91; objectivity, 90; overreach, accusation of, 90; tokenism at, 64; vision of, 63–64
McGill University, 15, 19, 52–55, 61, 66, 68, 70–74, 80, 83, 86, 94, 99, 107–8, 113;
McGill mafia, 1, 9
McGill University Press, 72
Meaning and End of Religion, The (Smith), 68
Mecca, 24–25, 27, 29, 31–32, 79, 83–84, 127
Media Dakwah (magazine), 177, 198, 225n95; academic claims to neutrality, rejection of, 181; "answering Liddle," 178–79, 183–84, 194–95; anti-Semitic language in, 178–79; Western academic, attack on, 180, 183
Ministry of Religious Affairs, 16, 33, 38, 45–46, 48, 69, 94, 102, 108, 110, 113, 116, 150–51, 153, 215n60; creative minority, nurturing of, 104; culture, altering of, 104; Ford Foundation, relationship with, 121; as fusionist institution, 103, 121–22; Western-style academic disciplines, 105, 106, 109, 121
modernism, 7, 23–25, 31, 79, 98–99, 147, 149, 212–13n15; rational thinking, 101–2

modernity, 5, 29, 63, 124, 126, 143; as secular enlightenment, 127
modernization, 16, 93, 97, 103; and Islam, 128, 130; secularization, as integral to, 127; as word, 127. *See also* Americanization, Westernization
modernization theory, 16, 189, 192; in Cold War politics, 126; development, 126, 143; and Islam, 127–28; mobile sensibility, 127; modern society, 124; as objective, 189; objectivity, 125; as pro-American, 126; traditional society, 124
Montreal (Quebec), 53, 66, 92
Morgan, Kenneth, 66, 70
Morocco, 127, 132
Moslem World, The (magazine), 55
Mudzhar, Atho, 152, 164
Muhammad, 4, 9, 12, 29, 36, 58, 71, 76, 78, 111–12, 134, 141, 170, 172, 180–81, 188–89; creative agency, 77
Muhammadan Anglo-Oriental College, 23
Muhammadiyah movement, 1, 19–20, 25–26, 31, 69, 81, 93, 98, 100, 115, 123, 141–42, 144–45, 146–49, 152, 159–61, 168, 185; academic revitalization of, 165; Pancasila, 158
Mujani, Saiful, 162, 178
Müller, Max, 81–82
Munhanif, Ali, 162, 213n32
Murji'ah, 110
Murtopo, Ali, 97, 102, 121, 212n14, 213n32
Muslim Brotherhood, 142; Islamic authenticity, claims to, 143; pan-Islamism, conception of, 144
Muslim College Student Association (HMI), 98–100
Muʿtazilism, 84–86, 101, 110–11, 113, 118, 175

Naharong, Abdul Muis, 151
Nahdlatul Ulama (NU), 31–32, 46–50, 93, 97, 100, 102–3, 144
Naim, Mochtar, 53
Naisbatt, John, 170
NASAKOM, 46
Nasr, Seyyed Hossein, 2
Nasution, Harun, 1, 18–19, 53, 55, 83, 90, 93, 99–101, 108, 111–14, 116–21, 139, 150, 155–56, 162, 164, 168, 174, 215n62; as fusionist, 74, 84–86, 94, 110; Muʿtazilism, adherence to, 84–85; New Order, support of, 109; and objectivity, 84–85
National Development Planning Agency (Bappenas), 96, 101–3
Natsir, Mohammad, 18, 23–24, 30–31, 35, 45–46, 51, 72, 93, 114, 148; as influential figure, 99; intellectual dualism, wrestling with, 39–40; Islam, civilizational conception of, 41; Islam, essentialist vision of, 40–41; PERSIS-affiliated school system, 39–40; Western Orientalists, deferring to, 41–44
Near/Middle Eastern Area Studies, 55, 225–26n7
Nehru, Jawaharlal, 60
neo-modernism, 212–13n15
Netherlands, 10, 106–8
Newton, John, 175
New York University (NYU), 151
Ngusman, H. Abu, 47
9/11 attacks, 12–13, 17, 199
Noer, Deliar, 98
Northern Illinois University, 146
Novick, Peter, 54

objectivity, 18, 43, 55, 60, 76, 78, 81–82, 84–85, 90–91, 123, 169, 173, 192, 194, 211n135; challenging of, 54, 59, 61–62, 89, 180; Christian missionaries and Muslim apologists, 56; as contested concept, 13, 54; dissenting version of, 59, 61–62; doubts about, 166; Islam, civilizational critiques of, 58–59; modernization theory, 125; and Orientalism, 57, 59

Office of Religious Research and Development, 106. *See also* Litbang Agama
Ohio State University, 177–78
Ohio University, 146–47
Omar, Toha Yahya, 108, 215n62
Orientalism, 5–6, 13–14, 40, 42, 50, 56, 61, 65–66, 89–90, 123, 151, 180, 183, 225–26n7; critique of, 72, 155–56, 165, 189, 195; East, inferiority of, 156; new Orientalism, 164; and objectivity, 57, 59; Western imperialism, 156
Orientalism (Said), 12, 155
Origins of Muhammadan Jurisprudence, The (Schacht), 58, 75
Orsi, Robert, 11
Other, 156; Othered tradition, 88; otherness, of Muslims, 12
Otto, Rudolph, 170
Oxford University, 56–57

Pahlavi, Shah Mohammad, 128–29
Pakistan, 9, 11, 15–16, 63, 70, 73, 79–80, 87, 128, 132; creation of, 61; partition of, 60–61
Palestine, 11
Palmach-Haganah, 128
Pancasila, 158, 212n14; and Suharto, 144–45, 153, 181–82, 212n14; and Sukarno, 33, 46
pan-Islamism, 144
Paramadina (think tank), 161–62
Parsons, Talcott, 125
Passing of Traditional Society, The (Lerner), 127
Patton, Laurie, 225n1, 227n49
Peacock, James, 98
Perwiranegara, Alamsjah Ratu, 121
pesantren, 31–32, 36
Pirenne, Henri, 43
Plato, 36–37
positivism, 70, 74
postcolonial theory, 11–12, 14, 136, 164–69, 173, 177, 189–92; fusionist thinkers, 156–57

postmodernism, 136, 157, 163–64, 177, 190, 192; Islamic thought, 173–74, 176
Prawiro, Radius, 96
Preachers Council, 159–60
Princeton University, 55–56, 59, 90
Pustaka Press, 152

Quraish tribe, 112
Qurʿan, 3, 9, 12, 21, 25, 37, 41, 57, 61, 75–79, 83, 90, 101, 108–9, 135–36, 138, 140–41, 144–45, 147, 149, 169–70, 173, 180–81; ethics, emphasis on, 148; finality, 82; hermeneutics, 8, 16, 124, 152–53, 165; Islamic authenticity, 133; Islamic state, 148; misinterpretations of, 73–74; Qurʿanic revelation, as Islamic truths, 4; universality of, 134, 167–68, 171–72, 224n77
Qutb, Sayyid, 42, 135, 206n79

Rahardjo, Dawam, 98–99, 101, 152, 161–63, 173–74
Rahbar, Daud, 64–66
Rahman, Fazlur, 2, 9, 18–19, 55, 68, 89, 122, 135, 139, 140–41, 143, 146–48, 150, 154, 160, 165, 168, 169–71, 174, 180, 188, 192, 211n135, 219n76, 223n48; bimodal approach of, 130–31, 133–34; death of, 136, 151–52; double movement theory, 133–34, 167; fieldwork, conducting of, 132; as fusionist, 74–75, 77, 79, 87, 90, 129, 149; fusionist alliance between social sciences and Islamic thought, 124; Islamic thought, critique of, 133; Islamic thought, impact on, 152; Muslim community, role in, 137–38; objectivity, belief in, 78; researchers, recruiting of, 131–32; Schacht revisionist historiography, rejection of, 76–77; social sciences and Islamic thought, blurring of lines, 123–24; Sunnah, conceptual history of, 77–78, 88

Rais, Amien, 1, 19–20, 123–24, 132, 141, 147–49, 154, 156–57, 161, 169, 173–74, 177–79, 182–83, 223n48, 218n48; academic imperialism, critic of, 166; as fusionist, 138, 146, 168; Islamic authenticity, importance of, 143; Islamic state, 144–45, 220n95, 220n112; as kingmaker, 185; Muhammadiyah, ascending ranks of, 158–60; Muhammadiyah, championing of, 165; Muslim Brotherhood, critique of, 143–44; Muslim charity tax, reconceptualizing of, 168; objectivity, doubts about, 166; Orientalism, criticism of, 165; as pragmatist, 167–68; social monotheism, vision of, 167–68, 223n44; Suharto, criticism of, 163, 184–85; University of Chicago, alienation from, 142, 165; Western academia, discontent with, 155, 165–66
Ramadan, Tariq, 188
Rangkuti, Bahrum, 102
Rasjidi, Mohamad, 18–20, 69–70, 73, 76, 83–84, 115–21, 141, 155–56, 180, 189; apologetics, embrace of, 71–72; cancelled classes, 71, 209n81; as intellectual misfit, 71; Nasution, criticism of, 94; Orientalism, critique of, 72; Schacht, confrontation with, 71
Rasyid, Daud, 180–81, 183
rationality, 8–9, 62, 84, 101
Reformasi, 185
Reformation, 127–28
Religious Research Training Program, 106–7
religious studies: insider-outsider problem, 10–13
Religious Studies Club, 161
Ricketts, Mac, 88
Ricklefs, M. C., 157
Ridwan, Kafrawi, 1, 48, 53, 92–94, 99–100, 102–4, 121–22, 213n32
Rockefeller Foundation, 16, 56, 63, 67–70, 73, 75, 89, 142, 182
Roem, Mohammad, 145–46, 220n95
Roman empire, 43
Rostow, Walt, 125–26

Sadat, Anwar, 16
Safi, Omid, 188
Said, Edward, 12–13, 155, 164, 166, 168–69, 177, 189, 192, 195; and discourse, 156
Saleh, Fauzan, 167
Salim, Agus, 29–30, 83
Saudi Arabia, 108, 115, 145, 215n60
Schacht, Joseph, 57, 75–77, 87–88, 90, 170, 188, 192; ex silencio rule, 58; Rasjidi, confrontation with, 71
Schimmel, Annmarie, 87
science, 108–9, 120, 125, 176; of development, 96; value neutral status of, 205n62
secularism, 130, 135, 145; in Indonesia, 70; v. secularization, 100, 116
secularization, 126, 182; as defined, 100; Indonesian Islam, revitalization of, 100; Indonesian Muslims, 100, 102; modernization, as integral to, 127; v. secularism, 100, 116
September 30 Movement, 95
Serjeant, R. B., 87
Shafi'i school of law, 31
Shahrur, Muhammad, 137
shari'a, 197
Shariati, Ali, 166–69, 223n44
Shi'a, 111
Shihab, Quraish, 162
Shils, Edward, 126, 128
silsila, 140
Simpson, Brad, 97
Sjadzali, Munawir, 150, 152–53, 160–62, 183
Smith, Jonathan Z., 187
Smith, Wilfred Cantwell, 14–15, 18, 52–53, 56, 60, 63–64, 67, 69–70, 73–74, 80–81, 84, 90, 105–6, 113, 155, 172, 211n135; critique of, 88; goldfish analogy, 62, 65, 123; Muslim apologetics,

254 INDEX

Smith, Wilfred Cantwell (*continued*) criticizing of, 65–66, 71–72; objectivity, challenging of, 54, 59, 61–62, 89; Orientalist model of history writing, 65–66; religious essentialism, arguing against, 68; resignation of, 89; subjective-objective vision of, 66
social monotheism, 167–68, 223n44
Social Science Research Training Program, 105, 107
Soenarjo, R. H. A., 47
soft power, 15, 17, 180, 182–83
Souroush, Abdolkarim, 137
Soviet Union, 55–56
Stanford University, 56
State Department: Foreign Service Institute, 178
State Islamic Institute (IAIN) system, 17–18, 44, 48–49, 79, 86, 94, 100, 108, 114, 142, 153, 176, 215n62, 221n152; curriculum, overhaul of, 109–10, 122; fusionist initiatives, 106; intellectual dualism, challenging of, 51; partisan conflicts, 45, 50; proliferation of, 46–47; reforming of, 104–5, 150–51; social sciences, integrating of, 105; Western academic influence in, 106. *See also* Islamic College
State Islamic Institute (PTAIN), 34–36, 44
STOVIA medical school, 28
Structure of Ethical Terms in the Koran, The (Izutsu), 73–74
subjectivism, 89
Sufi order, 25–26, 31, 57
Suharto, 9, 18–19, 92, 99, 103–4, 121, 149–50, 158; developmentalist agenda, 93, 95–96, 102, 109, 174; Masyumi, relationship with, 93; Muslim intellectuals, partnership with, 94; New Order, 15, 95–98, 109, 126, 144–45, 152, 163, 182, 184–85; Nahdlatul Ulama (NU), relationship with, 93; Pancasila policies, 144–45, 153, 181–82, 212n14; power seize of, 94–95; resignation of, 185
Sukarno, 30, 34, 40, 44, 47, 53, 84, 93, 95, 97, 99, 109; Guided Democracy, concept of, 45–46, 52; and Pancasila, 33, 46
Sumardi, Mulyanto, 103–8, 110, 121–22, 213n32, 214n56
Sunnah, 8–9, 58, 75–78, 140–41, 144–45, 147
Sunni Muslims, 23, 85, 111–12, 153–54
Surabaya, 1, 46
Syamsuddin, Din, 1, 152, 161
Syamsuri, Untung, 94–95

tafsir, 2, 27, 51
Taliban, 23
taqlid, 8, 25–26, 31–32, 99, 140
tawhid, 223n44
Tebuireng Pesantren, 31–32
Third World, 55
Toynbee, Arnold, 104
Trueblood, David Elton, 70
Turkey, 15, 132

ul-Haq, Muhamad Zia, 16
Ulumul Qur'an (Qur'anic Studies) (journal), 173–74, 178–79, 184, 194
Umar, 141
United Nations (UN), 95
United States Agency for International Development (USAID), 16, 151, 178
Universitas Gadjah Mada (UGM), 142, 158, 168
University of Beirut, 59
University of California, Berkeley, 56, 96; Berkeley Boys, 126
University of California at Los Angeles (UCLA), 57, 151–52, 165
University of Chicago, 19, 55, 57, 90, 107–8, 122, 128–29, 131–33, 136, 142, 146–47, 150–52, 154–55, 157, 161, 166, 168, 182,

184–86; fusionist culture of, 123–24, 137–38, 141, 149; Muslim community, 137–38; Muslim university students, growth of, 219n75
University of Indonesia, 70, 96
University of Michigan, 56
urbanization, 125
Usman, K. H. Fakih, 45

van Niel, Robert, 29
Venture of Islam, The (Hodgson), 169
von Grunebaum, Gustave, 57–59

Wahib, Ahmad, 98–99, 101
Wahid, Abdurrahman, 163, 185
war on terror, 17, 185, 199
Watt, W. Montgomery, 58, 113
Webster, David, 56
Westernization, 102, 127. *See also* modernization
Westoxification, 166

West Sumatra, 24, 26–28, 46, 84
Wiebe, Donald, 89
Wilhelmina, Queen, 28
Wolfowitz, Paul, 151
World War II, 36, 55, 83, 225–26n7
Wright, Robin, 137

Yahya, Mukhtar, 35
Ya'kub, Iljas, 28
Yogyakarta (Java), 25, 34, 92
Young Islamic Union (JIB), 29–30, 40
Young, T. Cuyler, 59
Yudhoyono, Susilo Bambang, 185
Yunus, Mahmud, 18, 23–24, 27–28, 35–36, 47, 51, 81; as education reformer, 37–39; mixed-curriculum model, endorsement of, 38, 44

zakat, 168, 223n48
Zaman, Muhammad Qasim, 23
Zuhri, K. H. Saifuddin, 46, 48

ENCOUNTERING TRADITIONS

Natalie Carnes, *Motherhood: A Confession*

Paul J. Griffiths, *Christian Flesh*

Rumee Ahmed, *Sharia Compliant: A User's Guide to Hacking Islamic Law*

Natalie Carnes, *Image and Presence: A Christological Reflection on Iconoclasm and Iconophilia*

Shaul Magid, *Hasidism Incarnate: Hasidism, Christianity, and the Construction of Modern Judaism*

Ted A. Smith, *Weird John Brown: Divine Violence and the Limits of Ethics*

David Decosimo, *Ethics as a Work of Charity: Thomas Aquinas and Pagan Virtue*

Francis X. Clooney, SJ, *His Hiding Place Is Darkness: A Hindu-Catholic Theopoetics of Divine Absence*

Muhammad Iqbal, *Reconstruction of Religious Thought in Islam*